Acclaim for *I'll Have The Liver, Please!*

"Food! Travel! Organ transplants! There's never been a book like this surprisingly witty account of a near-death experience. And it's a fair bet, there never will be another! Written with much humor, and even more appetite! Bradley Ross will make you hungry—and remind you of the importance of a yearly checkup!"
—*Merrill Shindler, Longtime Zagat Editor, Raconteur and Man About Town.*

"Bradley Ross shares his illness, fears, challenges, transplant journey, and ultimately gratitude and good health especially poignantly and insightfully. Uniquely and deliciously he reminds us of the value of appreciating every day...especially those days made possible by the gift of a stranger."
—*Thomas Mone, Chief Executive Office, OneLegacy*

"Delicious, funny and insightful! Bradley gives a glimpse on how travelling foodies travel, including the relatable woes when being with non-foodies."
—*Raymond Cua, Founder of Travelling Foodie*

I'LL HAVE THE LIVER, PLEASE!

a love story

BRADLEY D. ROSS

Fressers Publishing

Fressers Publishing
An imprint of Woo Enterprises
Los Angeles, California
1liverplease@gmail.com
First Edition
ISBN: 978-0-578-68826-8
Cover design by Bailey McGinn

For Helene,
with love forever

CONTENTS

"Enjoy every sandwich."

Singer-songwriter Warren Zevon's advice shortly before his death

PROLOGUE

November 29, 2016, 9:00 a.m.

My hospital room sounds like the first day of band practice in fourth grade. The IV drips with a rhythmic plunk. Compression pumps whoosh and squeeze completely out of sync with the IV. The dialysis machine whirs to its own beat. The nurses rush in when an alarm goes off. I have been here long enough to know not to become distressed at the sound of alarms. Unless the nurses have that look in their eyes. The nurses are trained to remain calm and not look panicked, but sometimes I can see it in their eyes.

I no longer have the energy or strength to move my torso much, but I can still wiggle my fingers and toes in silent protest against my deteriorating condition. It feels empowering to manipulate my digits. In my little hospital world, it is a bold act of defiance. A declaration that I am still alive and kicking. Or at least twitching.

My brain is not faring any better than the rest of my body. Names, faces, events. They are all slowly slip slidin' away. Any concept of time has turned to dust. As an attorney I spent decades billing time in one tenth of an hour increments. Now I have no clue what day of the week it is. Thoughts dance into my head, swirl around for a brief fling, then scamper away into the fog.

I have no control over what has been happening to my body, but everything else being equal I would just as soon not lose my mind too. The future is not looking so rosy, so I try to focus on pleasant thoughts from the past. I spent almost half my life planning for this moment, determined to create as many lasting memories as a person could jam into one lifetime. Few people can remember what they did on any random day last month or last year. It is only the supremely special days that we remember forever. In the game of life, whoever creates the greatest number of memorable days, wins. The payoff comes when for no extra charge, you get to snatch those moments right back and savor them again and again whenever you need them most.

I need them now. My most vivid and warming memories are of our family vacations. When my mind wanders off for an unscheduled stroll I try to reel it back in and center my brain by recalling every possible detail about our trips to faraway places where we mangled foreign languages, found ourselves lost on desolate trails, peed in places where no Ross had ever gone before, and most importantly for me dined on unsightly creatures that caused my wife Helene to recoil in horror. What was the name of that restaurant in Paris where I ended up ordering veal head by mistake, only to later hear our waiter speaking to another table in perfect English? I can picture our son Matthew sitting on a bench eating a chocolate gelato cone that was half in his stomach and half all over his face. Was that in Italy or in Switzerland? Where did we go on that cruise where our daughter Jessica became completely and utterly smitten both with our assigned waiter and the all-you-can eat chocolate tarts?

As I exhaust everything I can recall about one vacation, I start in on another. Is it just a coincidence that they all seem to involve a memorable meal? I think not.

My time in the hospital has passed quickly. In a way too quickly because I am in a bit of a time crunch.

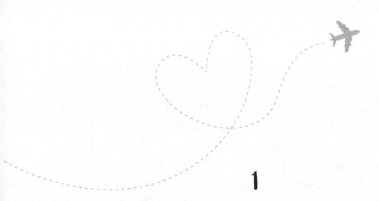

1

THE BOUILLABAISSE INCIDENT

1985

In the spring of 1985 I began research into the first of my culinary adventures. Naturally I started with France, and no trip to France is complete without a grand bouillabaisse expedition. My investigation suggested that the Michelin-starred Restaurant de Bacon in Cap d'Antibes was just the place to kick off our trip. A few months in advance I sent off a letter requesting dinner reservations from our home in Los Angeles and impatiently awaited a response. A month later my efforts were rewarded when an exotic-looking envelope with a blue Republique Francaise stamp arrived at my door. It was confirmation of a table for two! This would be my first real bouillabaisse, not like those served in most restaurants where a fry cook throws some limp, glassy-eyed fish into a canned broth and zaps it in a commercial microwave.

While still standing at our front door holding my prized reservation confirmation, I pictured what that precious moment would be like when Helene and I were escorted to our table at Restaurant de Bacon.

"*Bouillabaisse, s'il vous plaît,*" I say to our server, who will give me a slight smile and nod, instantly recognizing me as a man of discerning sophistication. I sip from my glass of Domaine de la Begude Bandol Rose and discretely sneak a peek at the nearby tables to determine if the other diners have ordered as wisely as I have. With my chin slightly raised to show off my best side, I gaze out the window as the sun sets over the perfect beryl blue ocean hugging the yachts lazing in the harbor. Our server approaches and carefully places before me a steaming bowl of liquid Provence heaped with seafood that was still flopping only moments before. I inhale the intoxicating fragrance a bit too deeply and get slightly woozy. After three cleansing breaths, I show off to Helene by pointing out the farm-fresh garlic, onions, tomatoes, and wondrous herbs delicately removed only a few hours earlier from a local weed- and pest-free garden. These garden delights were tenderly slow cooked with rockfish humanely caught that very morning by a nimble local fisherman. Gently pressed olive oil from hundred-year-old sun-drenched trees was drizzled over the top as the mélange reduced into an intoxicating stock. The chef nestled in prized examples of John Dory, red scorpion fish, monkfish, and perhaps moray that will flake apart with only a hint of encouragement from my fork, tenderly coaxed in perfectly proportioned waxy potatoes, lovingly simmered, meticulously deboned, tested a small spoonful with knowing satisfaction, and voila! I adjust my bib, maneuver a piece of baguette into position to sop up every stubborn drop in the bowl, and get ready to dig in.

My reverie ended abruptly when a most familiar voice thundered in from the living room of our home: "You're letting all the flies in, close the front door!" yelled Helene.

"Yes, dear."

* * *

After many years of hard work, I was on a roll. I was on track to become a partner at a law firm in a few years and our son Matthew was a healthy toddler. With Matthew safely ensconced in the loving arms of my parents back home, Helene and I were finally on a romantic getaway. It was summertime in France, we were about to wine and dine at some of the finest restaurants in the world, and my bouillabaisse dream was about to become a reality. Standing at water's edge, we turned our faces toward the afternoon sun of the Côte d'Azur. Anything was possible and we were unstoppable.

We arrived in Cap D'Antibes the day before our restaurant reservation. I whispered in Helene's ear that I wanted to take her for a romantic drive along the ocean to welcome ourselves to the South of France. She was not the least bit surprised when a few kilometers later I parked the car directly across the street from Restaurant de Bacon. My anticipation of the following evening's bouillabaisse spectacular was simply too much to endure. I rolled down the car window, hoping that a favorable onshore breeze would allow me to draw in just a whisper of that shimmering bouillabaisse.

"Some big romantic you are," Helene scoffed.

"The ocean is right there across the street, just like I said," I responded with false indignation. "Now that you've had a look," I continued, "let's hop over to the restaurant and take a quick peak at the menu."

I got out and started to walk across the street as Helene hurried after me. *Le menu* was posted near the entrance. There was not much to study as there were only two main courses on the menu: bouillabaisse, and bouillabaisse with lobster.

"What am I going to eat?" Helene asked with a tremor in her voice. "You know I don't eat fish."

The horror! No grilled chicken breast for Helene? Not even some lousy *coq au vin*?

A large group of diners with normal taste buds brushed past me as they entered the restaurant. After a few moments, I gathered myself up and followed them inside. The aroma of fresh fish and musky spices rushed at me like a surging stream of saffron. White linen-clad tables were laid out almost to the ocean's edge. Refined waiters glided about refilling wine glasses with practiced flair. Directly in front of me a laughing couple wearing giant plastic bibs coaxed sweet, sweet lobster meat from enormous jagged claws dripping with shimmering broth. The *maitre d'* with exquisitely pomaded hair and a smile as broad as the nearby beach rushed over to greet me.

I looked back at Helene, who appeared crestfallen but trying mightily to force a smile. I had promised her a romantic dinner overlooking the water in the South of France. Would she be forced to fight back hunger pangs while I sat across the table gleefully licking garlicky broth from my fingers? Was she to remain alone back at the hotel, staving off starvation by foraging Pringles from the minibar in our room? Throughout our five-year marriage I was a dedicated and caring husband. Dine without my wife while on vacation? Unthinkable. With bone-crushing regret and a final whimper, I canceled our reservations. *Merde!*

I slunk back into the car and turned it toward our motel. We could not afford to stay in Cap d'Antibes or in Cannes, but I was able to book a room in nearby Juan-les-Pins, a rather garish unwashed stepchild of a town catering to the younger unmoneyed set. Instead of the majestic hotels of Cannes offering access to a private beach, twenty-four-hour butler service, and balcony views of mega-yachts bobbing in the bay, our Juan-les-Pins motel offered a front row panorama of T-shirt shops, fast food bars, and a rundown disco. But Cannes can keep its international film festival because only Juan-les-Pins offers a battle of the Brazilian bands ice cream bar bonanza.

Just follow the pulsating sound and you will arrive. On one corner a Brazilian samba band has its amps turned up all the way at the Festival, an open-air bar/ice cream establishment with a Latin theme. Waitstaff samba their way through the throng while carrying mountainous ice cream concoctions that shoot off sparks from blazing sparklers planted in the heaping mounds of *glace*. Normally, one would be transfixed by such a sight on the otherwise tranquil beaches of the Côte d'Azur. But we could not gawk too long at the raucous Festival scene, because directly across the street the Pam-Pam beckoned.

The Pam-Pam is an open-air bar/ice cream establishment with a Latin theme, featuring a Brazilian samba band with its amps turned up all the way, because you just cannot have too many of these at a single intersection. In fact, I believe the Pam-Pam's amps were newer, bigger and even louder, but I'm sure the Festival will remedy that before too long. Aside from the simultaneous blasting of the bands, both the Festival and the Pam-Pam checked all the boxes you could want in a Brazilian ice cream bar. Garish lighting in reds and yellows, palm trees inside and out, carved tikis everywhere, samba dancers wearing little more than a feathered headdress, a youthful crowd packed around tiny outdoor tables under a shading canopy, and the pounding base beat from Brazilian *surdo* drums.

Helene and I snatched two bentwood chairs crowded around one of the Pam-Pam's outdoor tables. Do not embarrass yourself, as Helene did, by trying to order a cone with a single scoop of vanilla ice cream. Instead, you must try something like the Pampam, a massive creation larger than your head which includes sorbets of strawberry, mango, pineapple and banana under a canopy of fresh fruits, drenched in Grand Marnier, topped with Chantilly, drizzled with a berry sauce, and finally capped with sliced almonds. Yes, your ice cream with have some type of plant poking out of the side. Or a wooden monkey clinging to a spoon. Or a carved butterfly or tiki wedged in for no apparent reason. If you are lucky it will have all of those things. Want something to drink? Be prepared to sip through a coconut chiseled into the shape of a baboon wearing a silly hat. And wear goggles because those sparklers can put your eye out!

Samba music is wildly frenetic and in Juan-les-Pins is best presented at the loudest volume that the local electrical current will allow. Samba music in stereo is even more exhilarating. Samba music in stereo with each ear hearing a different song from competing Brazilian bands is a little too much excitement for me. Helene and I watched the youthful crowd at the Festival watching us, spooned up ice cream until we were on the verge of permanent brain freeze, and finally headed to our motel before our ears started to bleed. When we retired for the night I tried, without much success, to push The Bouillabaisse Incident out of my throbbing head.

I was beaten but not broken. The first course had ended in a bruising blow to my bouillabaisse dreams, but the ice cream had cleansed our palates, and the music had cleaned out our ear drums as well. The main course still awaited a days' drive away, a confirmed reservation at a three Michelin starred restaurant in the charming French hamlet of Lyon.

* * *

Lyon is to France as Velveeta is to Camembert de Normandie AOC. Sorry, but somebody has to step up and speak the truth. It is an ugly city. There, I said it. So what if I piss off half a million Lyonnais?

The unsightly city of Lyon has quite deservedly been awarded the nickname of "Black Lyon" due to the filthy caked grime streaked on its buildings. Take a look around. Lyon is a proud producer of birth defect-inducing chemicals and toxic metals spewing from smoke-choked foundries. Every competent urban planner must have fled long ago, as demonstrated by the city's riverbanks being used as common car parks. Yeah, Lyon has some dusty Roman ruins here and there. Big deal. You can hardly walk anywhere in France without tripping over some Roman ruins.

Ah, but Lyon has a precious treasure that no other place is the world possesses. Lyon has Chef Paul Bocuse. The Maestro of *Morue*. The Virtuoso of *Veau*. The Connoisseur of *Caneton*. Chef Bocuse was one of the original innovators of nouvelle cuisine and was as responsible as anyone for introducing French gastronomy around the world. Voted Chef of the Century, he created the world's top international food competition, modestly naming it Bocuse d'Or. His flagship restaurant tragically lies near the city of Lyon. But what is a little soot when one has the opportunity to make a pilgrimage to this holy bistro.

Helene and I climbed the steps of the stone building to enter the chandelier-laden dining room adorned with French antique furniture, fresh roses, and linens so crisply starched that you could remove the table out from under them and the tablecloth would still stand at attention and salute. As we settled into sumptuously uphol-stered chairs, I wondered what delectable trio of amuse-bouches might levitate from the Bocuse kitchen along with a lighter than air *gougère* choux pastry. Perhaps delicately smoked salmon with fresh dill and cream cheese? A sweet lobster salad?

I searched the menu until I found the four most glorious words in French cooking—*Menu Grande Tradition Classique*. By selecting this most regal of set menus, a life-altering journey commences with pan-seared scallop of foie gras in a passion fruit sauce. The foie gras will be perfectly caramelized with a soft creamy center, while just dipping its toe in the slightly sweet passion fruit bath.

Then things will start to get serious. *Soupe aux truffes noires V.G.E.* This black truffle soup was created by Chef Bocuse back in 1975 for the visit of then French President Valéry Giscard d'Estaing and has been featured on the menu ever since. The soup will arrive in an oversized puff pastry containing half of the annual butter output of Normandy. The earthy gnarled black truffles were no doubt harvested by an earthy gnarled truffle hunter who dug beneath an earthy gnarled oak tree that has looked out upon the Dordogne for hundreds of years. One of the monumental moments in life occurs when you crack open the pastry and suck in the rich musky fragrance ascending to the heavens from the steaming soup below. Magic.

At that point we will still be at the warm-up stage of this gastronomic godsend. I planned to lick every drop from the bottom of that bowl (those snobbish Parisians on holiday can stare all they like). After a brief pause to allow one of the line cooks to mop Chef Bocuse's brow, Chef Bocuse will personally send out to me his Filet of Sole "A La Fernand Point," a caramelized filet in a cream sauce nestled softly atop a bed of lightly cooked tagliatelle.

I will no doubt need a refreshing break during such a pageant, if only to compose myself for the main event. Anticipating my every desire, the Great Chef will insure a proper palate cleansing by delivery of a cooling Beaujolais sherbet.

But I will not be disposed to pause too long. Just as my already high expectations will be mounting to a point of near delirium, my bladder will overflow. Not to fret, because this will be an entirely different bladder than the one in my stomach fighting to hold in one too many glasses of Châteauneuf-du-Pape. Rather, picture a pig's bladder bloated to the size of a basketball. This, my friends, is Chef Bocuse's *Volaille de Bresse A La Mère Fillioux*, a truffle-stuffed Bresse hen cooked in the pig's bladder and carved tableside with vegetables and glorious truffle-kissed juices from the hen. How can mere human hands create such an unearthly treasure?

Cheese tray? *Oui, oui, oui!*

Will I still have room for dessert? Of course not. Will that stop me? Of course not. A massive dessert cart will wondrously appear. Fresh fruits, creams, tarts...*oui, oui* and *oui!* Will it be a culinary faux pas to leap naked onto the dessert cart and roll among the cakes and chocolates? There is only one way to find out.

But I am getting a bit ahead of myself. You see, I am not permitted to order the *Menu Grande Tradition Classique*. Like almost all fine set menus in the world, chefs require that every diner at the same table partake of the same menu. Chef Bocuse is no exception as his *Menu Grande Tradition Classique* makes it quite clear: "PREPARED FOR THE ENTIRE TABLE." Oh yes, and there she is, sitting directly across from me. My own personal epicurean dagger to the taste buds. There is no need to make inquiry of Helene. We have covered this soiled ground many times before.

Foie gras? The liver of a force-fed duckling? "No thank you."

Black truffle soup? "Truffles smell like an old pair of unwashed socks."

Filet of sole? "Too fishy!"

Hen prepared in a pig's bladder? "Surely you jest."

My orgasmic dream of partaking in the *Menu Grande Tradition Classique* was gutted like the carcass of that Bresse hen at the next table. I glared at my spouse. She smiled back at me. Was it time to simply give up without a fight, like the French in World War II?

A back-up plan was needed and of course I had one. *Loup en croûte, farci mousse de homard*, with *sauce choron*. Chef Bocuse's celebrated sea bass cooked in a pastry. But this is not just any pastry.

The pastry that lovingly caresses this sea bass is intricately carved to show each of the fish's fins and individual scales! A masterpiece worthy of Monet, with lobster mousse sauce instead of water lilies. Quite a meal could be built around such a chef d'oeuvre masterwork. Yes, a plan was forming and I could still frolic among the desserts afterwards. But then I noticed in the description of the *loup* on the menu, three little words designed to empty my hopes and dreams quicker than that punctured pig's bladder—"FOR TWO PERSONS."

My wife had impaled me on a razor sharp Laguiole chef's knife yet again. She remained sitting across the table trying to appear as if she were innocent of any culinary crime. Angelic, calm, patient, smiling sweetly. Few knew, as I did, that she was a cold-blooded *assassin gastronomique.*

"What are you going to have to eat, sweetie?" she asked.

"I'll see if I can get the truffle soup *à la carte* to start," I grumbled. "Then maybe the lamb."

"I'm a little tired of chicken breast. I might try something else."

I ducked under the table, peaking out only to see if a thunderbolt had struck our table or whether a fiery chasm had split the restaurant in two, belching out sulfuric clouds from the flaming bowels of hell. But no, everything seemed calm. Was there still a glimmer of hope for this woman? Had she finally seen the grotesque error of her timid dining ways and now wanted to repent?

"What are you thinking of ordering?" I bravely asked.

"It looks like they have a beef filet with bone marrow sauce. Do you think they can just grill the filet plain without the bone marrow?"

I found myself biting the back of my hand.

* * *

Was our much-anticipated meal with Chef Bocuse a success, in spite of Helene's defective palate? I am happy to report it was. Waving a magic wand cleverly disguised as a ladle, the Wizard Bocuse had taken humble soup and infused it with the very essence of thousands of years of French *terrior* while at the same time rendering it unworldly. The dinner was masterful and I should have been on a truffle-infused high, but as is my nature I still could not push The Bouillabaisse Incident out of my head. I do not deny that I have brought up The Bouillabaisse Incident to my beloved on occasion over the years, reminding her of the remarkable sacrifice that left me with a culinary scar that will never heal. Those occasions may have included anytime the word "bouillabaisse" came up in conversation. Or the word "France." Or "restaurant." Or "bacon."

I knew only too well that Helene was unwavering in her self-imposed dining limitations. My easy-going and otherwise open-minded wife will not eat any fish or seafood product. This includes anything that ever lived in, swam in, or accidently fell into a body of water. The lone exception to this rule is tuna fish out of a can, which we all know is not a fish. Additionally, nothing passes her lips that is spicier than an unseasoned chicken breast that has been boiled until the final hint of flavor has waved a white flag and leapt from the pan. Finally, Helene will not eat anything that she has not eaten before, which raises a thought-provoking "chicken or the egg" question. In the interest of fairness, she will eat both chicken and eggs. As long as they are not spicy and as long as they are presented in a familiar form.

My petite wife has innumerable fine qualities, not the least of which is that she is supernaturally patient, ever cheerful, and has followed me to the ends of the earth in a futile effort to keep me out of trouble. However, when it comes to food, Helene is to fine dining as a water spot is to a Riedel wineglass.

On the other hand, eating malodourous jungle animals, bulbous insects with hairy legs, and riled up deep-sea crustaceans with snapping pincers is my passion. I lust for the opportunity to catch and eat a ravenous piranha in the Amazon before it eats me first. My final deathbed wish will be to expire slumped over with my head face-first on a plate of lion steak simmered in a hyena reduction sauce with a side of gazelle foam.

Helene and I are the perfectly mismatched epicurean travel team. Yet, my dream is to partake of exotic cuisine on six different continents. I am boycotting Antarctica until it receives higher scores on Yelp or until someone smuggles in a hickory burning Meadow Creek barbeque so that I can smoke some Emperor Penguin. Sweet and smoky sauce or tangy vinegar-based? The guidebooks do not say which pairs better with penguin.

The author's prized autographed menu.

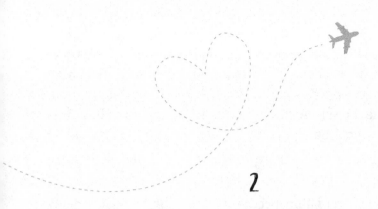

2

FAA WHAT?

1993

"We're going to have to postpone your surgery. Your pre-op blood test results have a glitch," my foot surgeon explained. I was scheduled to have minor surgery on my right foot a few days later. "It may be nothing," he continued, "but the test for your liver function came back too high. You're going to need to get that checked with a liver specialist before we can proceed."

"Helene and I are going out to a French restaurant next week that specializes in foie gras. Will that count?" I quipped.

"No."

My foot doctor was not known for his sense of humor. I guess that is understandable if you spend each day scraping away strangers' toenail fungus and removing plantar warts.

There are two words I never want to hear from a doctor. One is "diet." The other is "glitch," particularly when used in the same conversation as surgery. I thought the worst thing that would happen regarding my foot procedure was that I would not be able to eat or drink for twelve hours before the surgery. Not even a modest slice of gruyere, pancetta, and scallion frittata.

* * *

The liver specialist Dr. Ford came directly to the point. "You've got a liver disease called primary sclerosing cholangitis. We don't have all the answers about this disease but many doctors believe it is autoimmune related. We don't know how or why people get it, and at this time there is no known cure. All we can do right now is continue to monitor you."

"So what happens if there's no cure?" I asked with some foreboding.

"Sometimes liver failure occurs quickly but often it takes many years for the liver to fail. At some point you may suffer from fatigue, loss of muscle mass, jaundice, weight loss and even confusion. The liver acts as a filter for your entire body and if it is not doing the job, your other organs may suffer as well. Ultimately, you'll need a liver transplant to survive."

"Wow." It took me a few moments to process this. "How do I go about getting a new liver?"

"When you get sick enough you can get on a waiting list. Unfortunately, there just aren't enough livers to go around."

"How many people are on the list?"

"Currently close to seventeen thousand."

Seventeen thousand? That was almost as long as the wait list to get into Damon Baehrel's restaurant in New York! It was also an inconvenient time to die. Matthew and his younger sister Jessica were just small kids and if I died soon they would barely remember me. I still had little league games, dance recitals and school plays to attend, not to mention weddings and grandchildren to babysit. Waiting until retirement age to start working on my travel bucket list was no longer an option. Would there even be a retirement? And what about Helene? My training tactics to advance her palate were still at the embryonic stage.

"So where do we go from here?" I asked.

"Well, this disease carries a higher risk from viruses, infections and of developing cancer, so you'll need to stay out of the sun, have regular blood tests and check-ups."

"Okay."

"We should also get you in for a liver biopsy so we can have a better idea of what is going on in there."

"Got it."

"And you need to change your diet. Cut down on fats and fried or spicy foods. No more of those cheeseburgers with fries. Eat lean meats."

No more Double-Double combos with a chocolate shake from In-N-Out Burger? Was I simply supposed to go cold turkey on Jodi Maroni Sausage Kingdom's Hot Italian Pork Sausage? What of Langer's Deli's iconic #19 pastrami, swiss and coleslaw sandwich? This was sadistic. My body felt perfectly fine.

I went home and gave Helene the news. She had the same initial reaction.

"Wow," she said. "How do you feel?" she quickly added.

"My liver feels good as new," I replied. "Wherever it is. Left side of my stomach? No, right side maybe. Do you know?"

"I'm not sure."

"I bet you it's probably hanging out with my spleen, shootin' the breeze and gossiping about my kidneys."

"You need to take this seriously."

"I am. I'm also serious about wanting to travel more while we can. I want to create some lasting memories for all of us by taking the kids on our vacations, at least until they become teenagers and refuse to have anything to do with us. I want to eat as many new foods as I can slip past my doctor. I want to stalk lions in the Serengeti and paddle down rapids in the Amazon and stare down polar bears in the Arctic. My middle name is 'Danger' you know."

"So you've told me many times, but always from the safety of our home."

"Are you with me?"

"Absolutely. Wherever you go, I go."

"And I want us to go bungee jumping."

"You're on your own."

* * *

1994

I moped around the house for almost a decade trying to overcome the dual blows of The Bouillabaisse Incident and missing out on Chef Bocuse's *Menu Grande Tradition Classique.* But with my new medical news there was no more time to waste and I planned my triumphant return to France with the full family in tow. I hoped to instill in the kids the utter joy and delight of discovering new places and particularly new foods, in breaking bread in a culture entirely different than the one fostered at McDonalds, in partaking of a magnificent meal prepared at the highest level of skill by a world-class chef. A three-star Michelin restaurant in France is a considerable step up from Applebee's, but we decided to hope for the best. At worst, we could just flee the country.

Warm weather and a gentle breeze greeted the Ross family when we arrived in Paris. As a tune up to French culture Helene and I pointed out to the kids the sights from atop the Eiffel Tower, laughed at the street performers juggling their way to stardom outside the strikingly modern Centre Pompidou, tried to explain to Matthew and Jessica what the big deal was about the Mona Lisa at the Louvre, and shaded the kids' eyes as we walked past the world's oldest prostitutes on our way to the Moulin Rouge. New memories indeed! With the preliminaries finally out of the way, the four of us departed Paris and presented ourselves to the sun-kissed south of France, my taste buds on high alert.

Nearly seven-year-old Jessica looked resplendent in her brand-new sapphire satin dress with sequined accents. She skipped and twirled about as we made our way up the stone path to the sixteenth century olive pressing mill that now housed one of the greatest restaurants in the world. Cradled in an ancient hill town above the French Riviera, Le Moulin de Mougins was home to one of the architects of *nouvelle cuisine*, the great chef Roger Vergé. Most importantly, Jessica got a new dress out of the deal. Ten-year-old Matthew was not quite as excited as his sister was about dressing up, but still looked pretty sharp in his navy blazer and used his new dress shoes to kick loose stones on the walkway.

Jessica skipped ahead of the rest of us to the front desk of the restaurant and announced our arrival using her very best *"bonsoir."* When we caught up the four of us were escorted to our table. The sommelier handed me a tome entitled "Vin" that was heavy enough to have been used as the cornerstone for the original foundation of the mill. I commenced a serious examination of the wine list, starting with Alsace and working through the alphabet.

Of course, because Helene had inexplicably been seated at the same table as the rest of us, *Le Menu Tradition* was out of the question. However, at significant additional cost I was able to cobble together a reasonable facsimile from the *à la carte* menu. Nothing like some *foie gras frais de canard des landes en gelée de poivre noir et jus de groseilles* to jump start a meal, particularly when I already had liver on my mind. The kick from the pepper was the perfect foil for the sweet currants spread over the richness of the foie gras. Then on to crisp-skinned roast duck in a juniper berry sauce. Of course, everything tastes even better with a glass of Château Haut-Brion—Graves. The doctors had assured me that an occasional glass of wine would not do me any harm and I did not want to waste a single opportunity.

"What's that?" Jessica asked as the first course arrived.

"Foie gras," I replied.

"Faa what?"

"Foie gras."

"What's it made of?"

"First they take a baby duckling."

"I like baby ducklings."

"Me too. So does the duck farmer. He likes his ducklings so much that he feeds them twice a day. As you know, ducks have wings instead of hands, so the farmer helps the ducks eat by sticking a tube down their throats. After a few days each little duckling gets big and strong, especially their livers, and then the ducks go off to the big pond in the sky so that we can enjoy foie gras."

"That's cool," piped in Matthew. Clearly the boy had inherited just the right genes from the correct parent.

"That's cruel force-feeding," my spouse the buzzkill joined in.

"Let's eat," I said.

Chef Vergé's silky-smooth seared foie gras was artistry with liver! Jessica and I both decided to order the rest of the duck as well. Fortunately for her, Jessica didn't ask me how the duck was prepared and I didn't have to explain to her that Chef Vergé insists that his ducks be suffocated by having their necks pulled rather than being bled, how after singeing the body he uses a special technique to cut off the feet, wing tips and neck for use in the pan, and how he prefers to cook the duck with the heart, lungs and liver remaining in the cavity only to be removed later for thickening the sauce.

Jessica was duly impressed when her duck arrived and the waiter cut it into pieces easy for her to manage. After a few bites, Jessica declared: "This is the best duck I ever ate." It may have been the first duck that she ever ate, but nonetheless there was hope for that kid yet. If I could only keep her away from her mother for the next decade or so. Truth be told, it was the best duck that I ever ate as well.

Matthew dined on *fricassée de volaille aux herbes vertes du jardin*, stewed chicken with green herb sauce. The green sauce looked wonderful on top of the chicken, not quite as nice on the sleeve of his new blazer.

Next was a surprise delivery to our table. A white-toqued and white-mustachioed Roger Vergé presented himself to our party. He politely smiled at each of us, settled his gaze upon Jessica in her new dress, and exclaimed: *"Oh la la!"* Jessica blushed and melted like a slab of Normandy butter in a hot Matfer Bourgeat saucepan. Chef Vergé welcomed us, bid us *"bon appetite"* and then he was gone. He had Jessica at *"Oh la la."*

Ultimately, there was cheese. Much cheese. There was lemon soufflé. There were petit fours and tarts and cookies. There was an empty glass of Haut-Brion at my place setting. *Oh la la* indeed!

* * *

"I don't think you were supposed to turn off here, hon," Helene warned. "The sign said that the Loire Valley is the other way." We were supposed to be heading to the land of chateau, and more importantly pyramid-shaped Valencay goat cheese and chilled Sancerre. But I was a man on a mission, and both the goat and Sancerre would have to wait.

"I just want to take a short detour for a little snack," I explained.

"Gee Dad, again?" piped in Matthew from the back seat. Drive one hundred miles out of my way just to eat a pastry? In a heartbeat. Of course, I am not referring to just any old misshapen croissant but rather to the glory of the *pithivier*. In a wondrous and fortuitous coincidence, the *pithivier* is thought to have been created in Pithiviers, France. Where better to introduce my family to the unadulterated glories of this perfectly flaky and rich treat?

For those of you who haven't had the pleasure of driving one hundred and fifty miles out of your way with a carload of culinary heathens just to sample a pastry, a *pithivier* is a round scalloped-edged golden puff pastry bursting with copious amounts of butter and silky almond paste. What is a mere two hundred miles when the prize at the end of the journey is one of the world's great dessert treats? Particularly when I can share the journey with my loving family: My wife who gets carsick at each minor bump in the road and my two beautiful children who read books in the back seat while refusing to even glance out the window at the stunning French countryside.

My finely-honed navigational skills led us like a laser-guided baguette to the center of this small town and my nose took it from there, depositing us right at the front door of a boulangerie/patisserie whose windows were bursting with the golden round treasures. As the entire Ross family entered the shop, we were surrounded by *pithiviers* of every size, each one contributing to the intoxicating scent of butter, almonds and freshly baked puff pastry. Using my very finest unaccented French gesticulations, I pointed at a large just-out-of-the-oven *pithivier* and nodded my head. The store clerk wrapped it up in a bow and that warm *pithivier* was now all mine.

The four of us walked across the street to a small deserted park and sat down at a wooden picnic table. Helene had neglected to pack a freshly ironed Schweitzer linen tablecloth and silver cutlery for such an important event, but my Wisconsin—Who cut the cheese? pocketknife and corkscrew was at the ready. After sterilizing it by wiping it on my pants leg, I generously carved several thick slices. The *pithivier* was still warm as the flaky crust and silky center harmonized to melt on my tongue. I wanted that moment to last forever.

However, the spell of the *pithivier* quickly evaporated when Jessica announced mid-bite that she had to go to the bathroom. A quick look around revealed a public brick bathroom only a few steps away in the park. Helene pointed Jessica in the right direction and we watched her go into the bathroom. Only seconds later Jessica came bursting out of the bathroom crying and pointed back toward the bathroom. We raced over to her and visually confirmed that she had not suffered any apparent injuries.

Helene, who has a soothing effect on everyone, calmed her down and held her hand as they walked back into the bathroom to investigate. Meanwhile, I stood watch guarding the *pithivier*. A few moments later Helene came out giggling while holding Jessica's hand, and yelled over to me: "The bathroom doesn't have a commode, only a hole in the ground and two indentations for your feet."

It was in Pithiviers that Jessica received her first lesson in squatting. Many years later she insists that she was traumatized by this event, the details of which she can still recite with great clarity. Yet another lifelong memory! I was still on a roll.

As for me, I still lust over that *pithivier*, the taste of which I can recall with great clarity. It was worth every one of the four hundred miles that I drove to partake in its delights. However, whenever I recall our minor detour to Pithiviers, my mind inevitably drifts to that rustic hole in the ground with the footholds, throwing off a scent that was emphatically unpastry-like.

* * *

It was late afternoon at the end of a long drive when we finally arrived under the canopy of two-hundred-year-old lime trees leading to the Château de Colliers in the Loire Valley. Our travel agent reserved a large family room for us at this beautiful chateau that has been in the Gelis family since 1783. Before we could remove our luggage from the car, Jessica and Matthew had already made friends with Goldie, the golden retriever who had the run of the house.

The owner Madame Gelis came outside to greet us in the parking area. When we told her we were the Ross family, we received a blank look in return. It turned out that our soon-to-be-fired travel agent never confirmed our reservation and we were not expected. But Madame Gelis leaped into action and in no time we gratefully settled into two rooms adorned with four-poster beds, fireplaces and period furniture. Jessica in particular could not contain her excitement. Tomorrow was her seventh birthday.

Breakfast at the chateau was around an antique oval table set in a large dining room. The walls were decorated with museum quality paintings and tapestries that had no doubt been passed down through many generations. Madame Gelis must have overheard Jessica talking about her birthday because during breakfast Jessica received a peach with a lit candle on top. A wonderful way to start the day!

During breakfast Jessica mentioned that she loved her room, in part because there was a special kid-sized sink where she washed her hands. Yes, Jessica continued to be completely flummoxed by French plumbing. She had been using the bidet.

We drove through the Loire Valley exploring the French Renaissance architecture of Chambord along with the horse show in the old stables, then on to Château de Cheverny to watch the feeding of the hounds. Since the 17th century, the hounds of Cheverny have led the hunt over hill and dale for fox and other feisty beasts. Over seventy hunting dogs, a mix of foxhound and French hound, were clearly ready for their only meal of the day. The brown, black and white splashed dogs knew the routine and were jumping, baying and yelping as if it were their last meal. Over seventy hound heads swiveled as one when the trainer used a shovel to scoop their mush into long troughs. It looked like slop to us but it must have looked like filet mignon to the hounds. Suddenly, the hounds were released and it was dogs gone wild. They rushed in all directions for prime slurping position, hopping over and diving beneath each other, convinced that the slop was always grayer on the other side. Food flew everywhere including all over the dogs, but the hounds were more than happy to clean up, licking each other's fur until they could see their reflection. In a mere two minutes it was over and tired dogs now lolled about as others settled in for a nap. A few came over to Matthew and Jessica to receive a well-deserved pat on the head and to deliver a very wet kiss.

A casual dinner in Blois followed and the birthday girl enjoyed her new favorite dish, breast of duck with potato pancakes followed by chocolate mousse and chocolate ice cream. The four-poster beds looked very inviting by the time we made it back to Goldie and the Château de Colliers.

I find it impossible to pass by a street market in France without stopping to browse, and the one we stumbled upon the next day in Selles-sur-Cher was no exception. Everything one could possibly want for a world-class picnic was on display and we could not resist. We moved from stall to stall, taking in the colors and scents and shouts of the farmers. Jessica was in charge of carrying the fresh baguette that was almost as tall as she was. Matthew acquired a new blue beret which he proudly wore while he carried the *saucisson* that we bought from the *boucher*. I was not going to let anyone else carry the wonderfully pungent Valencay goat cheese that I acquired from the farmer's wife at her stand, and Helene cradled some peaches and a small French Charentais melon with bright green ribbing.

On the way to Valencay we spotted it, an inviting shaded picnic table at the edge of the forest. The scent of pine battled with the musk of the soil, as a particularly amorous cuckoo cooed away somewhere out of sight. Those smells and sounds quickly gave way as we readied our lunch. The goat cheese was tangy and fresh, the sausage slightly coarse and deliciously smoky, and the melon was the sweetest in all of France. It was the most perfect of meals.

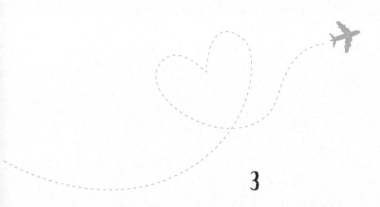

3

PORCUPINE AT THE PALIO

1997

My dedicated speed dial buttons filled up with doctors' numbers. One of my new physicians burrowed in again through my abdomen and carved off a few chunks of my liver for intense examination. Another snaked a camera down my throat and through my esophagus to have a looksee. Leaving no orifice unprobed, my gastroenterologist scheduled me for frequent colonoscopies. Another doctor periodically scanned the latest medical journals and papers to see if any new trials or studies might be promising.

I went online to start reading some of them myself to see if I could shed any further light on my situation. The first one started out like this:

> "We conducted a multicenter, randomized, double-blind, placebo-controlled trial. The diagnosis of primary sclerosing cholangitis required a chronic cholestatic liver disease of at least six months' duration; a serum alkaline phosphatase level at least 1.5 times the upper limit of normal; retrograde, operative, or percutaneous cholangiographic findings of intrahepatic or extrahepatic biliary-duct obstruction, beading, or narrowing consistent

with primary sclerosing cholangitis; and a liver biopsy in the previous three months with compatible findings. (New England Journal of Medicine 1997; 336:691, Ursodiol for Primary Schlerosing Cholangitis by Keith D. Lindor, M.D.)

I felt like I was back in college trying without success to decipher Beowulf in the original Old English. At least there was a CliffsNotes for Beowulf. With no offense to Dr. Lindor, I decided to wait for the movie adaptation of his work.

I visited my primary care physician Dr. Bart every couple of months and started taking some prescribed medicines as a precaution. Admittedly, my blood tests continued to show abnormally high liver scores, but with no symptoms the whole thing was merely an annoyance. I did learn that my liver is on the right side of my lower abdomen because Dr. Bart pushed and poked at it during examinations like he was kneading bread dough. Judging from his technique, it is a good thing he did not become a baker.

I tried to convince myself that Dr. Ford had made a mistake. I felt fine, working at least fifty to sixty stressful hours a week racing to court hearings, battling opponents at trials, berating witnesses at depositions. If I had the stamina to do that, I could not be that sick, could I?

*   *   *

1976

I can still picture the cute brown-haired girl seated in the front row of the lecture hall. It was Fall semester 1976, the first day of Sociology class at UCLA and students were ambling in wearing worn jeans with colorful sewn-on patches, grubby Earth shoes and faded T-shirts proclaiming allegiance to their favorite bands. She wore a conservative skirt and blouse, her make-up was carefully applied and every hair had been sprayed precisely in place, because she was headed to her job at the department store cosmetic counter directly after class. I did not notice her at first. I was busy scanning the back of the classroom to see if the professor had laid out any welcome cookies. He had not.

Someone was waving at me from the front row. It was Jeff, a friend of mine who I had not seen since high school. I walked over and took the seat next to him. He was talking to the cute girl on his right, both of them smiling and laughing. It was her. Jeff introduced us. Her name was Helene.

Over the next several weeks I often caught her staring at me in class. She always seemed to be smiling, not only with her mouth but also with her eyes. She often caught me staring at her in class. I thought about her all the time. One day I even forgot to eat lunch and I knew then that this was serious. I met up with her one night at the department store and made my move. She agreed to a date on Saturday night!

I picked her up in my backfiring, backbreaking, and only occasionally functioning Orient Blue Fiat Spider convertible. We stood in line to buy tickets for a Woody Allen movie, my arm around her shoulder, hugging her as close as I dared. I was so smitten with her that I even bought her a medium plain popcorn. If there was a second date, I might even consider getting her a popcorn with butter, which cost extra. After the movie, it was time to put her to the test. We went to La Barbera's Italian Restaurant in West Los Angeles, an institution among local students looking for the best pizza in town. Italian food was my go-to cuisine under such circumstances. Would she pick up her pizza with her hands or use a knife and fork? Would she slurp the spaghetti? Would she twirl her pasta clockwise or counterclockwise? The very existence of our future children depended on her next few moves.

Over the noise of the bustling restaurant we talked about the classes we were taking together, my job working as a file clerk in a small law office, the celebrities that she waited on at the cosmetic counter in the department store, and Helene offered to bring me cologne samples from work. She smiled and laughed easily. Most importantly, she ordered pepperoni pizza that she picked up with her hands. We were a perfect match!

We were inseparable after that, taking as many classes together as possible, studying together, and frequently ending up at a tiny local spaghetti hangout hiding behind a red awning. Classic torn red leather booths, scattered sawdust on the floor, checkered plastic tablecloths with ancient red sauce stains, unsterilized used Chianti bottles wrapped in straw that had been cleverly turned into salt and pepper shakers. To this day, I greatly miss that dump.

A few months after our first date her birthday was approaching. Little did I realize at the time that it was the first of many, many, many birthdays we would share together. I dug around in the Fiat for loose change, worked a couple of extra shifts at work, told her to get dressed up, and made reservations at Harry's Bar & American Grill in Century City. The restaurant was based on the famous Harry's Bar in Italy and was well known for its annual International Imitation Hemingway Competition. Whoever wrote the finest page of "really bad Hemingway" won a trip to Italy. But Hemingway was the last thing on my mind that night. When I went to her parents' house to pick her up she was the most beautiful girl I had ever seen, in her long blue dress with her short brown hair set off against a white crocheted shawl. I must concede that I looked exceedingly dapper myself in a white turtleneck sweater underneath a blue checkered sports coat. After her parents took a picture of us all dressed up, we hopped in the Fiat and prayed that it would not break down as we lurched our way to the restaurant. That night we dined on warm Italian bread, al dente pasta, a bottle of Harry's least expensive wine, and tiramisu for dessert. And we talked about what it would be like to visit Italy one day.

* * *

1996

A mere twenty years later, Helene and I were gazing out on the red tile roofs of Florence from Brunelleschi's cupola at the top of the Duomo, trying to catch our breath from scaling the 463 steps up from the *piazza* below. Our two jet-lagged kids were back at the hotel with a babysitter, prudently missing out on all the climbing. From our perch Helene tried to spot the Uffizi Gallery containing the greatest collection of Italian Renaissance art in the world including Michelangelo's Doni Tondo, Raphael's Madonna of the Goldfinch, Bacchus's Caravaggio and Helene's all-time favorite painting Botticelli's The Birth of Venus. She gushed about whether we should visit it first or go see the Accademia Gallery featuring Michelangelo's The David and some other old rocks. Meanwhile, I was scanning the horizon for Via Rosina, home to the very top sight in town, a spectacle that can make a grown man tremble and weep with joy—two open seats at Trattoria Mario.

The family-owned trattoria is small and cramped, open only for lunch, does not take reservations, hasn't been redecorated since it opened in 1953, does not take credit cards, requires you to sit at long tables on hard stools butt-cheek-to-butt-cheek with strangers who may or may not be drenched in cologne strong enough to stop a stampeding *Chianina* steer, has a limited butcher paper menu taped to a wall just far enough away to be unreadable unless you squint, usually requires you to wait outside for an hour or so alongside dozens of chain-smoking locals cranky from hunger, and doesn't suffer fools gladly. It also has the most succulent *Bistecca alla Fiorentina* around.

"Can't we grab a quick bite near the museum and go see The Birth of Venus first?" Helene pleaded.

"Not until I've seen The Birth of a Perfectly Seared T-Bone Steak," I said.

"Look at the line! We'll be waiting forever to get a table."

"Don't you worry. They know me here."

"That can't possibly be a good thing."

I opened the door to enter but froze in mid-step. My eyes involuntarily closed so as not to interfere with what was happening to my nose and ears. The tang of fruity olive oil, the slight acidic aroma of fresh tomatoes, beef fat striking a sizzling grill and magically transforming into savory smoke, lit cigarettes magically transforming into noxious smoke, all swirling together in a slow dance amid a cacophony of joyful diners.

"*Scusa!*"

An irritable sounding voice jolted me to attention. One of the diners was not so joyful. He was trying to leave and I was blocking the doorway. I let him squeeze by as I approached the Keeper of the List, a closely cropped young man wearing a white T-shirt and guarding the all-important waiting list.

"*Buon giorno*. About how long is the wait?" I asked him, using my hands for emphasis while hoping not to mistakenly signal some Italian curse word.

"How many people?" he asked.

"Two."

"One hour. Name?"

"Antonio." It was my "Starbucks name" while in Italy.

"Outside. We call you."

I rejoined my spouse outside in the throng on the sidewalk. We leaned against the faded buttermilk-colored stone building, slowly working our way up until we caught some shade under the turquoise and white striped awning. We killed time reading and rereading the dozens of newspaper articles, notices, stickers and bulletins pasted to the window. I wish I understood Italian. After shifting from one leg to the other and then back again for an hour and twenty-five minutes, we were finally called inside where the host pointed us in the direction of two empty stools across from each other in the middle of a communal table where half a dozen or so hungry diners were crammed in like Italian sausage in a pig's intestine casing. The woman to my right was so close to me that for a moment I thought we were sharing a kidney. But I had to keep my focus on the gentleman to my left whose wild gesticulations came alarmingly close to smacking me on the side of my head.

"I thought we were going to get our own table for two," Helene yelled to me above the din.

"This is a good table," I yelled back, "so long as the guy next to me doesn't stab me with his fork."

"They sure seat you close in here."

"That's part of the charm. By the way, you obviously did not get the dress code memo," I continued.

"You didn't tell me about any dress code. I look alright, don't I? This looks like a casual place."

"I'm shocked that they let you in without a black leather jacket. Please don't commit any more *faux pas* while we're here, ok?"

"Stop it. Where are our menus? I'm getting really hungry."

"It's on the wall over there," I said, pointing.

"I can't read that from here."

"Don't worry. I'll order for you."

"Not a chance. I'll end up with grilled oxen penis in a black truffle sauce."

"Don't be silly. Only a fool would order anything other than the house specialty here, *Bistecca alla Fiorentina*. A big fat T-bone specially prepared."

"I prefer a petite filet, as you well know."

"Their *Fiorentina* is world renown. It would be a culinary crime not to order one. They cut them in-house so that one order is over two pounds and feeds at least two people. We can also share a pasta with meat ragu. How's that?"

"I want to know exactly what kind of meat is in the ragu, right now before you order anything."

"Relax, its beef. No funny parts, I swear," I said with my fingers crossed under the table. We were wedged in so tight my fingers were the only part of me I could move.

"Make sure they cook the pasta soft all the way through."

"They only cook it one way, *al dente*."

"Is there anything else I should know?"

"Not yet. I'm keeping it a surprise."

"Great. I can't wait," she replied with a hint of familiar exasperation.

Our waitress squeezed mightily between the rows of diners until she finally reached us, yelling to us just slightly above the din: "*Buon giorno.* To eat?"

"We will have a *Bistecca alla Fiorentina* and a *Tortelli di patate al ragù,*" I yelled back.

"*Eccellente.*" She turned to my wife. "To drink?" she asked.

"I'll have a Coca-Co...."

Our waitress started to frown. "Noooooo!" I yelled to cut Helene off. "You can't order Coke here. They'll kick your butt right to the curb."

"Okay, okay. I didn't know," she said.

"Didn't I ask you to follow the rules just this once?" I pleaded. I turned to the waitress: "*Chianti, per favore.*" She gave Helene a stern look, wrote down our order and fled.

Now that we were settled in, I took a look around. The woman to my right was cutting into a T-bone steak the size of Sardinia. The lively gentleman to my left was sharing a *Bistecca alla Fiorentina* with another man across the table. Chewing did not seem to slow his spirited conversation, only now he had a steak knife in his right hand that he waved wildly in broad arcs that regularly passed within a millimeter of my jugular vein. With his other hand, he periodically punched the air with his fork to literally make a point. As I tried to make myself as small as possible, that familiar voice cut through the growing clangor like, well like a steak knife through a jugular vein.

"I just realized that the waitress didn't ask us how we wanted our steak prepared," hollered Helene.

"That's because they only prepare steaks one way here," I hollered back.

"Well, you know I like my steaks cooked well-done."

"Oh yes, I know."

Just a few minutes later our waitress bullied her way hips first through the stool-balancing mob to deliver our food. She not so delicately plopped our *Bistecca alla Fiorentina* between us in the middle of the table, causing the scarred wood to sag just a bit. The perfectly seared sizzling slab stood at least three fingers high and was a certified beauty. Gentleman that I am, I offered Helene the first cut of the steak. She took one look at the beef's ruby red interior and recoiled.

"That thing is still mooing," she said.

"It's rare. Seared on the outside and cool in the center. That's the only proper way to cook *Bistecca alla Fiorentina,*" I explained.

"They must have cooked this by holding a match underneath it for a few seconds."

"Would you please just try it?"

She cut a tiny piece off of the very end of the steak that was slightly less bloody and spooned herself a large helping of pasta. I moved in for a close-up inspection. This steak had better marbling than the Trevi fountain. Perfectly aligned grill marks and a ring of sizzling fat socked in the juices. The smoky crust had just the right amount of salty goodness, giving way to the cool red beefy center. It took a manly man to devour that entire steak but I was more than up to the task. The perfect lunch. Helene stuck mostly to the pasta and wonderfully chewy bread. Finally, I looked up and asked her: "Are you finished with your meal?"

"I am."

"Good, we have to hurry or we'll miss out on our afternoon snack."

"You've got to be kidding."

"You know I never kid about something as serious as food."

* * *

Caffè Rivoire sits on the corner of the famous Piazza della Signoria in Florence. The L-shaped piazza is the center of civic activity in the city. Ringed by amazing sculptures, the crenellated tower of the Palazzo Vecchio, and the Uffizi Gallery, it is the perfect place to sit at an outside table and observe the parade of fashion-conscious locals and camera-toting tourists from around the world. Far more importantly, it is also the place to delight in what is perhaps the greatest hot chocolate in the world.

Helene has a sweet tooth. More specifically, she has the very same sweet tooth that she had when she was ten years old. Only at the risk of serious bodily injury should you stand between Helene and cotton candy, caramel apples, snow cones, ice cream drumsticks, candy corn, Cracker Jack, or Peeps marshmallows in the shape of ducks. Helene received a lifetime ban from the Texas State Fair for wreaking havoc at the deep-fried chocolate sheet cake stand. Speaking of chocolate, I have been dragged into well over a thousand fudge shops on several continents. Helene will stand at the fudge counter, spending several minutes bending this way and that with her nose up against the glass to scrutinize every flavor of fudge on each shelf. Then she buys plain chocolate fudge. Every time.

As much fun as it is endlessly torturing Helene over blood red slabs of beef, I hoped that for a least one time we could share a moment of mutual gastronomic bliss. Was it even possible? I was determined to give it my best shot.

Helene and I grabbed a prime outside table protected by a large cream-colored umbrella. It would cost more to dine at a table than standing inside at the bar but it was well worth it. Particularly because I would deduct the additional cost from my wife's daily meal stipend. A black-vested waiter strolled over to take our order. He mumbled a brusque *"buon giorno"* and stood there with his pencil and pad at the ready. No, "Hi, my name is Jason and I'll be your server today." No, "Would you like to join our frequent diner club so that you can earn points for a free stuffed potato skin appetizer?" This guy was ready to get down to business and so was I.

"Two *cioccolate calde con panna montata,*" I said.

He strode off, appropriately impressed with my impeccable accent.

"Pig's blood shake, right?" Helene asked. I don't think she was kidding.

"I ordered you the nectar of the gods with whipped cream."

"Yeah, I can't wait."

Surprisingly, she didn't have to wait too long. A tray with two whipped cream topped china cups and saucers made their way to our table along with tiny silver spoons and napkins.

"This looks good and smells amazing. What's the trick?"

"Why do you always think the worst of me?" I replied, avoiding her question.

"By the time I could answer that we'd be back home."

"Dig in," I said. I wanted to see her face when she tried that first taste.

She tipped the edge of her spoon into the cup like she was barely dipping her toe in the ocean, tried a miniscule taste of the whipped cream and nodded with begrudging approval. She dug in deeper and her tiny spoon stood at attention by itself in the cup. Emboldened, she tried a small taste of the chocolate. "Oooooh!" was all she could muster as her eyes started to roll back in her head. As soon as she regained partial control of her limbs she dove in again.

"This is incredible! It's like a thick liquid chocolate bar, only chocolatier if that's even possible," she cooed. She attacked the contents of the cup like General Patton took Sicily during World War II, showing no mercy. "My god, I never knew it could be like this." Her voice had lowered into a seductive moan.

"Alright, don't get overheated," I said.

"I love you so much," she purred.

"I love you too, sweetie," I said with pride.

"I was talking to my hot chocolate," she explained without a hint of shame. "But I love you too," she hastily added.

"Never mind. But please hurry up, we'll be late for dinner."

* * *

To call the Palio di Siena a horse race is to call Prosciutto di San Daniele a slab of ham. Twice a year, the outer ring of the Piazza del Campo in the center of Siena is layered with dirt for a no-holds-barred bareback race that dates back to the seventeenth century. The first of ten horses to circle the track three times, with or without its rider, earns eternal glory for its *contrade* or neighborhood. Riders can use their whips made out of dried and stretched bull penises to flog a rival horse or if they prefer to whip another rider. Heck, why not do both? Everything is fair game in this race where riders are routinely thrown down beneath the trampling hoofs and where horses are often injured or killed trying to circle the mis-shapen track. Up to seventy-five thousand spectators cram shoulder to shoulder in the center of the piazza to watch the horses race around them. You must arrive many hours early if you want access to the piazza on racing day. It is scorching hot. There are no bathrooms. You may not bring chairs. You may not reserve a space. You may not place children on your shoulders because it will block the view of others, although if someone passes out from the heat it is perfectly acceptable to stand on top of them to get a better view of the race. This potential sweaty mosh pit did not appear to be the perfect spot to stand for many hours with our two kids, particularly Jessica who was only nine years old.

Fortunately, the race can also be viewed by a select few from balconies attached to private apartments that ring the outer edge of the piazza. But how does one obtain an invitation to view the race from one of the private homes? Today, anyone with a laptop can score tickets online. But back in the good old days when we visited it took a bit more creativity. I wrote a letter to the Siena CCI Chamber of Commerce asking for information about acquiring tickets to see the Palio. The Chamber responded with a list containing names and telephone numbers of Sienese families that owned apartments overlooking the piazza.

I telephoned the first family on the list. Stealing from the "Useful Phrases" portion of my Fodor's Italy guidebook, I tried to explain that I was calling from Los Angeles to inquire about viewing the Palio from their balcony. The woman that answered the phone hung up. I had a similar experience with the next name.

It occurred to me that perhaps I might have better luck if I asked an Italian friend to place the call. I enlisted the help of a colleague in my office named Piero who had relatives in Rome, claimed to know some Italian and was even an amateur opera singer. Using the speaker phone he called the next name on the list. It was then that I learned that Piero's mastery of Italian consisted of placing an "a" or "o" on the end of English words and adding in some Spanish for emphasis.

"*Buon giorno*," he said when a man answered the phone. We were obviously off to a smooth start. Piero continued in his usual booming opera voice: "I am callinga to visita you fora *Il* Palio."

"*Non capisco*," the man replied.

Piero muted the phone and turned to me: "Now we're making progress." He unmuted and continued on the phone: "*Il* Palio."

"*Si.*"

"Tickets, err, *biglietti* fora your *balcone*?"

"*Non capisco.*" Click.

Piero turned back to me: "He's going to be out of town that day. Let's try the next name."

We were well down on the list and Piero was working up quite a sweat when a pleasant-sounding woman named Signora Bianchi answered the phone. Luck was with us that day as Signora Bianchi spoke more English than Piero spoke Italian. Curiously, Piero was now in a groove and continued to translate Signora Bianchi's English words for me, even though I understood her better than I understood him.

"She said that she's a willing to sella you four tickets to her third-floor balcony overlooking the Palio," translated Piero into something resembling English.

"Ask her the price of the tickets."

She quoted us a price and I used my calculator to convert the lira into dollars. I ran the numbers a second time. "She doesn't understand," I told Piero. "Tell her I just want to buy four tickets to see the Palio from her balcony. I don't want to buy her entire apartment building,"

"That's the price she wants for the tickets," Piero confirmed.

"I can bribe every jockey in the race for that amount," I groused.

"She says she's firm on the price," said Piero.

"Ask her if she was in that heist movie The Italian Job. Nah, never mind. Tell her I'll take the tickets."

I sold the claiming rights to our next two children on eBay and forwarded the money to Signora Bianchi. I received a return letter instructing me to go to her family's store on the Piazza del Campo the morning of the race where I would receive tickets and be escorted to her apartment. She also asked whether my family preferred snails, goose, tortoise, owl or porcupine. Knowing full well how prickly my wife is regarding meals, I wrote back that we all enjoyed *istrice*, medium rare and preferably with the quills removed. I wondered to myself what Super Tuscan wine she intended to serve with the porcupine. Well, for the price we were paying at least we would be well fed.

* * *

We arrived a day before the Palio, renting an apartment in a renovated ancient villa in nearby Castellina in Chianti northwest of Siena. Surveying the vista through our apartment window, Helene and I gazed out over undulating hills striped with meandering rows of vines as far as one could see.

"This is just gorgeous here," she said.

"Nothing but the finest for you, sweetness," I replied.

"Let's go out on the patio and enjoy that cool breeze."

"Sounds good to me."

As Matthew and Jessica played inside, Helene and I stretched out on two lounges set out on the patio and took in the

Chianti-scented countryside. We nibbled on some local cheese, watched a large brown hare dance between the rows of vines on the hillside, and soon succumbed to the serenity and a nap.

Race day was not quite so serene. That morning I presented myself at Signora Bianchi's family's store on the piazza. A middle-aged man weighed down by enough gold chains and rings to recoat the dome of the Siena Cathedral twice over greeted me with an overly friendly *"buon giorno"* and started to pull out trays of rings for me to inspect. I introduced myself, explaining in a combination of English and "helpful phrases" Italian that I was not interested in any jewelry but rather had come to get access to Signora Bianchi's apartment. The man, who apparently spoke no English, became quite agitated. I calmly but firmly explained again. Our interaction was growing louder when a shopper in the store who seemed to know the gentleman interceded and offered to interpret.

"I purchased tickets back home for my family of four to see the Palio from Signora Bianchi's apartment," I explained to the woman. "I was instructed to come here to pick up the tickets and be escorted to the apartment. This gentleman became upset for some reason."

"Let me see if I can help," she said.

She spoke to the man in Italian. He replied emphatically and pointed angrily at me.

"He says that he doesn't know who you are and that you made vulgar comments about his cousin Signora Bianchi."

"I did no such thing. I merely want to pick up my tickets that we already paid for," I explained again.

She tried him again, resulting in more gesticulating. "He says if you bought tickets, you must present your voucher."

"I paid for the tickets but there was never a discussion of any voucher with Signora Biachi."

She spoke to the man again in Italian but after a few more words the man crossed his arms in defiance. "He says no voucher, no tickets," the woman translated.

"I have a confirming letter from Signora Bianchi," which I held up and then handed to the woman to read. She tried to hand it to him to inspect but he barely glanced at it and remained with his arms firmly crossed.

They exchanged more words. The woman then explained to me: "He says it is in English which he doesn't understand. I read it to him but he says if you don't have a voucher, you need to get out."

"I'm not leaving without the tickets," I said, planting my feet.

Thus commenced a stare down. The man stood there with his arms folded across the multitude of gold chains that were the only things keeping his massive chest hair from exploding through the exposed part of his shirt and filling the room. I folded my arms and stared back for almost a full minute. I was laser focused and was not going to budge. A wild Tuscan horse could not have dragged me out of that shop without the tickets. The man finally broke down and blinked. He pushed four tickets across the counter and begrudgingly pointed to an apartment door across the way.

With the precious tickets in my pocket, I went back to collect my beloved family. Although it was morning and the Palio festivities did not start until late in the afternoon, a crowd was already forming in the center of the piazza, jostling to get in prime position before the piazza was closed off for the race. We started to work our way back through the narrow cobblestone streets to shop for some supplies for the long day. As we walked colorful flags with depictions of different animals were flying above every shop and apartment, locals were adorned with animal scarves, and a feverous festive mood pervaded the streets. The color and design of the flags changed as we walked through different neighborhoods and we learned that each *contrade* had its own nickname, animal symbol, and horse to represent it in the race.

The streets were packed with locals and tourists alike waving flags, chanting and cheering. Drums pounded rhythmically as marching bands passed by, participants in the pre-race festivities wearing ceremonial medieval costumes joined in the fun, and Sienese children shouted down from open apartment windows while waving scarves, hats and anything else they could find. We found ourselves swimming upstream against the crowd without much luck. Suddenly the crowd pushed against the ancient buildings lining the street, parting to allow a parading group to pass by including one of the racehorses dressed in its costumed finest. We followed the crowd, that followed the horse, that followed the marchers, who all ultimately stopped in front of an ancient church. A priest appeared on the church balcony and gave a benediction over the horse and rider, drawing cheers from the already high-spirited crowd. A similar fete was no doubt taking place in nine other *contrades* that morning.

As the crowds grew thicker than Piero's fake Italian accent, we made our way to Signora Bianchi's apartment and used the ancient brass knocker on the centuries-old dual wooden doors. Signora Bianchi opened the door and warmly invited us in. It was clear that her side of the family had received all of the charm. She escorted us up a stairway to a third-floor balcony overlooking the piazza. The balcony was approximately three feet wide and fifteen feet long, "protected" only by a three-foot-high ornately carved railing that was thirty percent wrought iron and seventy percent rust. Lean too far over the crumbling railing and we might wind up bareback on a horse that was already pissed off from being whipped with a bull's penis. Lined up neatly on the balcony were ten or so tiny metal folding chairs. The only thing keeping the balcony attached to the ancient cracked plaster building was centuries of pigeon poop. Would the decrepit balcony hold all four of us? Surely it could not possibly hold the weight of ten people.

We were the first to arrive and inched our way over to sit down in four of the seats before any of us plunged to our death. It was a tight fit. There was no room for even a cup holder. I assumed Signora Bianchi was planning a buffet downstairs for later. The balcony was without a speck of shade and as the sun bore down on us, I started to daydream about antipasto and a cooling glass of Vernaccia. *Salumi. Crostini di fegato. Proscuitto crudo.* Pecorino Toscano cheese. A smattering of local Leccino olives, perhaps.

Jolted out of my reverie by sweat running down my forehead, I cautiously left my seat and threw my back against the wall as I crab-walked across the balcony to the doorway. I followed the now entrancing scent of garlic and olive oil down the stairway to inquire of Signora Bianchi when supper might be served. She was seated with some friends at a floral sofa in the living area around a large platter of freshly made bruschetta and drinking what looked to be a crisp white Vermentino. Not a bad choice.

Signora Bianchi looked up at me and smiled. "*Si?*" she asked.

"Signora Bianchi, might I inquire as to when we will be eating?" I asked.

"*Scusami?* I don't understand?"

All of a sudden her command of English faded. "Food and drinks? Antipasto?"

"Ah, antipasto! No antipasto today."

No antipasto today? What day might we expect it? Tomorrow after we had left Siena? This may be the first time in recorded history that Italians gathered at a celebration with no antipasto.

"What about the porcupine?" I asked with trepidation.

"Porcupine?"

"The *istrice?*"

"Ah, *istrice!*" she exclaimed with a smile. Finally, a look of recognition. She continued: "*Istrice,* I bring to you on *il balcone.*"

"*Eccellente!*" I said. We were finally making some progress and I knew Helene would be excited.

I climbed up the stairway and carefully maneuvered back to my seat on the narrow balcony.

"Don't worry, food will be here soon," I reassured my loving family.

"What are we getting to eat?" Matthew asked.

"One of your favorites. *Istrice.*"

"What's *istrice?*"

"It tastes just like chicken," I said.

"I prefer my chicken to taste like chicken," Helene chimed in. "The last time you told me something tasted like chicken I was gagging for a week."

"It's a local delicacy. Porcupine."

"Please tell me you're joking," she gasped.

"Not really, and you should feel lucky to get that. Signora Bianchi and her friends scarfed down all the bruschetta, but she assures me that the porcupine is on its way."

"If any porcupine shows up here, you'll be picking quills out of your you-know-what for the rest of the trip!"

Charming.

A few minutes later Signora Bianchi arrived with four small *contrade* flags featuring a golden crowned porcupine on a background of red, blue, white and black, the colors of the *Istrice contrade*.

"What's this?" I asked.

"You wave, for the race," she said, and with great enthusiasm she shook the flags in front of my face. She handed a flag to each of us and disappeared down the stairway.

Matthew, Jessica and Helene were the only ones smiling.

A little while later additional guests began arriving on *il balcone*. A group of four came over to us, nodded in greeting, showed us their tickets and indicated with their hands that we were sitting in their seats. There were no numbers on the chairs and I did not expect assigned seats in this informal setting. However, congenial fellow that I am, I motioned for our family to move down four seats so that the new group would not get their Speedos in a twist by being deprived of their favorite seats. Yet, as soon as we sat down again a group of four women arrived and similarly pointed to their tickets and our new seats, indicating that we were once again in the wrong place.

No cupholders, no antipasto, I was expected to chew on a flag instead of roasted loin of porcupine, and now I was being bounced around the seating area like a *bocce* ball. I showed the new group our tickets and shrugged my shoulders. Whatever the seating formalities were, I had no clue. A few moments later Signora Bianchi arrived yet again but this time she left her smile downstairs. She asked to see our tickets and then pointed at some fine print in Italian at the bottom of the stubs: "Standing tickets, no seats. You stand here." She pointed to the six inches of space behind the folding chairs.

"My shoes are longer than that!" I said.

"Standing."

She blew a strand of hair out of her eyes, exhaled a second exasperated breath and went downstairs. The woman who had been waiting to be seated with her three accomplices assumed a look of smug satisfaction as we got up to go stand behind the seats. Hours to go until the race, in the blazing sun, with no food or drink, and two small children, each of us digging our fingernails into the ancient plaster of the tilting building to keep from being blown off the balcony by a passing breeze. The only thing that kept me going was looking forward to having a chat with Piero after I returned home.

Much later in the afternoon and well after we had lost all feeling in our hands and legs, the pre-race *Corteo Storico* historical costume parade commenced. Into the piazza marched hundreds of representatives of the various *contrades*, dressed in traditional medieval costumes bearing their own unique color combinations. They carried flags of the *contrades* on long poles, which they flung at each other in a long-distance aerial ballet, skillfully catching the flags and then tossing them back in concert with rhythmic drummers. Each *contrade* tried to outdo the others with the height, distance and accuracy of their throws.

"Go long and try to catch my *Istrice* flag," I suggested to Helene, who had lost her sense of humor while clinging for dear life to the building. She was too paralyzed to even roll her eyes.

When the *Istrice contrade* representatives finally appeared in the parade, we used our remaining strength to cheer and wave our flags. If my flag happened to repeatedly hit the head of the woman seated in front of me, I am sure it was accidental.

The flag tossers down below were now joined by costumed riders on costumed horses, drummers, jousters, trumpeters, swordsmen, and religious authorities on wagons pulled by teams of oxen. The pre-race parade was almost overwhelming in its rush of colors, pageantry, skill and tradition. By the time it ended we were all exhausted and the race had not even started yet.

Once the course had been cleared a firecracker signaled that the horses were finally entering the track, but the loud bang was immediately drowned out by the roar of the crowd. The horses had barely lined up for the start when the race began as they leaped forward as one. Before a single circuit had been completed, one rider had already been knocked to the ground while his horse continued on in the race. Whips were flying at the horses and at other riders. On the second lap one of the horses smashed its head into a meagerly padded corner of the inside makeshift railing and went down in a clump. The other horses leaped over it. By the final lap, several riders were down and had been trampled, at least two horses were down, but the race carried on. The *Istrice contrade's* horse ran a good race, but ultimately the *Oca* goose *contrade's* horse won by a beak. When the victorious *Oca* rider crossed the finish line he was swarmed by members of his *contrade* as he leaped from his horse into their adoring arms like he was a rock star crowd-surfing at a concert. The young rider appeared to be a kid of maybe eighteen. His beaming smile could be seen clear across the piazza, showing off a moment of pride that will no doubt never be surpassed in his lifetime. In his short life he had already achieved a measure of greatness that he would brag about to his children and grandchildren for decades to come. He had successfully left his permanent mark on an enduring tradition. Almost as important, he would never again have to pay for a drink in his *contrade*.

I will not quickly forget the display of agility, athleticism and tenacity in the face of great danger that I witnessed that day. And that was just with respect to me clinging to the balcony for hours on end. The riders were impressive as well.

The kids loved the flag tossing and learning about the various *contrade* animal symbols. The race and the accompanying shouting from the crowd was a severe bolt of adrenaline that was over in an instant. The parade, combined with the race, was the greatest spectacle I ever witnessed. But my most lasting memory of that day was the look of pure ecstasy on the face of the winning rider when he dove off his horse into the outstretched arms of his friends and family.

For some there were toasts to be made and drinks to be downed. For others wagers to be collected. For most, all of the above. As for the exhausted Ross family, we were hungry. Tens of thousands of people were all flooding out of the piazza at the same time. There was no time to lose if we were to grab a table at a restaurant. I was certainly not counting on Signore Bianchi to offer any post-race snacks.

We joined the crowd below and streamed out looking for a restaurant with an available table. A friendly looking trattoria just off the main street invited us in with the smell of a long-simmering sauce and the sight of hanging strings of garlic and freshly made pastas. We took our seats at a sagging wooden table with simple wooden chairs that sat unevenly on the tiled floor. Some pizza Quattro Stagioni from the wood burning oven to start? Yes, please. This classic pizza is divided into four sections, each representing one of the four seasons. Artichokes for spring, tomatoes and basil for summer, mushrooms for the fall, and ham for winter. Then the specialty of the house was delivered to the table. Pappardelle with *cinghiale* wild boar ragu that had been simmering for hours. At that moment, it tasted even better than loin of porcupine.

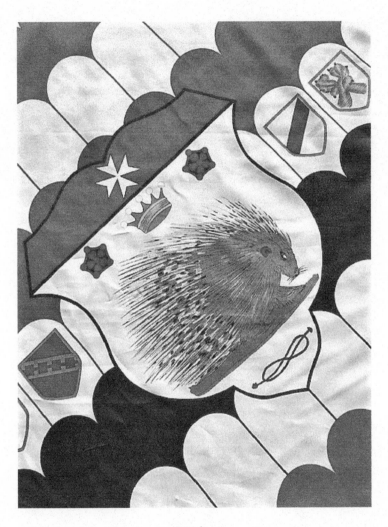

Istrice

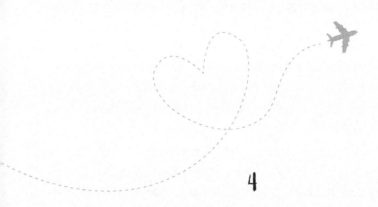

4

A SUNNY MIDNIGHT MEAL

1998

If you ask him, my father will steadfastly deny that he is superstitious. But if his baseball team is on a winning streak, you can be sure that he will wear the same socks every day. If his dog gets up and moves about during a football game while his team is winning, he will grab it and put it back in its original place so that it does not jinx the game. He taught me that wearing the color of the rival team at any time is awfully bad luck. To this day you will not find a single stitch of red clothing in my closet, although of course I am not superstitious either.

My father does readily admit to believing in premonitions. He has retold the story many times of the night when his mother leaped out of bed screaming that something terrible had happened to his older brother. Shortly thereafter they learned that his brother had been injured on Iwo Jima that very night.

It seemed innocent enough when a family friend gave my parents a special candle to celebrate my birth. It was well over a foot tall and thick enough to require two hands to circumnavigate its circumference. The white wax was decorated on one side by blue numbers that ran top to bottom from one to twenty-one. On each of my birthdays, after the smaller birthday candles atop the cake had been blown out and the cake devoured, my father would light the larger candle and allow it to flicker in the kitchen until the recently reached milestone number had melted away, at which time my special birthday candle was extinguished and put away to await the following year. The burning candle made me feel just a bit more special on each birthday.

Not so much for my father. When my birthday candle was taken down from the closet in anticipation of my fourth birthday, a large crack was visible cutting directly through the number twelve. No one knew how it happened, but my father was absolutely convinced that the crack marked an evil omen that something terrible would befall me on my twelfth birthday. He did not reveal this to anyone until I was well into my teenage years, when he admitted that he worried about this prophecy constantly until my twelfth birthday had passed without incident. For good measure, he continued to worry for an additional few years just in case the candle's internal clock was off.

My birthday candle tradition finally burned itself out and expired by natural causes on my twenty-first birthday. But my father was not finished worrying. He was always a considerable worrier, particularly where the well-being of his family was involved. After I married and started my own family, he moved with my mother about a hundred miles away to Oceanside, California. Whenever I visit him, he insists that the moment I return home from the drive back to Los Angeles I call him to let him know that I arrived safety. If I fail to call, he will stay awake waiting. This tradition has continued unabated.

My father hates that I travel. It does not matter the location or means of transportation. Planes, trains and automobiles will crash in a massive fireball, whatever ship I am on will sink to the very bottom of the deepest part of the ocean. Thieves, bandits and terrorists lie in wait around every corner thirsting to commit mayhem. Foreign countries will erupt in riots and revolutions if I travel there. He claims he does not sleep at all when I am on a vacation, whether I am away for three days or three weeks. I learned not to alert him of my travel plans too far in advance, trying to lessen his total worry time. I do not know whether that works or not, but I try not to give him more than two weeks' notice of any trip. Of course, I am required to call him the minute I touch ground on each return home from vacation. Otherwise, he will worry in perpetuity. Which he does anyway.

When I learned of my potentially fatal liver disease, one of my greatest concerns was how to deal with my father.

"I've decided not to tell my father or mother about my liver," I told Helene.

"Are you sure?" she replied.

"He already worries if I tell him I'm going to the market. What's he going to do if he learns I have a liver disease with no cure?"

"I understand."

"I don't want to tell your family either, in case they leak the news. This way my liver won't be the sole topic of conversation every time we get together for a family event."

"Okay."

"There's no reason to worry everyone when nothing might happen for years. We can deal with it when the time comes. I might even die of old age."

"I won't say a thing."

*   *   *

1998

One hundred and fifty kilometers per hour. The forest whizzed by in a blur of green like freshly picked dill weed going through a Thermomix food processor. One seventy-five. The entire above average looking Ross family was moving quickly. This in and of itself violated most of the laws of physics. Moving in on two hundred kilometers per hour. We sat back in our airplane-style seats watching the overhead speedometer on our high speed X2 train for the three-hour trip from Stockholm to a small village in central Sweden. If my father knew we were on a high-speed train he would never close his eyes again. But our family's summer vacation had officially commenced.

I first met Viktor a few years earlier on business in Los Angeles. After our final meeting, as he was readying to depart L.A. and return to his home in Sweden, he offered up the seemingly obligatory "if you are ever out my way please come and stay at our place." When I travel, I always studiously refrain from making this offer to others out of fear that some long-forgotten acquaintance, along with his extended family and pet llama, might actually show up at my doorstep. I graciously thanked Viktor and falsely assured him that I would keep his offer in mind.

It turned out that Viktor was not only alarmingly genuine but persistent as well. Over the next couple of years he contacted me periodically to reiterate his invitation for our family to come stay with him on his family's homestead in rural Sweden, particularly if we could time our visit during his village's Midsummer festival. I politely declined, citing the crush of work I had to do in Los Angeles. Viktor told me that his family's property sat next to a lake and there would be fresh perch to eat. I told him that I wished I could join him but the timing just was not right. He told me there would be pickled herring in abundance and fresh baked pastries for the festival. I began to weaken.

"And at midnight on Midsummer we cook a big traditional dinner over an open fire with the sun blazing overhead," he said.

"What time should we be there?" I asked.

* * *

"You signed me up to be part of a pagan festival?" Helene asked incredulously. "This may be a new low, even for you."

"Those freezing winters get awful long in Sweden. Midsummer is an ancient pagan celebration of the birth of summer. Most importantly, there will be food and dancing," I promised.

"Yeah, and I suppose you offered me up as the human sacrifice for the occasion?"

"Only if you keep this up, sweetness," I said with a smile. "Look, the Midsummer celebration has been taking place every June on the summer solstice since before Christianity. We'll be in Viktor's home village, we get to watch the festival, and we'll probably be the only tourists for a hundred miles around. Then we share in a midnight meal under the sun."

"You mean under the stars?"

"No, it's the longest day of the year and the sun never sets."

"Do me a favor. Don't tell me what the pagans eat at this meal. I want to be surprised."

"No problem."

* * *

Viktor met us at the red tile roof train station and drove us the short distance to the property that has been owned by his family since the 1600's. Along the way the unspoiled emerald countryside was dotted with *falu* red barns, grazing sheep and fat lazy cows. Viktor's family home turned out to be a fascinating compound consisting of a cottage built hundreds of years ago, two ancient barns, a main contemporary house, and a couple of roughly hewn wood cabins. A canoe and small boat lay overturned on the grass, waiting to be put to work. A crude handmade fence comprised of cut tree branches set out the property boundaries.

We exchanged greetings with Viktor's many family members who had returned home from various parts of Sweden for the festival. The Ross family got settled quickly into one of the old cabins, which featured double-decked timbered beds with modesty curtains. Not a moment too soon we were called to lunch. Viktor's parents prepared a traditional mid-day meal for Midsummer including pickled herrings and potato salad. To Helene's great relief, they also made delicious homemade Swedish meatballs, a green salad and home-baked bread. After enjoying a second helping of everything, I considered asking if I could move into the cabin permanently.

While Viktor went outside to demonstrate some of the finer points of soccer to Matthew and Jessica out on an expansive lawn that separates the cabins, Helene and I slid into our cabin for a brief rest. Victor had warned us that we would need to conserve some energy for later. He was so right.

Following our nap, it was time to prepare the *majstång* or maypole to be placed near the main house. The maypole consisted of a cut and trimmed tree trunk about ten feet high with two wooden crosses set on a beam near the top. Matthew helped decorate the maypole by wrapping it with birch leaves to bring good fortune and health to the occupants of the house and to their animals. Jessica, Helene and I plucked yellow and purple wildflowers by the lake to help make colorful round wreaths to hang on the maypole. Viktor told Helene and I that the long poles and circular wreaths prepared during Midsummer had mating significance to the pagans. Helene shot me a look, wondering what else I had not told her.

I found out that making wreaths can be exhausting, but Viktor's parents came through once again. A snack break to enjoy a buttery homemade rhubarb tart with vanilla sauce! This was definitely shaping up to be my kind of a festival. I heard a motorboat engine roar to life as Viktor, Matthew and Jessica sped out onto the lake to see what could be caught for dinner. A little while later the boat returned with Matthew proudly holding up several prized perch. Jessica, who was now eleven, came running up to me as soon as the boat reached land.

"Daddy, those fish we caught were staring at me in the boat!" she cried out with concern.

"They were just happy to see you," I reassured her.

The decoration of the maypole at the house turned out to be just a warm-up for the major celebration in town. It was time to get dressed and leave for the main event. For many of the men it was "come as you are," which included various sizes of ill-concealed flasks as the main fashion accessory. Others, including our entire chic family, wore wildflower covered wreaths on their heads— something I do not often do when dining at Spago in Los Angeles.

When the women of the house emerged for the short walk into the town center, they had changed into traditional Midsummer folk costumes in a style that had been worn at the festival for countless generations. Homemade black skirts, red aprons with gold embroidery, hanging red and gold pockets, white shirts and red vests, red stockings, black shoes with gold trim. The colors of the village for as long as anyone could remember.

As we started walking to the center of town we joined a growing informal parade of townsfolk working their way on the same path that had no doubt been used for centuries. Male fiddlers appeared wearing traditional gold pants bunched just below the knee, red-topped stockings that leaked out of the top of tall shiny black boots, and long white shirts with dark vests festooned with bright gold buttons. A strumming guitarist and a man playing the fiddle-like *nyckelharpa* joined in as traditional Swedish music filled the air. The crowd parted to make way for a long line of festively adorned women walking twenty feet apart carrying a seemingly mile long rope woven of fresh greenery to wrap around the town's maypole like a barber pole. As we reached the town center I got my first look at the main white wooden maypole itself, a behemoth at least seventy-five feet long and well over a foot in diameter laying horizontally and supported by sawhorses. When the Swedes design a phallic symbol they do not mess around!

With the women's hard work of carrying the long greenery into town completed, the men took over and wrapped the green rope around the maypole while affixing a leafy covered cross and rings near one end. The pole, which was still laying across the sawhorses, was topped with a wooden rooster and the blue and gold Swedish flag. I had watched the women spending the day cooking, gathering greenery and wildflowers, getting dressed up, and carrying the decorations into town. I could not imagine how the village women were going to hoist that massive maypole upright without a hundred-foot-high crane and hoist.

They were not.

Without warning I was ripped away from my precious family and dragged into a chainless gang of dozens of men placed one behind the other along the maypole. Once everyone was in position, an ex-drill sergeant who had been dishonorably discharged from the Swedish special forces for unspecified acts of excessive brutality gave the order and we were forced to lift the maypole up from the sawhorses and carry it over our heads to lay it down into ready position in the center of the square. The pole was now properly decorated in the center of the square, but it was still lying flat on the ground. How was a seventy-five-foot-long solid wooden pole that weighed more than a Volvo eighteen-wheeler filled with herring going to be set upright by a ragtag group of mostly intoxicated Swedes and one American with a bad back?

Under bellowed orders that would make a Viking warrior soil himself, the men at one end of the maypole groaned as one and lifted it up over their heads as far as they could reach. Even for the unusually tall Swedes this only achieved an eight-foot heft of one end of the pole. It would not be long before I learned the rest of the terrible secret. From seemingly nowhere the real instruments of torture appeared. Long wooden sticks of various sizes bound together near the top to form an X shape that could cradle a massive maypole. Starting at one end, two men on either side of the maypole maneuvered the sticks under the very top of the maypole and grunting on cue heaved upward. The maypole jerked a few degrees upright. The two men would hold it in place as another set of men rushed just underneath the first two men to heft up the pole with another set of sticks. This process was repeated until dozens of men with similar sticks were wrestling with the maypole, groaning, heaving and inching the maypole slowly skyward. Very slowly. Over twenty minutes later the unforgiving sun had stubbornly refused to set, instead continuing to baste us from overhead. Should even a single man falter in his appointed position, the entire pole could come crashing down and no doubt result in an embarrassing folktale to be told to future generations of Swedes about the interloping weak-armed American who caused the entire male population of the town to be crushed to death. I hoped my father was not having a premonition about this.

Fortunately for the future of the town, I held my own despite this being my first erection (of a maypole). I did notice that a number of my fellow prisoners down the line were beginning to weave from side to side as they struggled to keep their sticks aloft, so to speak. At first, I thought this was from fatigue but I learned differently when the grizzled older Swede next to me thrust a flask in my face. "For fuel," he slurred in my general direction. What was in the flask? Perhaps some fine Karlsson's Gold Vodka? I took a gulp and violently started to cough up a lung and part of my spleen. Had I misunderstood and the fluid was actually tractor fuel? My guess was remarkably close. It turned out to be homemade potato aquavit that had been filtered through the rusted radiator of a 1972 Saab that I saw up on blocks in a nearby front yard. I passed the flask on down the line for the next victim.

Strangely fortified by the fiery home brew and under renewed extreme threats by the drill sergeant, the manly crew gave one final gasp and thrust as the maypole lurched upwards. It not only became completely vertical but its momentum caused it to momentarily threaten to career down the other side, sending a number of women and children scurrying out of the way for their lives. After a series of dramatic wobbles that brought "oohs" and "aahs" from the crowd, the pole softly nestled into place perfectly upright. A joyful cry arose from those in the crowd still strong enough to speak, applause rang through the square, and musical instruments came to life.

Ring dancing erupted as the costumed villagers paired up and danced around the maypole. This culminated in the "frog dance" *Små Grodorna*, a cursed tradition that has stunted the growth of many a Swedish child and filled the coffers of Swedish mental health care practitioners throughout the country. Adults and children alike hop about like frogs, singing and using their hands to pretend to wave frog ears and tails, even though those body parts have always been completely absent from frogs. I received no explanation.

At least the mayor stopped hopping long enough to give a well-received short speech about the harvest, the importance of preserving ancient customs and local dialects, and noted the welcome presence at the festivities of the strong good-looking American and his family. Babies were kissed, flasks were emptied and refilled, the fiddlers fiddled, and the pole dancers pole danced.

Midnight approached as the maypole festivities eventually wound down and we all made our way back to the compound. Along the way, Viktor motioned for young Jessica to join him. "Jessica, do you want to hear about an important tradition we have during Midsummer?" he asked her.

"Tell me, Viktor," said an already quite smitten Jessica.

"It is said that on Midsummer, if a young girl pets seven lambs, climbs seven fences, and places seven newly picked wildflowers under her pillow that night, she will dream of the man that she will marry. Would you like to try it?"

"Oh yes," squealed Jessica. Then she got a worried look on her face. "But I'm not much of a climber and I don't have any lambs," she said dejectedly.

"Don't worry. I'll help you," winked Viktor, and off they went. He lifted her up over seven short wooden fences that separated the properties, took her to visit with lambs grazing near the lake, and helped her gather more yellow and purple wildflowers which she clutched closely all the way back to our cabin as if they were made of gold.

With everyone back at the compound, Viktor invited the neighbors to come over along with some fiddlers to help raise the smaller maypole at the house. More joyful dancing, fine fiddling, and enthusiastic singing of traditional Swedish folksongs. Just as exhaustion was setting in, it was time for dinner. We were invited into one of the old seventeenth century barns. It had not been redecorated since then, which was a good thing. The walls were black from soot, the culprit being the original fireplace which was now burning brightly. In the center of the room was an ancient wooden spinning wheel. An antique butter churn, old bibles, ancient eyeglasses and rusty tools lay about, seemingly just as they had been left hundreds of years ago. An old Viking calendar that had been discovered under the house now lay on a heavily scarred wooden table. Who knew that the Vikings were so organized, scheduling the third Thursday of every month at 10:00 a.m. for pillaging an unprotected village? I had a flashback of polishing my *spangenhelm* iron Viking helmet (with nose guard) which I had not taken out since our wedding night, but I tried to push that out of my mind and focus on the meal before us.

The glowing fireplace produced freshly grilled perch that were set out for dinner. Potatoes, salad, and fresh bread were also ready for the final part of the celebration. I watched with amusement as Helene's eyes darted around the array of food looking for something familiar. Then she brightened. Could it be? Yes! Fire-grilled hot dogs, buns and chips! Viktor's parents were certified geniuses.

We drank, we talked, we laughed. One of the elderly neighbors asked me if I knew any Indians in America. I assured her that Indians in feathered headdresses riding horses were commonplace on Sunset Boulevard in Los Angeles but that we had signed a peace treaty with them and we did not have to worry about being scalped. She expressed relief.

At around 1:00 a.m. we made our way back to our cabin to go to sleep. It was the longest day of our lives, literally, and one of the best. With the sun still high in the sky, Jessica gently placed seven wildflowers under her pillow and drifted off to sleep.

*   *   *

As soon as Jessica awoke in the morning, everyone wanted to know if she had dreamed of the man she would marry.

"I think so," she said. She described a man from her dream that sounded suspiciously like the lead singer from Jessica's favorite boy band. Like the rest of our family, Jessica remembers her Midsummer experience joyfully to this day.

After breakfast, it was tight hugs and teary good-byes. Viktor drove us back to the train station and for the first time ever I told someone with all sincerity: "If you are ever out my way please come and stay with us."

In the smallest of ways, we had become part of a special tradition lasting thousands of years. It was not a commercial enterprise designed to sell T-shirts and coffee mugs. It was not a stunt to be posted on YouTube. Rather, it was a lasting connection honoring hundreds of generations of Swedes through the traditions of clothing, dancing, songs and of course food. It was our most memorable family vacation ever.

Only six more lambs to go, Jessica

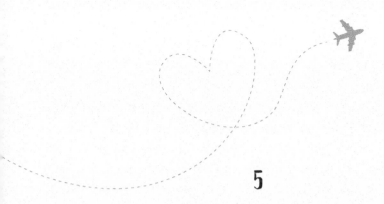

5

HARD OF HERRING

2000

Although it had been several years, I kept envisioning the look of pure ecstasy on the face of that winning Palio rider. He did not just win a horse race. He made his mark in something much greater than himself, much greater than even his *contrade*. He had forged his place of honor in a remarkable centuries-old tradition.

Victor was helping to preserve his family's property from the time of the Vikings. Yes, those Vikings! Every man, woman and child in his village knows the ceremonial dress, the songs, the dances and the importance of their traditional meals. They preserve the pagan maypole ceremony year after year, knowing with absolute certainty that it will be carried on by their children and their children's children.

I found myself humming the song from Fiddler on the Roof. "Tradition!" the Jewish dairyman Tevye belts out time and again. There is tremendous comfort not only in connecting with the past but also in knowing that you are part of an enduring connection to future generations. Tevye was shaken to his core that his traditions would be lost. I was soberly questioning whether I had any lasting connections at all.

I had not made my mark. If I died tomorrow, two generations from now no one would remember my name. What would I leave behind that would endure? I did not have any answers and I did not know how long I would have to search for them. I now had symptoms I could not ignore and they were getting worse.

In the two years since our vacation in Sweden, fatigue had slowly enveloped my entire body, often making any kind of movement a chore. Fevers, night sweats, shakiness, uncontrollable itching. They came, they went, they came again. Sometimes it felt like the notorious Toxin Gang had blown a hole through my liver, made a daring escape by tunneling through my deteriorating bile ducts, drove a getaway platelet through my bloodstream, and was hiding out in my brain holding my memory hostage. My skin became thin, bringing on the cold and causing me to bleed whenever I even brush against a piece of furniture. Beloved wines, fatty meats and spicy foods sent my newly delicate stomach to churning. Peppery New Orleans-style barbeque shrimp? Out. Merry Edwards Meredith Estate Pinot Noir? Nope. Caramelized fatty pork belly with jalapeno vinaigrette? Not if I wanted to live until morning. Moist brisket from City Market barbeque in Luling, Texas? Well, maybe once in a great while some things are worth dying for.

The people we met in Sweden had welcomed us like family and allowed us to share their most treasured traditions. I missed that warm feeling of connection, of adding an additional small link to an endless chain. There was so much more of Scandinavia to discover. What to do when you are seeking answers to your place in the universe? Flee back to Scandinavia for some smorgasbord, of course.

* * *

2000

An ill-tempered drizzle rudely greeted us early one morning as our cruise ship carved its way through the heavy mist toward Helsinki's harbor. As those warm-blooded Finns are fond of saying:

"Helsinki has only two seasons. Nine months of winter followed by three months waiting for summer." But it was not the weather that had my throbbing head in a fog. Last night the walls of our ship cabin had been no match for the reverberating roar of hundreds of drunken Scandinavians singing with as much gusto as they could muster before the ship ran out of vodka. As these early rejects from the Scandinavian version of American Idol launched into the seventeenth round of their favorite drinking song Helan Går, Helene and the kids and I struggled to get some rest.

Our two-day quickie cruise started innocently enough, leaving Stockholm at dusk. We arrived the next morning in Helsinki to spend the day. At dusk we would reboard the ship and return to Stockholm the next morning. Two noteworthy events occurred during our brief voyage.

One was a smorgasbord large enough to threaten the seaworthiness of the ship. Smorgasbord started out in the 1500's as a small side table buffet for the wealthy. Some bread, butter, cheese and cold fish to keep them busy before dinner while they debated the price of herring futures. The word comes from "*smörgås*" meaning sandwich and "*bord*" meaning table. Over the years the side table inched over to become the main table, adding hot dishes as well. Visitors to the 1912 Stockholm Olympic Games came away raving about the astonishing variety of hot and cold dishes at the table. Smorgasbord really took off internationally when it was introduced to America at the Swedish delegation's exhibit at the 1939 World's Fair. Today, smorgasbord has reached its pinnacle in the form of HomeTown Buffet where you can get all your Scandinavian favorites like hard shell ground beef tacos topped with fried jalapenos, spicy buffalo wings and a slice of Snickerdoodle cookie pizza.

My newest Nordic friend the ship's chef had set out a buffet table as impressive as any Viking's plunder. There was *knäckebröd* open sandwiches with shrimp, eggs, and cold cuts, boiled potatoes in dill, a mosaic of carefully arranged cheeses, meatballs in a dense dark gravy, sliced roast beef, pork and reindeer, dozens of salads, salmon, eel and of course lingonberries. Then there was the herring. *Senapssill* herring with mustard, another herring dish with pepper. *Matjessill* pickled herring. Herring in sour cream. Herring in herring.

Speaking of herring, those "feeling no pain" singers were causing me to lose my hearing. What had delivered them to such a state of awesome inebriation? Why, duty free shopping! Once the ship entered international waters, a buzzer announced the opening of the duty-free onboard store, and the ship turned into the site of a rugby scrum as passengers raced to fill their shopping carts with Svedka vodka before the ship docked. With high taxes, particularly on alcohol, Swedish and Finnish hordes descend on these cruise ships for two days of duty-free spirits shopping and non-stop alcohol enhanced partying. Those still standing at the end of the cruise can be seen careening from side to side trying to keep overloaded shopping carts from running away down the gangplank.

I was in a different kind of stupor from the herring, but with some assistance from my spouse, the Ross family disembarked in Helsinki and we found ourselves at the colorful harbor fish market. All in all, not a bad place to be. Local fishermen docked their small boats right up to the steps of the harbor promenade. Crates topped with the fresh catch of the day were set out under yellow and red umbrellas on the back of the boats. Seagulls kept a respectful distance, waiting to swoop over and snatch up a scrap of fish at the first opportunity. The yellow and blue flags on the nearby ferryboats snapped crisply in the breeze. The four of us strolled along the water's edge, checking out the wares. Salmon, shrimp, and...wait for it...more herring.

I had already consumed twice my body weight in herring on the ship and Helene did not seem to be in a raw herring tasting mood, so we kept walking across the way to the Kauppatori market square. Not far from the Havis Amanda mermaid fountain with its dancing sea lions, the market spreads out under sky-high curved lights among outdoor cafes that could conceivably be useful if the sun ever returns to this part of the world. Farmers and tourists alike crowded together under colorful tents that also sheltered carefully balanced mounds of fresh fruits and vegetables. Berries seemed to be particularly popular. We spotted strawberries, blackberries, raspberries, blueberries, bright red lingonberries and golden cloudberries.

We continued on to the ornately decorated brick Old Market Hall built in 1889. It was old and contained a market situated in a hall. I wondered how much the developers paid the marketing team to come up with that name. We entered through the arched doorway to find beautiful wood-paneled stalls, lighted glass display cases, and...all together now...herring! There were just as many types of salmon. Salted salmon, peppered salmon, lemon salmon, salmon smoked in different types of woods. For variety I sampled some reindeer jerky on the way out and found myself staring at a rather deflated version of Rudolph.

"Hey, check this out," I called to my group. "Reindeer hides. We should definitely get some of these."

"Yeah Dad, those are cool," said Matthew.

"That poor reindeer," chimed in Jessica.

Then the boss spoke. "Really? What are you going to do with them?" Helene asked.

"I don't know."

"That's what I thought."

"Maybe we could put one over the couch as a throw and use another one as a rug."

"Just what I was hoping for, a living room that smells like a horned animal."

"Back in the old days, every man hunted his dinner and had a hide in his house."

She just gave me The Look.

It seemed like Helene would need a little time to warm up to the idea of a genuine reindeer hide. Perhaps a little something to eat would put her in a better mood. "How about a little snack, sweetie?" I suggested. "You must be hungry after all of that herring that you didn't eat on the ship."

"Yeah, I know, you're going to try to get me to eat an elk butt sandwich or something."

"You know I wouldn't do that. How about a nice piece of pie?"

"I know this is a trick question." But she could not help herself. "What kind of pie?"

"I see lingonberry pie over there."

"I don't like lingonberries."

"I never would have guessed. How about cloudberry pie?"

"You're making that up."

"I'm not. It's a real pie."

"No thanks."

"Ok, you can't possibly say no to a fresh slice of *kalakukko* pie."

"Whatever sick thing that is, no thank you."

"Well, I'm going to get one. I'm sure after you smell it you'll want a bite."

"Don't wait for me."

I ordered a piece of *kalakukko* pie from one of the vendors. A traditional Finnish treat, this pie was filled with pieces of salmon and perch wrapped in a thick rye bread crust. It was much more filling than I had thought it would be. I barely had room for a slice of cloudberry pie afterwards.

* * *

It remained wet and dreary outside as the entire afternoon beckoned. It was up to me to give the Ross family an energizing boost.

"Do you guys know what time it is?" I chirped with forced enthusiasm.

"Oh no, let's not do this now," interrupted Helene, "or ever for that matter." She had been down this road a time or two.

"What time is it?" Matthew and Jessica responded in unison. The youngest Rosses were still quite gullible, thank goodness.

"It's pick an activity time," I said perkily.

"I want to pet dogs," Jessica pleaded.

"Well, you only get an advisory vote to help your mother pick. Today she gets to select from three very carefully curated opportunities," I explained.

"I'm ready to go shopping," Helene interrupted again.

In fact, Helene was ready to do just about anything else. Helene hates making decisions. Big decisions, little decisions. It does not matter. Where to go for dinner? What movie do you want to see? What is your favorite animal? Good luck getting any kind of easy answer from Helene. So I knew she would be enthusiastic for this game.

"You're going to have to wait and hear the choices," I said. "You know how this works. I will describe one possible activity. You either accept it or you pass on it. If you pass, it is gone forever. You can't come back to it later. Are you ready?"

"Wake me when this is over."

"Come on, I worked hard on these just for you. You can tell because none of them involve food. We can eat directly afterwards."

"Okay, let's hear them Dad," Matthew urged.

"Ready? Here is choice number one. You guys know what a sauna is, right?" I asked.

"Is that where they put mud on your face and cucumbers over your eyes?" Jessica asked.

"Not quite. That's a spa, Pumpkin. A sauna is a small room they heat up by pouring boiling water over hot stones and you sweat a lot. Here in Finland they hold the Sauna World Championships every year where they have a contest to see who can stay in the sauna the longest. To make it even more fun, they give you a bundle of birch twigs to hit yourself with so you can increase the blood circulation."

"Can I have the wooden switches now to practice on someone?" Helene asked with a smile.

"Concentrate. Do you want to take activity number one or try for the next activity?" I asked.

"With great reluctance, I'll pass on activity number one."

"Okay, the sauna activity is gone. You can't come back to it."

"I'll try to get over any aching regret."

"What's the next one, Daddy?" Jessica asked impatiently.

"Activity number two. You skipped your chance to train for the sauna competition but never fear, you can still get in on the exciting traditional post-sauna activity called *jäähy*."

"I'm only going to ask so we can move this along. What is it?" Helene asked wearily.

I could feel the excitement building. "Well, technically it means penalty, but in real life it is the pleasant cooling period after you get out of the sauna."

"I know there's more. Go on."

"You get all hot and sweaty during the sauna, so you need an opportunity to just chill out in the traditional way here in Finland. You get a choice. You can jump into a nearby freezing lake or run naked and dive into a pile of snow."

"Exactly how much time did you spend curating this list?"

"I will go to any length for your pleasure."

"Pass, obviously."

"You understand that if you pass on this one you have to take activity number three no matter what. I'd think this over carefully if I were you," I said.

"Keep moving," Helene replied.

"Alrighty then, congratulations on selecting activity number three."

"What is it, Dad?" Jessica implored.

"*Eukonkanto*," I said.

"Yukon Tonto. Like the Lone Ranger?" Matthew joked. I think.

"Right here in Finland they invented a new sport call *eukonkanto*. Wife carrying."

Helene finally coughed out a laugh. She was not holding any birch sticks so I continued. "This is a serious competition. You have to carry your wife over an obstacle course that includes a log hurdle and running through a water hazard. It started back in the nineteenth century when a local robber and his gang went to a neighboring village and stole another man's wife by throwing her over his back. So there you go. Now that you selected this activity, you need to decide which style of carrying you prefer. Some do the traditional piggyback method. Others like the sack-of-potatoes throw your wife over the shoulder technique. But I have always preferred to carry Estonian style."

"I swear, I am not going to ask," Helene insisted as she shook her head.

"What's Estonian style?" asked Jessica.

"Good girl," I said. "Estonian style is where the man holds onto the wife's legs draped over his shoulders and she dangles upside down on his back. You just have to watch your head on the log hurdle."

"I'm going shopping now," Helene declared.

My chance at immortality by winning the wife carrying competition had slipped through my fingers like a wet herring.

*　*　*

It seemed to be raining herring ever since we boarded the ship in Stockholm. Now, I enjoy a good piece of herring as much as the next person (as long as the next person is not my wife). But I cannot go too many days in a row without a thick brick of seared meat from a recently deceased hairy beast. Strolling through Helsinki's markets and in particular seeing the animal hide displays had me thinking about two of my favorite topics: dinner and meat. In Finland, one of the meatier specialties is bear.

Finland is famous for its brown bears which can be seen roaming the forests not far from Helsinki, and I thought that this trip might be just the right spot to try my first bite of bruin. But the cruise ship smorgasbord was filled with so many different types of herring that there was not enough room left over for even a single bear meatball, and not one vendor at the Kauppatori market was offering samples of bear salami. It was becoming unbearable.

In less than an hour we had to rejoin the ship for the two-hundred-and-fifty-mile cruise back to Stockholm. We had already strolled along the food carts at the harbor, toured the stalls at the Old Market Hall, and greeted nearly every vendor at the Kauppatori market square without finding anything that bore even the slightest resemblance to Yogi, Smokey or even Winnie.

While Helene and Jessica gave their feet a rest on a nearby park bench, the men of the family headed into a supermarket to pick up a few toiletries for the return trip, including earplugs. As I wandered the aisles expecting to find herring-flavored toothpaste, I saw a familiar picture of a hairy creature on a display of canned goods. I was not entirely sure what "Karhu Keitto" meant on the label, but I had a pretty darn good idea what "Bear Soup" was when I read the small print. I bought a can and could not wait to show it to Helene. I knew how excited she would be.

* * *

"Do not under any circumstances eat that bear soup." Dr. Bart was adamant on this during my post-trip check-up.

"Why not?" I protested. I liked to keep Dr. Bart sharp.

"Let's start with trichinosis, which is rampant in bears. Once the trichinosis cysts are eaten, they develop into adult worms that can eat holes in your brain."

"I don't usually like to start with trichinosis," I interrupted.

"Well, then start with diarrhea, nausea, vomiting, gastrointestinal pain, fever and chills, which are just some of the things that you'll have to look forward to if you eat that bear."

Dr. Bart was a fellow world traveler and we frequently compared travel notes during my check-ups. He was also quite a killjoy. The unopened can of bear soup remains in our pantry to this day.

6

DONKEYS AND DAGGERS

January 2014

"It only hurts when I breath." Old joke. New reality.

Some of the doctors at the hospital said I had pleurisy, an inflammation of the lung lining. Other doctors at the hospital said that it was not pleurisy, although they were not able to offer an alternative diagnosis. I was in too much pain to join in the lively discussion. Whenever I took more than half a breath, a shot of pain exploded on the left side of my chest just below my heart. This had been going on for months. I learned to take only very shallow breaths but any jarring motion, including even walking, had the same painful result.

They discharged me from the hospital with a gentle pat on the back and a bottle full of oxycodone. It was not a very satisfactory outcome, particularly because I had to be clear-headed to drive and work.

A few months later the identical pain started in on the right side of my chest, while the first area of pain on the left side was still going strong. Then the right side of my stomach joined in and a few weeks later the left side of my stomach as well. There are no lungs down there, so the second set of doctors that said it was not pleurisy won. Good for them.

Mr. Science will tell you that the immune system is your body's best friend. It provides a defense system against all types of pathogens, bacteria, viruses and other nasties. What is particularly impressive about the immune system is its ability to distinguish between good body cells and foreign bodies that need to be repelled. My immune system was not that clever.

One lobe of my liver had shrunk from my disease, the other lobe had compensated by expanding, and my connecting ducts that carry bile away from the liver were disintegrating, sending bile everywhere it was not supposed to be. As a result, my turncoat immune system went on DEFCON 1 and decided to attack. Me.

I thought that pain in the four quadrants of my upper torso was a pretty formidable assault, but my immune system was just getting warmed up. My latest blood test showed a significant abnormality with my bone marrow function. I was referred to yet another new doctor to receive a bone marrow test.

As I climbed up on the examination table and laid on my side, the doctor and his assistant explained the procedure.

"First, we're going to inject some local anesthetic to the skin area near your hipbone," said the doctor.

"Okay," I said. That sounded fine.

"Then I'm going to insert a larger needle through the bone and remove a bone marrow sample that we can send off for analysis."

The doctor gave me the first injection. Then the assistant moved in and started to hold me down as if they were going to saw off my leg with a rusty pocketknife. I looked up at him with a "what are you doing" look on my face.

"Don't worry," the assistant said, "it won't hurt much."

"Well, it's really not fair to say that," the doctor interrupted. "The anesthesia only works on the skin. Unfortunately, it won't help when we break through the bone."

That did not sound good. The next sound I heard was "crunch!" It was not good.

Oddly, the lab report came back as normal. Somehow, my immune system had thrown out a false signal. Shrewd psychological warfare.

My plucky immune system was a true warrior and continued to press the attack. A month or so later a fifth area of pain erupted in my left ear running down the side of my jaw. My ear, nose and throat doctor sent me to a radiologist for an MRI. It was late in the afternoon when I finished the procedure and was greeted by the radiologist in the reception area.

"Here's a copy of the MRI test," he said while handing me a CD. "Take this over to your ear, nose and throat doctor right now."

"Well, I'll have to take it in the morning," I said. "He's way across town and will be closed by the time I get there."

"No, I just spoke to him," the radiologist responded. "He's going to wait for you."

This did not sound promising. It took me over an hour to get to the ENT doctor's office and he was indeed keeping the office open to wait for me. He looked at the report, used a scope to examine in my ear, another scope to go up through my nose, and got on the phone with the radiologist. I could only hear one side of the conversation, which sounded more like an argument.

"I've examined the area thoroughly and there is no tumor in his ear canal."

"There is no large tumor there. There is no small tumor there. I just examined him. Are you sure that you're reading the MRI correctly?"

"I understand that you've been reading radiology reports for over twenty years. I have been examining ears for just as long. I know a tumor when I see one. There isn't anything there."

"Good-bye."

The ENT doctor turned to me. "The radiologist is adamant that the MRI shows a large tumor that he fears could be cancerous but I've looked carefully and there is absolutely nothing there."

I still cannot figure out how my crafty immune system pulled that one off, but I did not stop too long to ponder the issue. I could not breathe, walk or do anything else without searing pain.

* * *

2004

We had taken the kids on several trips to Europe, trying to infuse them with some old-world culture and create lasting family memories that they could cherish forever. I often pondered how much they would remember. Years from now, would Europe just be a hazy memory for them? Then one day I was rewarded with proof our travels had made an indelible imprint on their young minds.

For my parents' wedding anniversary our entire family, including sixteen-year-old Jessica, joined my parents on a cruise to Bermuda. At the cruise check-in counter we were greeted by an effervescent cruise representative wearing a festive uniform with a badge showing her name and hometown. Jessica leaned over the counter and read the information from the woman's badge.

"Oh, I've been to Bruges," Jessica said to the woman.

"Really? That's where I was born," the woman replied. "Did you enjoy Bruges?"

"Bruges was great! I ate chocolates until I got sick!"

"Oh my. Do you like to travel?"

"It depends on where we go but I've been to lots of places."

"Well, I was born in Bruges but I grew up in Normandy which is in France."

"I've been there too," Jessica exclaimed.

"My, you really have travelled about. Let me tell you something since you like to travel. When you are a bit older and ready, there is only one place in the whole world to get married."

"Really, where?"

"There is an island in Greece called Santorini. On the very Northern tip of the island is a tiny village called Oia. The village is partially carved into a cliff and its houses have wonderful whitewashed walls with bright blue roofs the same color as the ocean. Every night just before sunset all the people on the island gather at the very tip of Oia to sit on the rocks near the ocean and watch the sun go down. I think it is the most beautiful place on earth. Near the rocks in Oia there is the most precious little church. It is simple outside but inside it has gold and marble and frescos and beautiful paintings. That is the most wonderful place to be married."

"Yeah, the Church of Panagia. I've been there."

The one-upped cruise representative forced an even broader smile as she turned back to my parents, checked them in, and avoided any further eye contact with Jessica.

*　*　*

1999

My introduction to Greek food was a neighborhood restaurant in Los Angeles that has been operating for over thirty-five years. It was owned by a bulky Greek gentleman with a slick comb-over who could be found pacing out front on the sidewalk in his rumpled sport coat and suspenders, chain-smoking Sante unfiltered cigarettes. He always seemed excited to greet me and show me to a table. He was no doubt excited when any customer showed up. As of a couple of years ago I no longer saw him at the restaurant. I hope he is lazing on a sun-bathed beach in Mykonos enjoying occasional shots of ouzo, rather than his lungs having succumbed to those Santes.

The restaurant is still there. Inside it is whitewashed with blue trim and features the obligatory murals and pictures that are supposed to remind one of Greece. I have tried most of the items on the menu. The lamb and beef souvlaki are tough, the gyro is carved from an industrial grade slab of unrecognizable preformed meat, and the spinach spanakopita is limp and greasy. Ah, but the *taramasalata*. A smooth bright pink pillow of fish roe mixed with olive oil, some lemon juice and breadcrumbs. When spread generously on pita bread it reminds me of smoked salmon with cream cheese on a bagel, but in a Greek way. Our local Greek taverna outrageously charges extra for pita bread to accompany this addictive concoction, but for this *taramasalata* I dig deep and spare no expense. The pita bread is perfect for scooping up every last bit of the rosy dip and I refuse to waste even a single fish egg. I never had the opportunity to offer this dish to Helene and have her say "no thank you," because she refuses to even enter any restaurant serving Greek food.

No problem. Although the chances of her taking me up on an offer to try a dish made of raw fish eggs is about the same as finding a male Greek sunbather on the beach in Naxos with a waxed back and long board shorts, there was no way that I would run the risk of having to share one bit of the *taramasalata* with my wife.

After a number of years, I started to suspect that our local taverna's food was not entirely authentically Greek. My first clue might have been that the menu includes hamburgers and New York cheesecake. I also learned that the pink color of the *taramasalata* was the result of food coloring. *Malakas!* Yet, I still yearned to dip my pita into the salty mixture and let the olive oil run down my chin. I was deeply ashamed but I just could not stop sneaking in regularly for lunch. If this phony *taramasalata* was so addictive, imagine what real *taramasalata* must taste like in Greece! A plan was hatched to travel to Greece and find the true source of this delicacy, an authentic Greek *taramasalata* that would make me forget about the Americanized version dispensed at our local taverna. Following the siren's call, the Ross Family set out for the Land of the Gods.

* * *

Following the Trojan War, it took Odysseus ten years to finally return home to Ithaca in Greece. Along his tortuous journey, Odysseus and his crew were blown off course and subjected to the intoxicating drugs of the Lotus Eaters, fought off the cannibal Cyclopes, narrowly escaped the charms of Circe who turned Odysseus's men into swine, ventured into the depths of Hades, maneuvered past the song of the Sirens, fled Scylla who ate six of the crew alive, and were unable to use the ship's spa due to undisclosed renovations. Tragically, the ship was destroyed by a thunderbolt before the evening's dinner service had been completed.

But Odysseus's journey was like a five-star luxury cruise in a Concierge Class suite compared to the Ross Family's efforts to reach the Greek islands. Disaster struck before we even left home. Two weeks before our departure Matthew, who was now fifteen years old, broke his ankle while playing basketball. He was placed in a protective boot from foot to knee and could barely limp around on crutches, which was less than ideal for maneuvering through ancient ruins, cobblestone streets and sandy beaches.

We checked all our bags at LAX, only to learn an hour later that our flight was delayed. Every hour or so we checked the departure sign to learn that the flight was further delayed. Our original connecting flight had long since sped away into the friendly skies without us. There was no *taramasalata* in sight. A Burger King Whopper at the LAX food court, yes. Freshly grilled octopus drizzled with Lambda ultra-premium extra virgin olive oil pressed from hundred-year-old vines, no.

After a nine-hour delay, the ticketing agent at LAX finally grew weary of me scowling at her and put us on a plane to Heathrow Airport. A mere eleven hours later the bedraggled Ross Family was in rainy London, now facing an additional nine-hour layover. An agent in Heathrow informed us that the airline was "presently unable to locate" our luggage on the worldwide luggage tracking computer system.

How to spend our unexpected nine-hour layover in dreary rain-soaked London? Perhaps some blue lobster chowder at the

Grill At The Dorchester as a pick-me-up? Roast bone marrow and parsley salad at St. John's? Grilled filet of wild sea bass at Sketch? It turned out that the rest of the Ross Family were under the mistaken impression that our family operated as a democracy. Before I realized what had happened, I found myself cursing and shivering on the last remaining rain-soaked seats upon the top deck of a "hop-on hop-off" red London Big Bus with a mob of rowdy soccer fans from some remarkably unsophisticated village in Albania.

The bus started up. It stopped. It started again. Over fifty stops, each at an "exciting" London landmark. Three hours of canned narration pointed out important historical facts throughout London. Did you know that London's smallest house is only three and a half feet wide? Did you know that the legroom on the bus was only three and a half inches deep? Our two teenagers fell asleep within the first fifteen minutes. Asleep at Buckingham Palace. Asleep at the Tower of London. Asleep at Westminster Abbey. Meanwhile, my knees were gouging a hole through my jaw.

The resilient Albanians rallied, although their team had not, and started singing their team's fight song throughout the periodic rain showers. It was a rather remarkable song because it did not seem to have any ending. A couple of the Albanians started kicking a soccer ball back and forth, only striking me in the back of the head twice. I was shivering, wet and hungry. I maneuvered over to the edge of the top railing of the bus and peered over. I calculated that if I straddled the railing just so and timed my jump precisely, I could be instantly crushed by the wheels of the bus and not be simply wounded or disabled. However, my concentration was shattered when my all-time favorite voice called out to advise me that it was time for us to disembark this multi-level rowboat on wheels and take the tube back to Heathrow for our jolly old flight to Athens.

When we finally arrived back at Heathrow, Jessica needed to use the restroom, Matthew limped his way through the terminal, Helene wanted to shop for tea at the Harrod's store, and our luggage was still AWOL. So was our non-refundable room deposit for the first night of our vacation in Mykonos. But we finally boarded our plane bound for Greece.

It was well past midnight when we landed, day three of our vacation had officially commenced and the Athens airport was just where it was supposed to be. Our luggage was not. Suddenly I heard Jessica squeal. "Mickey D's!" she yelled and pointed at the mostly but not quite closed food court. I looked up and saw a window sign for some abomination called a "Greek Mac."

"No," I said wearily.

"I'm hungry," Matthew chimed in, using his crutches and sad face to paint as bleak a scene as possible.

I tried to remember what day it was when we had last eaten real food. "Go ahead, I'll stand watch in case our luggage materializes out of a worm hole."

"Do you want me to bring you something, hon?" Helene offered.

"Yeah, bring me a McCyanide."

Shortly before dawn we crawled onto our flight to Mykonos, with Matthew having to climb and then an hour later descend the narrow loading stairs with his crutches. Just for laughs we went over to the Mykonos baggage carousel where the incoming bags went around and round until all had been claimed. But on my way toward the lost baggage department I glimpsed an irresistibly beautiful vision off by itself in the far corner of the room. Was that truly Aphrodite arising from the sea foam in the Mykonos baggage claim area? *O'hi*, it was not the lovely Aphrodite. It was our luggage, by Zeus!

Although it was 6:30 a.m. and over a day later than planned, and although I could not attest with any level of certainty that we were even in Greece, a representative of the Petasos Beach Resort & Spa was somehow waiting for us at the airport with his van. I tried to leap into his arms and kiss him on the lips but I was so weak that all I could do was offer a feeble wave of gratitude. He delivered us to the reception area of the hotel, where we crawled the last fifty feet to the reception desk. We were in the same clothes that we started out in three days earlier. We had not bathed during that time (and truth be told my spouse was particularly "fragrant"). We were hungry and haggard. I gripped the reception desk with both hands to steady myself. On the other side of the desk was a vivacious young Greek woman with cascading tight curls of long black hair. She spread her arms out wide in a welcoming air hug, smiled warmly, and uttered five words that I will never forget:

"Relax, you are in Greece!"

And so we did.

* * *

We slept for a very, very long time. I am not completely sure what day we woke up, but when we did I knew that it was time to eat. We took a bus from the hotel and flew like Hermes toward Jimmy's Place. There it was, the savory smell of fat dripping from skewered meat, the master carvers armed and already in action, the tiny stools out front were filling up. Gyros, chicken souvlaki, tzatziki sauce ready to run down my arm. All was good again. Well, not quite everything.

"There's nothing here for me," Helene chimed in as I licked a bit of sauce off my elbow.

"Order the chicken souvlaki," I suggested.

"What is it?"

"It's broiled chicken on skewers, you'll like it."

"Is it spicy?"

"No."

"I don't like Greek food."

"What do you want to do, send out for Chinese? Order the souvlaki already."

She did.

"Hey, this souvlaki is good." she conceded.

"Yeah, I should have told you. My bad."

As much as I wanted to linger on the rickety stool at Jimmy's, now that the appetizers were out of the way it was time to get serious and explore the real Greek world of *taramasalata*. After a brief *mesimeri* Greek siesta, Restaurant Avli Tou Thodori was only a short stroll from our hotel, directly on Platis Gialos beach. When we arrived the music was in full swing, the waiters were starting to dance, and the aroma of roasting lamb drifted from the kitchen directly to my olfactory glands.

My order of *taramasalata* arrived. It was white, not pink like every *taramasalata* I had eaten in the states. Didn't they know about food coloring here in Greece? This *taramasalata* was coarse, not smooth and creamy. The fish roe tasted quite strong, not as delicate as I preferred at home. This was not the *taramasalata* of my dreams. Next my lamb *kleftiko* arrived, roasted perfectly with fresh vegetables. During this phase of her gastronomic development, Jessica refused to eat any animals that she thought were cute. Chickens? Okay to eat. Pigs? Never. Cows? Maybe. Lambs? No way. She started to object about the lamb on my plate.

"If you don't be quiet, I'll tell you exactly how they slaughter lambs here in Greece," I threatened. I have a way with kids.

Next to arrive was the biggest surprise of the evening. I took a closer look at a party that had just been seated nearby. The gentleman in the group looked strikingly like Adonis himself. To my astonishment it was my very own Dr. Bart, the bear soup killjoy but all-around good guy along with his family! I went over to greet him.

"What, did you travel seven thousand miles just to check on my cholesterol?" I asked him.

"Well, somebody's got to do it. I know how you eat," he replied.

Of all the places on the planet, both our families had independently decided to stay at the same Greek beach and eat at the very same restaurant at the same moment. Even the gods would be impressed! The waiters were now in a frenzy dancing the *syrtaki*, the music grew faster and louder. Dr. Bart's daughters joined in to dance with the waiters, the ouzo flowed, the *loukoumades* Greek donuts soaked in local honey were sweet and pure. It was a very small world. We were in Greece and we were relaxed, mostly. But I was already starting to worry about my next meal.

* * *

"That's quite a hairy ass you've got there," I called up to Helene.

"You'd better be referring to this donkey that I'm riding."

"Of course I am, sweetie.

"I bet you are."

"Alright, I promise. No more ass cracks."

As a result of a bout of temporary insanity, the Ross family were atop donkeys plodding up the steep and slippery path to the Acropolis on the Greek island of Rhodes. The donkeys, referred to locally as the Rhodes Taxi Service, must have been heavy smokers of unfiltered Greek cigarettes when they were young, because the beasts were all on the smallish side and chugged along quite slowly. This worked out fine for my petite wife and the kids, but I was fairly sure that I had my donkey outweighed by at least twenty pounds. Halfway up the hill my donkey was wheezing and kept asking for rest breaks. I had to verbally encourage my donkey the entire way by whispering in his ear my favorite recipe for donkey stew.

Later that evening I escorted my family up to the roof at Caesar's Meze Bar to continue my *taramasalata* studies at a poolside table under the stars. I had an excellent grilled *tsipoura* sea bream that tasted as if it had just been plucked from the water by a delicate sea nymph, but the coarse white *taramasalata* was similar to the one I tried on Mykonos. It had neither the smooth texture nor the delicate taste of the *taramasalata* that I enjoyed at home. My *taramasalata* quest would have to continue elsewhere.

* * *

The powerful alcoholic drink raki and Greek daggers with intricately carved bone handles are two cultural standouts on the Greek island of Crete. Only a Cretan, I mean cretin, would mix the two. Meet my family.

The day started innocently enough as I lounged early in the morning on the rooftop terrace of our rented Crete apartment overlooking the old Venetian harbor at Chania. Matthew, who had been clomping all around Greece on his crutches, was no doubt less than enthused to see that we were occupying an apartment on the third floor with no elevator. Far more excited was Jessica, as it was her twelfth birthday and we planned on celebrating later that evening. Matthew perked up when I explained that the Cretans were well known for their artistry with knives, going back hundreds of years. Matthew had assembled a small but diverse pocketknife collection back at home and a genuine Cretan knife would be a welcome addition.

That morning we made our way to Knife Street near the harbor and Matthew window-shopped until he found just the right *mahairakida* or knife craftsman. The mustachioed owner greeted us warmly and ushered us over to the knives displayed on the wall in order of size. At the far right side of the wall the owner took down a small pocketknife for Matthew to inspect. With great enthusiasm the owner described how the knife was made and its uses. Then the owner placed it back in its display, removed the next slightly larger knife in line and extolled its virtues and uses to Matthew. This went on for over a dozen knives, each one larger and more expensive than the last. Finally, the owner reached the very last knife in the display. It took two hands for him to remove it from the wall and with great care he drew the knife from its highly decorated metal sheath. The knife was enormous and curved toward a pinpoint sharp end. It was single edged with a "V" shaped manika handle made from the bone of some animal that was too dim-witted and slow of foot to escape. The owner now pointed with disdain toward the smaller knives in the display, commenting that they were primarily decorative. He nodded knowingly at Matthew, stating that a true adventurer like Matthew no doubt wanted a "real" knife. The owner then cradled the largest knife in the palms of his two hands, presented it for Matthew's inspection, and with barred teeth and a glint in his eye he proudly snarled and told Matthew, "and this one we call the Turk Killer."

"I'll take it," Matthew replied.

"He'll take the pocketknife," his wise father told the owner. Matthew completed his purchase of the pocketknife and we quickly left the store before he spotted some other maiming device to purchase.

"Let me see that knife," I said to him. "You obviously have to be very careful with a knife like this. I'll show you the safe way to open it."

I took the knife, pulled out the blade, and immediately cut my finger. It was a small cut with just a hint of blood, but Jessica almost instantly passed out on the street. Jessica is petrified of blood, injections, or anything having to do with medical issues. Getting her to a doctor is a major challenge that takes considerable planning. Fortunately, during her twelve years she had never had to be rushed to an emergency room. Helene and I could not even imagine how we would deal with that.

After some deep breathing exercises Jessica was mostly revived. We continued our inspection of the charming old Venetian harbor in Chania. A jumble of pastel-colored buildings crowded each other on a gray stone promenade rimmed by boisterous outdoor cafes and quaint shops. Vintage streetlights would later cast a warm glow in the evening when local families mesh with package-toting tourists to stroll while enjoying a gelato and working up an appetite for the next meal. Now it was just past noon as the sun played tricks with the water, the occasional stray dog scampered out of the way of a horse-drawn carriage, and a sailboat rounded the point past one of the oldest lighthouses in the world. It was exciting and peaceful at the same time. I spotted an empty bench overlooking a few moored boats in the water and was just about to suggest that we sit down to enjoy the scene when our children cried out in unison at the top of their lungs:

"PIZZA HUT!"

Yes, the city planners in their infinite wisdom had allowed a garish Pizza Hut franchise to foul the otherwise quaint beauty of the Chania harbor area. Not for the first time, I regretted my longstanding promise that each child could dine at the restaurant of their choosing on their birthday. "Are you sure that you wouldn't prefer some raw fish eggs or octopus tentacles for your birthday lunch?" I asked Jessica.

"Disgusting," was the answer.

I dutifully put on my sunglasses, tilted my Tilley hat low over my forehead, pulled up the collar on my shirt, and slunk into The Hut where my daughter joyfully dug into her "cheese pizza, light sauce" as a special birthday treat.

After lunch, it was Jessica's turn to go shopping and she shrieked with delight when she saw an enormous stuffed donkey for sale in one of the shops. It was not much smaller than the one I bonded with in Rhodes. Jessica cuddled it when we returned to the promenade later that evening as we strolled toward the restaurant at the Amphora Hotel for our last celebratory meal in Crete. We were seated outside in prime position to watch the people sauntering harborside. The red checkered tablecloths stood out boldly against the color of the chairs and the water of the harbor, both of which were trimmed in Aegean blue. Inside the restaurant traditional Cretan handmade rugs, possibly made in China, hung on the walls. The pizzas on the menu were just right for the rest of the family, but I was still searching for the *taramasalata* of my dreams. It was not to be. The *taramasalata* was the same as each of the others that I had tried in Greece, each missing the creamy delicate goodness served up only a few miles from my home.

When our quite sociable young waiter learned that it was Jessica's birthday, a fact that she had somehow communicated to everyone present in the restaurant as well as to every neighboring establishment on the promenade, he promptly returned with five glasses and a bottle of raki. Also known as Cretan moonshine, it tasted as if it had been fermented for seven minutes in an open bucket maintained in a not necessarily hygienic corner of the restaurant's basement. There was no doubt in my mind that the pressed grape residue used to create this highly alcoholic concoction had been fertilized by the dung produced by my Rhodes donkey as a form of revenge. That donkey was not as dumb as he looked.

The waiter toasted the birthday girl with raki. We toasted the waiter with raki. The beautiful city of Chania was toasted with raki. After finishing off chocolate brownies for dessert, we raki-ed and rolled all the way back to our apartment.

* * *

About five minutes after I fell asleep, the alarm clock went off. The raki was still sloshing around in my head. My tongue was dry as two-day old pita. But we had to make a red-eye flight to our last stop in Greece, the island of Santorini. We hurriedly dressed and flagged down a real taxi with wheels. A short flight later, we arrived at the Santorini airport in the middle of the night and piled into the one remaining cab for the ride to our hotel. In Greek mythology Helios drove the chariot of the sun across the sky each day to earth. One day his son Phaeton tried to drive his father's chariot but lost control and set the earth on fire. Our Santorini taxi driver must have been a distant relation. We were flying down a black hole of a narrow, weaving mountain road. At least I was told that it was a road. I searched deep into the upholstery for a seat belt but came up only with a handful of moldy feta crumbs. Occasionally, the taxi driver kept at least two of the taxi's wheels on the ground. We lurched to the left. We careened to the right. We bumped our heads on the roof of the cab. We were tossed deep into the seats of the shock-absorberless vehicle. Not until all of the blood had drained from my face did the taxi screech to a stop near our hotel.

"We are here," said the driver.

Truer words were never spoken. It was still darker than octopus ink when we climbed out of the cab. Much to my horror, some of the hotel staff loaded our luggage onto donkeys which we had no choice but to follow up a very dimly lit steep path as we climbed to the hotel.

"At least it's convenient," quipped Matthew as he struggled up the never-ending winding steps on his crutches. That's my boy!

Remarkably, the innkeeper was waiting for us even at this ridiculous hour. We followed his flashlight as he led us up the path to our rooms and brought in our luggage from atop those four-legged flea hotels. Our accommodations were quite nice but there was something odd. It finally occurred to me that there were no windows anywhere, not that we could see anything outside anyway in the dark. I pitched into the bed and fell asleep, trying hard not to dream about donkeys.

When I awoke in the morning I went to pull the curtain back on the window to check the weather. Then I remembered. No curtain. No window. I opened the front door, stepped out, and did a double take. It was one of the most spectacularly beautiful sights I had ever seen. I was peering into the center of a volcanic caldera. Thousands of years ago the island of Santorini, known then as Thera, blew its top in a massive eruption. The Aegean Sea rushed in to flood the core of the volcano, leaving only a semi-circle of rocky outcroppings poking up from the water. As I stood looking out, the brilliant sun bounced off the water and was warm against my face. Immediately below me was a flower-laden terrace, swimming pool, and steep cliffs leading down to coves and inlets dressed in teal, viridian and every color in between. Colorful boats floated in a small bay down below. Our room was literally a cave carved into the side of the caldera. Breakfast beckoned on the terrace, including a basket of croissants. I took in the biggest breath of my life, one massive gulp that captured the crisp sea air, blooming flowers and fresh baked pastries all at once. Nothing could break the spell of this tranquil scene.

A horrible sound reverberated off the rocks. For once it was not Helene's voice calling me but rather a donkey braying a greeting from down below. Eventually the donkey grew tired of torturing me and shut up. The Ross Family sat down and peacefully enjoyed an amazing breakfast overlooking this glorious scene. After breakfast, a little swim in the saltwater pool. A little *resto* out on a lounge. Another dip in the pool. I was starting to get the hang of this "Relax, you are in Greece" idea. Before I could say *"taramasalata"* it was almost time for dinner.

We were in the village of Oia on Santorini. This town used to be so poor that it could not even afford to buy a consonant. Yet now it was achingly beautiful with whitewashed houses trimmed in blue roofs perched precipitously on the edge of the volcano. It was almost sunset and time to stroll to the most Northern end of the island to sit on the rocks and watch Helios drag the sun into the sea. While strolling down the narrow path we came upon vendors grilling freshly caught octopus tentacles over open smoky coals. I purchased one and carried my snack away in a napkin. It was beautifully charred on the outside and turned out to be the sweetest octopus I had ever eaten. I finished the last bite just as our stroll brought us to the tip of the island. We lounged on the rocks until the final finger of light disappeared into the sea. As we started to walk back toward our hotel to get ready for dinner, we came upon a small blue-domed church.

"Do you guys want to check out the church?" I asked the family. "It says it's the Church of Panagia."

"Sure," said Jessica.

7

ZEBRA BREATH

September 2014

Property Brothers was on the television. Every time. I had never seen the show before but I was now involuntarily binging it for hours on end at least once a week. The brothers were desperately trying to find a suitable house for an ultra-picky family of four. The wife was a major diva, finding fault with every potential house. All of her requirements for the new house had to be accomplished on an improbable budget within an impossible time frame in a neighborhood that was out of their price range. As they completed their tours of over a dozen prospective houses, her favorite phrase was "I'm not impressed." Of course, the brothers came through in the end, gutting a house down to the studs and creating the beautiful home of her dreams. I suppose it was better than watching Bridezillas.

    I was comfortably reclined all the way back in my chair. Sheila was in her usual chair to my left with her caregiver on the other side. Sheila had cancer. Bud was in his chair on my right near his caregiver. Bud had cancer too. In fact, all the Tuesday regulars at the infusion center were being treated for cancer except me. Magically, Property Brothers was always on the television while we received our IV infusions. One week Sheila stopped coming. I never learned whether that was good news or bad news.

At first, I did not hit it off with my new rheumatologist Dr. Patel. Not after he immediately ordered a blood draw of twenty-three vials from my scrawny little arm. Rheumatologists have never seen a blood test they did not like and Dr. Patel was no exception. My immune system had been on the offensive for many months and it had taken its toll on me. I could barely remember what it was like to take a full breath of air without stabbing pains throughout my upper torso. I lost weight, any semblance of muscles had atrophied, my complexion was so pale it would scare a ghost, and I shuffled around like an old man trying my hardest to keep movement to a minimum.

Dr. Patel was a tiny man with a high sing-song voice. He was also brilliant, lecturing all over the world and performing cutting edge research on autoimmune disease. He was fascinated with my case because the onset of my liver disease seemed to be uniquely related to other autoimmune disorders that I was experiencing. During my office visits Dr. Patel would become excited and his voice would go up a full octave while describing how he had discussed my condition with colleagues at symposiums around the world. I had finally made my mark! One day I would be a footnote in a medical journal. Just dandy.

I came to think of Dr. Patel as somewhat of a mad scientist, but in a good way. His research had taught him to think outside the box and he came up with a desperate plan for a desperate man. The good news was that there was a drug available that was approved for other purposes and he thought it might help me. The bad news was that it was made from mouse DNA and most people suffered an allergic reaction to it sooner or later. There was a trial being conducted with a similar drug made without mouse DNA that did not cause that type of allergic reaction, but it had not yet been approved for any use. Was I willing to give the mouse DNA drug a try while we hoped for government approval of the other drug?

Sign me up!

Dr. Patel came to the infusion center and sat with me to test the first infusion. We watched Property Brothers together. My infusion went smoothly and the remodeling of the home went off without a hitch as well. After several infusion sessions almost ninety percent of my pain was gone. Thanks to Mickey Mouse and his progeny, I could move about and laugh and sneeze and breathe. Other than a constant craving for cheese, I had no apparent side effects.

I also learned a great number of helpful hints for how to renovate a house.

* * *

2006

The crisp white linen that enveloped the dining table had more starch than a platter of sautéed plantains. I picked up a spoon from the table. It was already warm from the high African sun and my lightly sunburned face stared back at me in reflection. Our dutiful waiter placed a simple azure vase bearing a single pink pyjama lily between Helene and I, adding a splash of color and romance. He then retreated a few feet away, allowing us to soak in the most intimate of alfresco dining experiences.

I told Helene that I was getting a bit teary-eyed dining with her in such an enchanting setting. However, the truth is that my eyes were watering from an unearthly stench. It was as if a crater has opened up to deliver a pungent primordial funk that had been festering since the Earth was young. I tried to hold my breath. Either our waiter had a flatulence problem worthy of inclusion in the New England Journal of Medicine, or some other remarkably malevolent odor was wafting in our general direction. I dabbed my eyes with my napkin as an excuse to cover my nose. Out of the corner of my eye I caught a couple shamelessly copulating in public only a hundred feet away, complete with moaning, groaning and grunting worthy of a pair of wildebeests in heat. Although I made a perfunctory showing of averting my eyes, upon closer examination it became clear that the couple was indeed a pair of wildebeests in heat! I did not know whether to be relieved, afraid, or in need of a cold shower.

With our open-roof Land Rover parked nearby, we had taken a break in our game driving while our driver and guide Yaro set up a folding picnic table in prime position on a large grassy plain deep in the Tanzanian Serengeti. By this time Matthew and Jessica had reached young adulthood where other commitments and/or lack of interest in travelling with their parents had left Helene and I alone for a romantic journey to the Mother Continent. Well, alone except for Yaro.

We first met Yaro just a few days earlier after our six-seat plane dodged a couple of loping giraffes and bounced several times before landing on a small dirt strip that marred an otherwise pleasant meadow. I was the first to spot Yaro through the plane window because Helene still had her eyes sealed shut from the flight. Yaro wore dark khaki pants with a T-shirt bearing the logo of our safari outfitter, along with a broad white smile to match his white visor. He had spent the previous day traveling twelve hours by slow train from his tiny village and family to be our private guide for the week. It was the height of the annual Great Migration when literally millions of animals including wildebeests, zebras, cheetahs, leopards, lions, elephants, giraffes, antelopes, gazelles, hyenas, and a daring American tourist follow the growing grass and each other in an "eat what you kill" parade of life and death. We were ostensibly in the Serengeti on a photo safari. That did not stop me from checking out the various animals to see which had the best marbling.

I always consider it pretentious when restaurant servers bring raw steaks or seafood directly to the dining table and make a big show of allowing the diner to select a specific one for cooking. However, with our picnic table completely surrounded by animals as far as we could see, I was now starting to see the merit of just pointing out an animal and having it massacred as lunch for us. The wildebeests—God's ugliest animal—were everywhere. They looked like they were put together from parts leftover after a post-holiday animal sale. An elongated face like a moose, horns from a steer, a few zebra stripes that abruptly ended halfway down the body for no good reason, a huge upper torso with a small rear like a buffalo, and a stench like, well, like nothing I had encountered before. Speedy gazelles were also in abundance. I imagined asking Yaro to try to run down one or two for a mid-afternoon snack. However, the vision of being served by a sweating waiter simultaneously scraping giraffe dung off of his shoes was not particularly appetizing. The zebras looked quite tasty, with well-rounded hindquarters, no horns to contend with, and there were over a quarter million of them in the moving feast of the migration. Certainly, no one would notice if a single zebra happened to go missing. But those zebras were smarter than they looked. We spotted a number of zebras standing with their necks intertwined, working as a team to be on the lookout in opposite directions for lions and hungry tourists.

I asked Yaro whether the local Maasai ate the nearby game, and how far it was to the closest gastropub to get a medium-rare tomahawk zebra steak. Yaro shook his head almost hard enough to cause his visor to fall off. "Boss, the Serengeti is wildlife preserve. The animals are protected. No one can eat them," he said. "I was park ranger here for over fifteen years, so I know."

Apparently, Yaro was a stickler for details. More importantly, any further discussion was unduly delaying my lunch. We opened the box lunches prepared by our lodge. Plain chicken breast sandwich, salad and fruit. Helene's eyes lit up with delight.

*　*　*

Yaro offered to take us to a nearby Maasai village and we readily agreed. Perhaps they would be serving some Hippo Cordon Bleu. At the very least, one of the villagers could give me some dining tips on where to enjoy an unusual game dish. I was not going to leave Tanzania without first trying something new and hairy to eat.

The Maasai, a semi-nomadic people of fierce warriors, are famous for raising cattle in the Serengeti. Cattle are a source of both food and wealth. The Maasai eat the meat, drink the milk, and even ritualistically drink blood from the cattle by stabbing them with an arrow near the jugular vein. Occasionally we spotted Maasai tending to a small herd of skinny cattle as we drove along.

The Maasai village came into view, several thatched-roof huts made of packed cow dung and a separate semi-open-air schoolroom made of long thin sticks bound together. The entire village was surrounded by a fence made of acacia thorns to keep out unwanted animals. As we bounced up the dirt path to the village, a group of stern looking Maasai men slowly gathered. They had closely cropped hair, beaded earrings and necklaces, and were resplendent in their crimson and blue ankle-length *shuka* blanketing their bodies. They watched silently as we approached. Yaro explained that we needed to pay to enter the village. Twenty-five dollars later the Maasai were posing for pictures, laughing, dancing, and jumping about. For twenty-five bucks, I hoped there would also be a buffet.

Standing to one side were a group of Maasai women in similar dress, all with colorful beaded neck rings and some with flat white beaded collars the size of a large pepperoni pizza. Two small barefoot children who could not have been more than three or four years old sat on the dirt in the shade of a hut. Similarly adorned with beaded necklaces and dressed in the same blue and crimson colors as the rest of the villagers, the children playfully entertained a small brown dog with a stick. In short order the prince of the village emerged from the pack to welcome us with a VIP tour. Yaro, who had no doubt witnessed this scene many times before, retired to the Land Rover for a well-deserved nap.

Helene and I followed the prince inside his hut, bending down low through the small opening and crawling inside on the dirt floor. There was no Property Brothers approved granite-topped island in the center of the kitchen. In fact, there was no kitchen. Just a fire burning in the center of the hut, creating a thick blanket of smoke that hung in the single windowless room. Through the smokiness we could detect the smell of dirt, dung and humans that had all been in close proximity for a long time without any ventilation. As it was nearly impossible to see, we made our way inside mostly by touch. Through a cloud of burnt carbon and sparks the prince motioned for us to sit down on what felt to be a rickety bed made of bound twigs. I perched precipitously on the edge of the wobbly bed while Helene sat down next to me.

I subtly felt around the twigs behind me with my right hand to stake out my territory. Instead I bumped into what felt to be a warm, hairy leg. I was sure that it was not mine and reasonably sure it did not belong to my wife because I had observed her using her epilator that very morning. I said a silent prayer that the leg would turn out to be human. A moment later Helene and I were both startled when the bed moved sharply. Unseen to us, there were several other royal family members already lying in the small bed, one of whom had just shifted in his sleep, causing a chain reaction in the Maasai spooning train. Helene and I crawled even closer to the edge of the bed.

The prince, unadorned by any bead work but wearing the same blue and crimson style *shuka,* squatted down directly in front of us. Without warning, he pulled out a three-foot-long double-edge knife with cow hide handle and thrust it directly in front of my face. Helene immediately dove into a self-induced coma, I could no longer see the exit through the smoke and the nearest cavalry was on another continent. But it turned out that the now smiling prince was simply immensely proud of his knife and was showing it off to me. I nodded approvingly.

Attempting to further ingratiate myself to the prince prior to what I hoped would be afternoon tea and at least antelope finger sandwiches, I used my camera to take a picture of him holding his knife. When I showed him the image on my camera he broke out in a wide smile that caused Helene to stop digging her fingernails into my thigh. Now that everyone had loosened up and was comfortable, I politely asked him for some recommendations on where I might be able to dine on zebra.

The prince did not understand a word I said. I pulled a twig from the bedding and tried to draw on the dirt floor a picture of a zebra leaping onto a Kalamazoo Hybrid Fire Grill. The prince laughed. We were not making much dining progress. I wedged the twig back into what I thought was the bed, causing one of my unseen bedmates to howl in pain. Helene became startled by the loud howl and abruptly stood up, causing the delicate balance of the bed to shift and it started to topple. From the other side of the bed came angry grumbling along with some words that I presume remain unprintable, even in the local dialect of Maa. It was time to take our leave.

As we exited the hut the prince waved goodbye at us with his knife. At least I thought it was a wave but he may have been calling for reinforcements. A small army of village women raced over to surround us, holding out bracelets and other handmade jewelry for sale as they vied for our attention. We were being jostled about as if it were Black Friday after Thanksgiving and the doors to Target had just opened. Without asking, several of the women placed bracelets on Helene's wrists. As Helene tried to remove the bracelets, more would take their place. I could see that my wife was becoming a bit overwhelmed while trying to remain polite. We bought a couple of bracelets in self-defense as we fought our way through the gauntlet, leaped for the Land Rover, and sped off with empty stomachs.

* * *

Yaro's ability to spot game was astonishing. He could spot an impala tail twitching a mile away. Unlike Snoring Dog, our Yellow Labrador who spends her entire life sleeping on our bed when she is not eating, Yaro was like an expertly trained retriever that had picked up the scent of some small unfortunate animal and was now eager for the chase. Without warning the Land Rover would come to a lurching halt as Yaro grabbed his never out of reach binoculars and intently scanned the vast Serengeti. We knew then that something with four legs was afoot.

"Leopard in tree," whispered Yaro as we skidded to yet another stop.

"I don't see anything," replied Helene.

"Leopard in tree," repeated Yaro while pointing up ahead.

"What tree?" asked Helene.

"I don't see a tree," I said, feigning support for my wife.

We drove on up a half mile or so until we were in the shade of the only tree for a mile around. "Leopard in tree," Yaro said firmly, once again pointing up toward a large branch.

"Where? I don't see anything," Helene confided to me.

"All I see is a tree," I whispered.

"Leopard in tree," Yaro repeated yet again, clearly exasperated.

"There it is," I confirmed. The perfectly camouflaged leopard was fifteen feet above us, fast asleep up on a branch. As the saying goes, if it were any closer it would bite us.

We drove on, repeating the process every half hour or so with elephants, cheetahs, hippos, ostriches, gazelles, hyenas, giraffes, water buffalo, and more. Meanwhile, I was still looking for a proper meal as our Land Rover bounced along kicking up more dust than the time I pretended to help Helene with housework. Near the only Acacia tree in sight we came upon a pride of five tawny lions lounging on the grass, shaded from the warming sun. Yaro explained that the two larger lions with magnificent manes were old brothers. I presumed that the smaller lions were their younger-looking "nieces." It is good to be king.

Standing up through the open roof of the Land Rover, Helene and I were only twenty feet or so away from the lions. One of the lions lay on its back with its front paws curled up like a lap dog waiting for a tummy rub. Another methodically licked its fur. We could hear them breathing as we watched their massive chests rise and fall. The nearby buzzing of a thousand flies caused me to turn and spot a half-eaten zebra off to the side. The lions had already eaten their fill and were taking a nap. It reminded me that I was still hungry. As we peered out through open air at the kings and nieces of the jungle, my stomach let out a rather loud and embarrassing growl. One of the lions slowly opened one eye and seemed to notice us for the first time. He sat up on his hind legs while staring at us, opened his jaws wide as if an MGM movie was about to start, and roared. It was the most primal, thunderous sound I had ever heard. It seemed to start from the beginning of time and blew us into the next week. Instinctively, Helene and I both dove for the floor of the Land Rover.

Yaro, who never flinched during this episode, laughed so hard that tears ran down his face.

* * *

While Yaro performed brilliantly spotting animals during the game drives, he continued to follow outmoded ideas regarding "preserving" the game. I had not been able to acquire any dining tips from the Maasai prince, and no zebra short ribs had yet passed my lips. I could only hope that the lodges and tented camps where we were staying would follow the migration-to-table dining formula and serve up some unusual local game dishes. After all, we were staying at some pretty great places. The Mbalageti Tented Lodge offered an astonishing view of the Dutwa Plains and we could watch the migration pass by right under our noses. At night we could hear the now all-too-familiar sound of wildebeests mating right outside our tent. Each night a Maasai guard carrying a long spear for protection against predatory animals escorted us from our tent to the main lodge for dinner, but he was incorruptible and declined to use his spear to impale one of the smaller appetizer-sized animals whose eyes winked at us out of the darkness. There was also a ridiculously large and quite irritable water buffalo with enormous curved horns that was often seen around camp but we were warned to steer clear of him. I imagined a major celebration at the lodge with the buffalo turning on a spear rotisserie over an open fire. But all I could do was dream.

The very intimate Mbuzi Mawe Tented Camp offers what they call "a ringside seat for one of the greatest wildlife spectacles on Earth." While the game viewing was indeed like having a front row seat to a National Geographic documentary, meals consisted of a typical "English breakfast" and a nicely prepared but routine continental dinner. Our well-appointed tented cabin came with a zippered front with a small lock. Small locks on a canvas tent in the middle of the Serengeti? For what, to stop a charging rhino?

Had the local giraffes been watching too many heist movies? Was the antelope motorcycle gang back in town? I inquired of the owners and learned that the local baboons had quickly learned how to unzip a tent and throw a wild animal-themed party inside. As of yet the baboons had not figured out the locks, but just give them a little time.

The Kusini Camp provided yet another spectacular setting including sundowners on a rock formation overlooking the Great Migration. Yet it never occurred to the owners that the evening campfire would be infinitely improved if we could roast flamingo s'mores.

Finally, the Ngorongoro Crater Lodge is one of the most stunning lodges in the world. It rests on the edge of a volcanic caldera that is littered with wildlife. Any place that provides your own private butler who has a hot bath with rose petals waiting for you after a game drive cannot be all bad.

Yet breakfast at each of these lodges, on the rare occasions when Yaro allowed it, was inevitably an English-style buffet. Lunches were usually boxed sandwiches prepared in the morning and eaten in one's lap while out on a game drive. Dinner, always ample and nicely prepared, included a fish dish (usually Nile perch from Lake Victoria) and simple chicken and beef dishes. Perhaps some local vegetables but not a single rack of gazelle in sight. The beef dishes were always described as filet mignon. However, the meat was sinewy and overcooked, with no hint of the delicate texture of the buttery filets that we are accustomed to at home. It has been said that Kobe beef from Japan is so extraordinary because the pampered cows are raised in a most tranquil atmosphere, fed beer, massaged daily with sake, and played soothing classical music for maximum relaxation. On the other hand, the beef in Tanzania tasted as if the cows were herded about by Maasai warriors prodding them with sharp spears, subjected nightly to the terrifying sounds of lions roaring and wildebeests bellowing at them, and then routinely stabbed in the neck to extract their blood for drinking. Which they were.

With not a single Giraffe Neck Wellington on the lodge menus, I stuck to the perch.

* * *

At the time that we booked our African adventure, the lodge brochures repeatedly emphasized the opportunity to relax and enjoy the well-appointed safari camps where we would be staying. As explained in one brochure, travelers could select between getting up at five in the morning for a game drive or choosing "a more leisurely morning with breakfast at the lodge." Then game drive for the rest of the day or "return to the lodge for a late lunch and some relaxation." Unfortunately, Yaro had not read any of the brochures. He had his own firm ideas about our visit and had independently determined that he would be an abject failure if he did not personally show us every animal in the migration. Not every type of animal mind you, but apparently every single one of the millions on the move.

Each evening before we retired, Yaro would inform us of the next day's schedule: "We leave tomorrow again at five a.m. The lodge will make a box breakfast and box lunch to take."

"How about we eat a hot breakfast at the lodge tomorrow and leave a little later," I suggested after consecutive twelve-hour days of dusty game drives battling rutted dirt roads (if we were lucky to find a road at all), without bathroom facilities, in a Land Rover barbarically fitted with cloth seats rather than leather.

"No, boss," Yaro would say. "We have to leave at five to see the antelopes perform synchronized calisthenics. They only do it at morning." At least that is what it sounded like to me.

Thus, each day we headed out before sunrise and did not return until dinner. While the game spotting was spectacular, a single afternoon relaxing in the lodge jacuzzi swirling a glass of South Africa's Hamilton Russell Pinot Noir and sampling from a cheeseboard filled with Dalewood Fromage Huguenot would have been delightful. Yaro did not agree.

It was midafternoon. We were precisely seven minutes away from the middle of nowhere. Yaro had shown us so many hundreds of zebras and gazelles that we no longer even turned our heads to look at them as we passed by. Yeah, there is another herd of hundreds of zebras being stalked by a deranged serial killer lion. Big deal. But the indefatigable Yaro was on a crusade and was not to be deterred. He kept checking his two-way radio, repeatedly swept the horizon with his binoculars, and drove like a ravenous lion chasing an obese gazelle. I thought perhaps some gentle hints might do the trick.

"How much longer to get back to the lodge?" I asked.

"Oh, a few hours away," replied Yaro, as he continued to drive in the opposite direction.

Several miles and mouthfuls of dust later: "Are we headed back toward the lodge?"

"Not yet, boss."

We continued our secret mission to oblivion, driving off-road for hours on unforgiving shock absorbers through vast treeless savannah. Even the animals knew better than to venture into this desolate area because we had not seen one in quite a while. I was getting calluses on my rear end from Mr. Toad's Wild Ride. We had to keep the roof open on the trampoline, I mean car, or we would have been knocked unconscious when we bounced up every few seconds. I had clearly been too subtle with Yaro because he was not getting the message. It was time to try a more direct approach.

"We are tired and would like to go back to the lodge to relax," I said.

There. At the risk of hurting his feelings, I could not be any clearer. But there was no response from Yaro. He kept driving, in what direction I had not a clue. I considered mutiny. However, I now had no idea how to get back to civilization.

After I had given up any hope of survival—or more importantly dinner—Yaro stopped the car, smiled broadly with great satisfaction and pointed to a small mound of dirt up ahead. Sitting atop the mound was a stunning mother cheetah and her litter of six fuzzy cubs that had been born only a few weeks earlier. Yaro beamed from ear to ear as he explained how rare it was for a litter of six to survive this long. We watched the cubs jumping about and playfully wrestling with each other from only a few car lengths away. But even more fascinating were the movements of the mother cheetah. She was sitting on her haunches intensely staring out into the barren savannah. She seemed to have that same look of forceful concentration that we had seen on Yaro's face for the last ten hours. From time to time she would crouch down in the tall grass as if to spring into action at any moment. But instead, each time she would slowly rise again and gaze out. Helene and I scanned the horizon but naturally saw nothing.

Yaro silently pointed up ahead and we could now see what had caught the mother cheetah's fancy. It was a Thomson's gazelle about a hundred yards away nibbling on a tiny thatch of grass. The gazelle, if properly simmered in a Pinotage reduction, would make a gourmet treat for a family of cheetahs. We watched the mother cheetah for perhaps an hour as she stalked the gazelle. She repeatedly crouched as if preparing to attack but that moment never came.

"I know gazelles are fast but aren't cheetahs the fastest animal out here?" I whispered to Yaro, showing off my vast knowledge of the animal kingdom.

"Yes."

"Then why doesn't the mother run and catch the gazelle?"

"That is why," replied the wise Yaro, pointing behind us. A couple of hundred feet behind us and the cubs sat a mangy hyena with a very hungry look on its face. "The hyena hopes the mother will chase the gazelle so the hyena can grab one of the little ones to eat," Yaro explained.

The life-and-death standoff illustrating Darwin's natural selection theory continued with the mother cheetah hoping the gazelle would come closer but not daring to run after it, the hyena hoping the mother would stray far enough away from the cubs, and the blissfully ignorant cubs playfully rolling around on each other.

Each species had adapted to survive, they were all intertwined, and the struggle continued day to day. As we finally departed the food chain scene in action, it looked like mother cheetah, cubs, and hyena would all go to sleep hungry that night. Yaro, whose mission for the day was finally complete, turned our vehicle back toward the lodge.

That evening a spear-carrying Maasai warrior escorted us as usual to a linen-covered candlelit table for dinner at the lodge. The waitstaff brought us multi-course meals served on fine china with shining cutlery. Wine from South Africa flowed, live music played softly in the background, and we ate until fully satiated.

I was feeling fatigued after a very long day. It was my liver's way of reminding me that it was still there seeking attention and that I had a doctor checkup as soon as we returned home. I thought about the two small Maasai children sitting in the dirt by their dung hut. When I returned to Los Angeles I would have access to a choice of world-class hospitals and medical centers employing the best doctors anywhere using the finest equipment available. My employer-provided health insurance would pay for any treatment I needed including cutting edge drug therapy if necessary. But for those kids and the others in the village, the nearest doctor was over fifty miles away. They had no transportation to reach the doctor and even if they did, no way to pay for any medical care. Should any Maasai develop even preventable illnesses like diarrhea, pink eye, or malaria from a mosquito bite, there is a good chance they would die.

I was a ridiculously lucky guy.

* * *

With our trip almost at an end, Yaro deposited us at our hotel in Dar es Salaam for an overnight stay before we commenced another series of long flights home. Helene and I exchanged hugs with the amazing Yaro and gave him a Hollywood T-shirt complete with sparkly klieg lights and colorful palm trees. Hopefully, he would be the first one in his village to be strutting around in such sartorial splendor.

Yet I felt a certain emptiness. When that happens it usually has something to do with my stomach and this occasion was no exception. Not a single morsel of zebra had nestled on my tongue. Meat is a luxury for many Tanzanians and the types most commonly enjoyed on special occasions are goat, beef or mutton. But I had heard that zebra farms existed somewhere in the country and that zebra meat was very lean and quite healthy. Our hotel concierge, who was used to requests for fine dining, was of no help. Directly outside of our hotel I approached a cabdriver that was standing near the curb leaning on a wheeled vehicle of questionable provenance. I explained my predicament.

"Get in, I take you," he replied. He assured me that he knew just the right place that served *mishkaki* skewers using farm-raised zebra meat.

Helene was less than enthusiastic about entering the taxi and it took me several attempts to coax her inside. The back seat smelled like a perch left out in the African sun just a few days too long. Helene vigorously wiped down the seat with disinfectant wipes in a cleaning frenzy that she rarely exhibited at home. The cabdriver drove quickly past walkways teeming with humanity. Dar es Salaam has over four million residents and every one of them seemed to be out on the streets waiting for buses, hawking fruits and vegetables, or walking to some destination. At each stoplight, dozens of beggars swarmed our car. The cabbie cautioned us to keep our windows up and the doors locked. Helene slunk down low in the back seat, pretending to look for loose change and hoping not to find anything.

After a short drive we came to a halt in front of a small sidewalk grill. No name out front. No "A" in the window signifying that the local health inspector had been greatly impressed by the cleanliness of this establishment. Indeed, no window. Just a soiled fabric covering overhead, a greasy grill spewing toxic smoke, skewers of roasting meat, and a couple of plastic chairs around a squat plastic table. Our cabdriver got out and I stayed close behind him. I noticed that Helene was still inside the cab.

"Are you coming out?" I asked her.

"No."

"If you don't want to eat that's fine but it's not safe for you to stay in there alone."

No response.

"Do you have any idea what has gone on in that back seat over the years?" I prodded.

She scurried out of the cab. Helene can be quick when properly motivated.

Our cab driver spoke to the owner, who nodded in return. The owner motioned for us to sit down at the table. Helene took one look at her chair and started to get her disinfectant wipes out again. I shook my head and motioned for her to put the wipes away.

"Please, just sit down and don't embarrass the owner. We can steam clean your backside later if you want to," I told her.

I heard a new skewer fat with meat plop and sizzle on the grill. A few minutes later the proprietor brought a plate over to our table. The zebra serving was not plated on Limoges with a smear of hyena blood reduction and seemingly random but in fact meticulously placed droplets of colorful gazelle foam, as I would have preferred. But it was grilled simply, accompanied by cornmeal based *ugali*. I inspected it to see if the zebra stripes ran all the way through the flesh. Nope.

I politely offered Helene the first bite.

"You have completely lost your mind," she declared. On this single occasion she was probably correct.

"One little taste?" I asked.

"Look at this place," she said with disgust and a dismissive wave of her hand, "and its zebra, for God's sake."

"Why do you have to view things so black and white?"

"You are one funny man," she said. "Let's see if you're still this funny when you and your zebra breath are locked out of our hotel room."

I took a bite and chewed it for a while. Helene looked up at me with an expression that combined expectancy and revulsion, waiting for the verdict. I wanted to give her an answer but I needed to chew some more. This was more exercise than I had anticipated. I needed something to cleanse my palate and used my hand to roll up a small ball of *ugali*. It was a bit sticky and smelled vaguely of roasted corn. The *ugali* tasted slightly salty and was pleasant for a starch. I turned once more to my zebra and took another bite from a different part of the skewer, just to confirm. Yes, it was still tough. And stringy. And gamey. And sweet, in a bad way. It made the filet mignon at the lodges taste like, well, like filet mignon.

With dinner concluded, we safely returned to our hotel. Helene even relented and let me into our room. Perhaps the hotel restaurant was still open and I could get a nice medium-rare filet mignon in peppercorn sauce.

Too smart to end up on a plate, watching in both directions for hungry lions and hungry tourists.

I was not the only one that was hungry on this trip.

8

SHOOTING THE PASS

April 2015

I was in the middle of receiving an infusion of mouse parts when a burn rushed over my body like a rogue wave. My heart began pounding like those Brazilian *surdo* drums as it tried to explode out of my chest, my brain swirled around in my head and my entire body trembled uncontrollably. I struggled to cry out but just like in a nightmare no sound came from my lips. Somehow I stood up and just froze in place in front of my recliner, the IV still dangling from my arm. A nurse saw me and came over to ask if I was alright. I tried to answer but could not form any words. That is when the alarm went off and people started running. I looked down and saw red blotches the size of pancakes covered my arms and in fact every part of my body. A doctor rushed in to stop the infusion. It was to be my last, because I had finally become allergic to the mouse DNA drug.

I went to the office the following week but I became so weak and disoriented at work that I did what any level-headed person would do. I got in the car and drove away. Luckily, both my car and I made it to Dr. Bart's office unscathed and Dr. Bart jammed me into his ferocious schedule.

"You've definitely gotten weaker and your cognitive functions are declining. You need to stop working immediately," Dr. Bart declared.

This hit me like a mackerel in a fish slapping contest. I worked part-time as a paperboy when I was twelve years old and had not stopped working since then. I got up every morning and went to work. It was just like breathing, although breathing was not as easy as it was supposed to be either. It suddenly struck me as odd that stopping work had never even entered my thought process. But I did not have the strength to argue with Dr. Bart.

"I hadn't even thought about it," I said feebly.

"Enough is enough. You should have quit a year ago. You've worked hard during a long career and accomplished a great deal. But now you've climbed the hill and planted the flag. It's time."

His words gave me great comfort at that moment. I knew that I had done my best to keep going as long as I could. I suppose that was some sort of achievement. I relented with a weak nod.

"You need to go back in the hospital, right now," he continued. "My nurse is going to walk you across the street to the ER and get you admitted for some testing. After that we need to get you a formal liver transplant evaluation."

I rested in the hospital for four days. That should make anyone feel like new. Except me. I was weak and declining. High dose infusions of the steroid Prednisone failed to give my fatigued adrenal glands a kickstart. Dr. Patel called with additional bad news. The non-mouse DNA drug trial had ended prematurely because one of the patient participants in the trial died. I thought about the deceased patient, someone who had been desperate enough to become a human guinea pig for an experimental drug that had not been approved for any purpose. I fully understood.

* * *

Helene and I walked into the conference room at the medical center and observed the dozen other couples as we each nervously took a seat around a large table. Some couples appeared to be comprised of spouses, others of a parent and a child, some patients were accompanied only by a caregiver. It was easy to tell the patients in the group. They looked old and withered. Some had eerie yellowed skin from jaundice, some looked downright skeletal. One was in a wheelchair, another used a cane. They all moved very deliberately with glacier-like speed.

"These people look really sick," I whispered to Helene. "I hope I never get like that."

"I was thinking the same thing," she replied. "I don't know how some of these people are going to make it through the day."

We were called to attention by a nurse standing at the head of the table.

"Good morning. Welcome to the medical center for your liver evaluations. We are going to show you a short orientation film that will explain the process today. At its conclusion I will give you some additional information and then you will be off to your scheduled medical appointments throughout the day as listed in your packets. I know it is 7:30 a.m. and you may still be sleepy, but it is important that everyone stays awake throughout the film and my talk. Please hold any questions until the very end of our program this morning as we have to keep on a tight schedule."

The film commenced on a large monitor at one end of the room. Within five minutes the sound of snoring erupted from one side of the table. The nurse walked over and gently shook the person awake. Five minutes later it happened again with a different patient.

At the film's conclusion the nurse spoke about the process of getting from one appointment to another. A patient quickly interrupted to ask a question about the evaluation process.

"We'll get to that later today. For now, please hold your questions until we finish giving you this important information."

Not two minutes later the same woman interrupted to ask the very same question. We all turned to look at her in astonishment. The nurse once again politely asked her to hold questions until the end. The woman was undeterred and interrupted with another question a few minutes later.

"That woman is so rude. What is she thinking?" I whispered to Helene.

"I don't think she understands or maybe her memory is completely shot," Helene replied.

We were all present for the same purpose, to obtain a formal liver evaluation and determine whether any of us should be added to the liver waiting list. Over the course of the next several days each patient was evaluated at the medical center by every type of doctor imaginable. Helene and I ran from office to office and building to building until nighttime consulting with a transplant hepatologist, liver surgeon, cardiologist, psychiatrist, social worker, pulmonologist, neurologist, rheumatologist and way too many more to remember. Then we got up early the next day and did it again with other doctors. There were more tests and doctors over the next two weeks as I went through cardiac testing including a nuclear medicine adenosine stress test, an abdominal MRI, pulmonary function tests, tuberculosis testing, x-rays, endless blood work, and much more. We also met with the medical center's financial and insurance experts after submitting exhaustive personal financial data. If the medical center was going to award a precious liver to a patient, it needed to make sure that the patient would be both medically and psychologically prepared to deal with the trauma of such a surgery and the rigorous recovery program that would last the rest of that person's life.

Helene and I were completely spent from running around. We had not even had a lunch break in two days.

"Those other liver patients are really sick. How do they get through this?" Helene asked as we ran to the next doctor's office.

"I don't know. I can hardly keep up and I'm in better shape than most of them," I said, shaking my head.

"How are you feeling overall?

"Well, everything else being equal, I'd just as soon be laying out on a beach in Tahiti."

"I'll go with you."

The golden ticket at the end of this process was receipt of a MELD score. Short for Model for End-Stage Liver Disease, it is a morbidity analysis based on a patient's blood workups. Using a 0-40 scale, MELD predicts a patient's chances of living for the next three months. If you have a score of fifteen or higher you are deemed sick enough and can get on the waiting list. But that is the easy part.

Livers are allocated throughout the United States to eleven different regions. Due to extremely high demand and low supply, a MELD score of thirty-six or higher was generally needed at the time to receive a liver in the Los Angeles region. Other regions with older populations had a greater supply of livers and were able to make livers available for patients with a MELD score as low as twenty. In consultation with my doctors, I knew one thing for sure. I was not going to wait until I was a few weeks from death to hope to get a transplant in Los Angeles.

"Let me be sure I understand this," Helene started. "Dr. Ford said that your chances of getting a liver one day in Los Angeles will be quite difficult but if we move out of state you have a much easier opportunity to get a liver?"

"Correct," I replied.

"Why is that?"

"Just supply and demand. Believe it or not, states with no helmet laws have a greater supply of healthy livers available."

"I don't want to even think about that," Helene said with a shudder. "So where do we have to go for a liver?"

"It depends because supplies change, but right now the quickest places are Indianapolis, Birmingham, Alabama and New Orleans."

"Do we have to establish residency or anything?"

"No, we just have to move there a few weeks ahead and make sure they accept our testing results from Los Angeles. Then we cross our fingers and wait. After the transplant, we have to stay there for at least six months to receive all follow-up care. Then we can move back."

"What do we do with Snoring Dog? And Jessica? And the house?"

My head was spinning just thinking about the logistics and how little I would be able to help. "I don't know but somehow we'll figure it out. We're incredibly lucky that we have the ability to move. Most people can't just pick up and move across country."

"Why can't they just send the extra livers around the country where they're needed most?"

"Once a liver becomes available it can only survive outside of the body for a short period of time. The recipient has to be close by."

"This whole situation is just crazy but we'll get through it."

"Finally, one of the requirements is that I have to bring a caregiver with me that will stay the entire time."

"I don't come cheap."

"Oh, I know."

Two weeks after the last medical appointment had been completed, a medical committee met to evaluate each patient's data and issue a MELD score. Dr. Ford called me with the news. I had been assigned a MELD score of fourteen, one shy of getting on the list. I would have to wait and be reevaluated when my condition worsened.

* * *

2007

Way back in 1980, in an unexpected display of loyalty Helene agreed to join me in Maui for our honeymoon. We soaked up the rays on Kaanapali Beach, shivered together under a blanket as we watched the sun rise over the Haleakala volcano crater, stuck our feet under a waterfall on the twisting drive to Hana, and attended a luau complete with fire dancers and hula girls wearing the ever-popular coconut bras. As we clinked our glasses of wine in front of a perfect sunset, I asked her if she wanted to go snorkeling with me the next day.

"No, thank you."

'Why not?"

"I don't like to snorkel."

"Have you ever been snorkeling before?"

"No."

"Then how do you know you don't like it?"

"I get seasick."

"You won't get seasick walking out into calm water to snorkel."

"No, thank you."

Careful readers may notice something familiar in this exchange. I did not realize it at the time but over the years I have come to admire how doggedly consistent my spouse is. Once I hear that "no, thank you," my brain knows that I should move on to another topic. But something inside of me just cannot let go. I believed that over several decades I could wear her down. This remains unchecked on my bucket list.

On each of our subsequent trips to island locations I engaged in virtually identical conversations with Helene regarding snorkeling. Yet, she remained firm in her conviction that she loathed snorkeling, notwithstanding the fact that she had never tried it.

Years later while vacationing in Poipu Beach, Kauai I became quite ill and by all accounts should have stayed in bed. However, I refused to waste a single day of precious vacation time and insisted on going snorkeling. When Helene could not dissuade me from going into the water alone, she astonished me by declaring that she would go snorkeling with me. She had grown fond of me by that time and wanted to keep an eye on me.

After snorkeling for ten minutes or so Helene suddenly surfaced and yelled out: "These fish are so colorful! This snorkeling is really great."

"My bad," I said. "I should have mentioned it to you earlier."

But Helene was right about one thing. Like me, she does easily succumb to seasickness. In so many ways, we are the perfect match.

* * *

We were both ready to try out a new snorkeling location as long as it did not involve bobbing on the ocean in a seafaring vessel. My research led me straight to Rangiroa, a coral atoll in Tahiti with the second largest lagoon on the planet. It is also known as one of the world's magnificent diving and snorkeling sites. Emerging from the remnants of a volcanic caldera, the coral rim has hundreds of open channels called *motus* that allow water and marine life to flow into and out of the lagoon. Two particular sets of *motus* on opposite sides of the island have created a surging liquid highway buffet packed with a bounty of sea life including rays, mantas, turtles and sharks. Divers and snorkelers can "shoot the pass" by starting at the *motu* that brings the fish in from outside the lagoon and then drift with the fish toward, but not out of, the *motu* on the other end of the lagoon. It is most desirable not to exit with the current through the second *motu* unless you want to try your luck at outswimming hungry killer whales in Antarctica.

The friendly lagoon welcomes all kinds of sharks. Black Tip reef sharks, White Tip reef sharks, the ever-grumpy hammerheads and even Tiger sharks. Tiger sharks are known to have the most perfect teeth structure of all sharks. Aside from having a great smile, Tiger sharks can successfully kill almost every category of prey including humans.

"Sweetie..." I started to call out to Helene from in front of my computer back home.

"I know," she interrupted after having peeked at my research. "You want me to fly for over nine hours, then get on some turboprop plane left over from World War II that will try it's hardest to land on an airstrip scraped onto a postage stamp-sized island in the middle of the Pacific, and then outswim hungry killer sharks while snorkeling in Rangiroa. Sure, no problem."

That's my girl!

A few short months later our ancient plane mercifully touched down on a humid and breezy Rangiroa runway late in the morning and I was a man with a plan. Relax on the sand that afternoon, get a good dinner and night's sleep, then shoot the pass in the morning. After that, fly on to Bora Bora for a few days and eventually to Morea where we had reserved an overwater bungalow with a small deck where we could dangle our feet in the water and feed the fish. Our brief visit to Rangiroa was for one purpose only—to shoot the pass. I had convinced Helene that the protected lagoon of Rangiroa offered a world-class snorkeling opportunity while still avoiding those pesky seasick-inducing waves. Simply drift with the current and shoot the pass in the calm lagoon without going out into that nasty open ocean. Even better, if I accidently forgot to tell Helene about exiting before the second *motu*, I would not have to share the banana Po'e dessert at dinner.

Upon arrival at the Hotel Kia Ora we were immediately greeted with a cold drink and chilled towel as we breezed through the open reception area, checked in while seated on a comfortable lounge and were whisked away to our room. After settling in we strolled over to the activities center to confirm our snorkeling trip scheduled for the next morning. We were shocked to see a sign posted stating that the drift trip to shoot the pass earlier that morning had been canceled. I went over to speak with the person in charge.

"Did today's trip get cancelled?" I asked.

"Yes, sir. Bad weather from a storm north of here that really messed up the current. Right now, the current in the pass is going shark ass-backward."

As much as I love local colloquialisms, that did not sound like a good thing. "We're signed up for tomorrow morning's trip. Do you expect it to go out?"

"No telling until tomorrow. Just check-in with us tomorrow morning."

"Aye, aye," I replied, showing off my maritime cred.

Helene and I walked out to the gleaming white beach overlooking the bluest lagoon ever and fell into a plush pair of blue lounges under a broad umbrella. The beach overlooked a long wooden pier with a small boat dock at the far end. I sighed with great satisfaction at this perfect scene, closed my eyes for a well-deserved nap and dreamed of dinner. Until a familiar voice knifed through the tranquility like a shucker slicing open a dozing oyster.

"Hon, you should put some sunscreen on," Helene cautioned.

"No thanks. We have an umbrella covering us and anyway, I don't burn."

"You always say that and then you burn. That umbrella doesn't keep out all the harmful rays."

"No, thank you."

Turnabout was fair play. I showed her. An hour later I woke up from my most pleasant nap under the umbrella. My back was red as a Tahitian prawn.

"I told you so," Helene reminded, as if I could possibly forget.

Dinner at the hotel was quite fine. I very gingerly sat down in the dining chair and enjoyed Rangiroa fish soup with garlicky croutons followed by my new soul mates, Tahitian prawns. Helene was delighted as well with her filet of beef followed by Tahitian vanilla crème brûlée. After dinner we retired to our room and were peacefully lulled to sleep by the sound of rolling waves.

In the morning we awoke to a strong breeze but clear skies, and the sand felt warm between our toes as we eagerly walked to the breakfast buffet. It was a large well-stocked bounty but my eyes quickly locked on one item. Freshly baked *pains au chocolat!* All I could eat! A thousand layers of croissant flakiness. Quality 70% cocoa dark chocolate. Two lines of chocolate, not just one like those lesser croissants. After giving silent thanks for French colonialism, I put on my game face and attacked.

But mid-breakfast my croissant fantasy sprung a leak. "Don't you think you've had enough?" my loving spouse interjected as I took a brief intermission from my chocolate binge to scarf down a cheese omelet and a few waffles.

"I need to keep my strength up to shoot the pass today," I said.

"You shouldn't eat too much right before you go in the water."

"Thanks, Mom."

Reeling just a bit from my *pain au chocolat* high, with some trepidation I slowly made my way to the activities center to see if our drift trip was on. "The current is still funky and it's pretty choppy outside the lagoon. Just go on over to the dock at 10:00 a.m. and the Captain will decide at that time," I was told.

Helene and I grabbed our snorkeling gear shortly before 10:00 a.m. and walked down the pier to where a small boat was docked. The watercraft looked to be the size of a base model Prius with bad brake linings. Six additional guests had signed up and were waiting to tempt fate on the boat as well. Captain Ahab knocked some sand off of his weathered leather sandals, scratched his multi-day-old salt and pepper beard and gave us the news: "The weather is still playing games with the current but climb aboard. We can go search for dolphins for an hour or so and see if the current settles down by then."

"Did he say search for dolphins?" I asked Helene as we climbed aboard the vessel whose seaworthiness remained an open question.

"That's what the man said."

"I didn't know there were any dolphins in the lagoon."

There were not. As the boat pulled away from the dock, we cut through the smooth as a polished abalone shell lagoon and exited one of the *motus* into malevolent ocean waters where our new dolphin friends might or might not be frolicking. I did not want to see any damn dolphins. I did not want to be outside the lagoon. I wanted to go home.

Now, I have seen my fair share of ocean disaster movies. You know the ones where the captain struggles at the wheel while waves the size of Mount Fuji relentlessly crash down upon him, half the crew is thrown overboard, the mast breaks in half and overall it is quite unpleasant. The Perfect Storm. The Poseidon Adventure. Moby Dick. Those were just child's play compared to our search for dolphins outside the lagoon. Our knot-holed boat flew up out of the water like a hooked marlin and then mashed straight down into the maw of that troubled ocean. Over and over and over and over and over. Our seafaring rust bucket got more air than an Olympic snowboarding team. I did not see a single dolphin and I sure didn't give a flying fish whether I saw one or not. This may have been because I spent the entire time with my head buried beneath my knees and a death grip on the seat.

When I dared to peek up, all of the passengers looked seaweed green except for the Captain, who by all appearances was having a grand old time. He eventually announced that it was time to head back to the lagoon to check on the current. If I could move, I would have kissed his dirty sandaled feet. We made it back to the lagoon mere moments before the boat was about to disintegrate, and the Captain announced that we would try to shoot the pass. "Everyone into the water and follow me closely. The current is quite strong today."

We put on our masks and snorkels and collapsed into the water. But I could not hold it any longer. Virtually upon impact with the water the previous night's prawns, a garlicky crouton or two, and at least half a dozen partially digested *pains au chocolat* spewed into the water. Just as quickly, hundreds of fish of every size and color suddenly appeared in a spirited feeding frenzy.

Helene and I feel truly fortunate to have visited so many extraordinary places during our travels. From the Arctic Circle to New Zealand and across six continents we have been infinitely enriched by dozens of different cultures and the wonderful people we have met. We also feel a strong commitment to not just take away souvenirs, photos and memories from each of our trips, but to give something back to each community that we visit. It was most gratifying then, that I was able to give back to the Rangiroa community by feeding every fish in that damn lagoon when I puked into the water.

As best I could tell, Helene seemed to be hanging in there while we shot the pass, although at that point as far as I was concerned it was every snorkeler for himself. For most of the run my eyes were closed tauter than the sphincter of a fat sea turtle being pursued by a great white shark, as the current hurled me toward a certain death which I readily welcomed. The next time I opened my eyes, some unknown hands were dragging me back into the boat. My somewhat queasy spouse sat down beside me and stated, in-between deep breaths, that we had shot the pass. It was news to me.

"Did you see that giant shark?" she asked excitedly.

"The only thing I saw was my life passing before my eyes and it wasn't pretty."

Somehow, the nearly exhausted Prius boat finally limped back to the dock. At the other end of the pier the many guests of Kia Ora were lounging on the beach watching the boat come in, which was the most exciting thing that happened on this lazy atoll. To say that Helene and I staggered out of the boat onto the dock would be an injustice to staggerers everywhere. We looked like we had just been rescued from forty days out at sea clinging to a plank after our ship sunk, and that we had eaten the other survivors to stave off starvation.

We careened from side to side, trying to find our footing on a pier that seemed to be mounted on roller skates. Helene had performed commendably on this adventure but even she had her limits. Just when we were only steps away from being in the clear, Helene projectile vomited all over the pier, directly in front of an entire beach of guests who had been quietly sipping their mai tais. Up on the beach I saw one rather rotund gentlemen in a red Speedo start to gag.

Once she got up off of her knees and came up for air, Helene completed her walk of shame down the pier and through the beachgoers, who by now had regrouped and gave her a lounging ovation. We crawled back to our room and onto the bed, covered our heads with pillows while trying to remain as still as possible and prayed that it would all just go away. We both remained so ill that we never made it down to the barbecue dinner buffet and Polynesian show that evening, although we greatly appreciated the pounding *pahu* bass drums that reverberated endlessly through the walls of our room as we tried to sleep it off.

Helene vomiting on the pier.

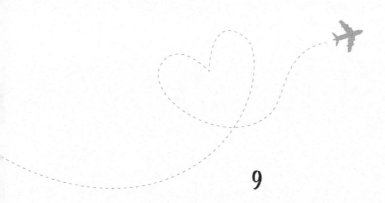

9

AN OLD WARRIOR

November 15, 2016

Since April, Dr. Patel had done his best, reaching deep into his wizard's bag of tricks. After my last aborted infusion attempt, Dr. Patel told me that there was another drug that might help. Once again, it was approved for other purposes and would be experimental for my condition. Instead of an infusion, I would have to inject it into my stomach every other week. It cost $2,500 per injection.

My insurance company said "no." Dr. Patel resubmitted the request. My insurance company said "no." Dr. Patel personally called my insurance company's adjuster to plead my case. My insurance company said "no." Dr. Patel wrote my insurance company a letter explaining the situation. My insurance company said "no." Finally, during an office visit I listened in as Dr. Patel got on the phone in a heated exchange with the adjuster and finally yelled that he was going to sue her personally! How preposterous! But my insurance company said "yes." I learned how to give myself injections of the drug. Unfortunately, it did not work and caused a mild allergic reaction to boot. After a few months I stopped taking it and watched helplessly as my body continued to deteriorate.

By November, my condition had taken another major turn for the worse. It felt like my liver had jumped off a cliff and was dragging the rest of me with it. Then Dr. Bart made it official.

"It's time for you to go for another liver transplant evaluation," he told me, shaking his head. "You're much worse than just a few weeks ago. You need to get on the list."

"I know. But there is no way in the world I can run around to two dozen different doctors' offices like last time and I don't think I can wait a month for a committee to meet and give me a new MELD score. I could barely make it up the elevator to your office today. Is it time to look into going out of state? I don't know what to do," I said. I was frustrated and dejected.

"Let me make some calls. Wait here."

"Believe me, I'm not going anywhere."

Dr. Bart returned a few minutes later. "I called the head of the liver transplant clinic at Cedars-Sinai Medical Center near West Hollywood. They can see you tomorrow at the liver clinic and evaluate you in one day," he declared.

"How is that possible? The entire process took a month last time. How can they do it in a single day?" I asked.

"They promise they can do it. You have an appointment at 8:00 a.m."

* * *

November 16, 2016

Helene held me steady by latching onto my upper arm as I shuffled very slowly into the conference room at the hospital's liver clinic. Despite daily protein drinks, any semblance of muscle mass had long since abandoned me. Severe jaundice had taken its place. Even the whites of my eyes had turned yellow, giving me an unfashionable werewolf vibe. Skin hung limply in sheets over my frail bones. Even the slightest movement was exhausting.

Helene and I waited in the reception area of the liver clinic, still not really believing that I would have a new MELD score and be on the list by the end of the day. I had little choice other than to have some faith. I watched as other couples entered the room and sat down. They all looked healthy compared to me. I chuckled at the contrast from when I was evaluated only last year. Then I stopped. It hurt to chuckle.

While waiting for the orientation to begin a volunteer who received a liver transplant came over to speak with Helene and me. She explained that when you near the top of the liver list you may receive an offer of a liver, and you have only a short time to decide whether to accept it or reject it.

"Why would anyone on the list reject an offer of a liver?" Helene asked her, while I slumped in the chair and just listened.

"Well, the livers are screened for blood type, size and condition before an offer is made. With some livers you know the history of the donor but with other donors you have no idea. Did they suffer from alcohol or drug abuse? Were they HIV-positive? Did they have hepatitis? Do you want to go through a major surgery and take such a risk? Do you accept an offer of a liver that is borderline small for your size or an older person's liver that may not last as long, or do you wait and hope you find one more suitable? These are life and death decisions that you need to deal with in a short amount of time. I rejected an offer before receiving my transplant."

"Wow. How long ago did you receive your transplant?"

"Over a year ago."

"That must have been a hard decision to reject the offer."

"Not really. The hardest part was that I accepted a number of different offers before actually getting a new liver."

"You're kidding! How did that happen?"

"Once you accept an offer, there are still a lot of variables. The liver is only viable out of the body for a few hours so it may not reach the hospital in time if it is coming from far away, sometimes they come from out of state. Also, the doctors may not know everything about a liver until it is removed from the donor. Sometimes the livers are too scarred or fatty. I was ready for surgery more than once only to have it fall through."

"I can't imagine the disappointment."

"It all turned out well. Good luck to you."

Helene and I sat through the brief orientation and then were ushered into an examination room where we met with a liver transplant surgeon. After an hour the surgeon got up to leave and told us to wait where we were. Helene and I looked at each other. We were not sure what would happen next. A moment later a cardiologist came in to examine me. I did not have to move at all. The different doctors were lined up and scheduled to come to me. The mastermind at the clinic even brought in food for a lunch break! For the first time I felt like I would make it through the day.

I was not concerned about getting on the list because I knew my condition had worsened dramatically since my last evaluation. I was not even thinking about getting a new liver or having major surgery. I was just so grateful that I did not have to move any more that day. It was an unexpected gift that I deeply needed to just get through another twenty-four hours. Surviving yet another day was a victory and I had won again.

Helene and I sat there as a parade of doctors and other professionals came and went. I told each of them the same story and answered the same questions that I had been answering through years of treatment.

Mid-afternoon a dose of reality hit me. In a few hours I would have a new MELD score. Helene and I would have to move to another part of the country. Quickly. Helene and I were born and raised in Los Angeles and lived there our entire lives. We resided in our current home for twenty years. How would we move cross-country for just six to eight months? What would we take with us? Who would take care of things at home while we were gone? I became exhausted putting my clothes on in the morning. How was I going to help pack, or carry a suitcase, or even think clearly? The suddenness of what was happening overwhelmed me. But I had always adhered to that old Chinese saying: "A journey of a thousand miles begins with a single step." I had a journey of two thousand miles in front of me and I needed to take that first wobbly step immediately.

During short breaks between examinations and without speaking but with the telepathy that comes from having been together for almost forty years, Helene got on her phone and started searching for apartments near the liver transplant hospital at The University of Alabama at Birmingham while I checked my phone for similar living arrangements near Ochsner Transplant Institute in New Orleans. I could likely get on a plane bound for either location and be in line for a new liver within days. I was already picturing the New Orleans shrimp po-boy sandwich from Parkway Bakery that I would have following surgery but I decided that it was not the right time to share this with Helene.

It was almost five o'clock in the afternoon. I was beaten down and looking forward to going home and crawling into my very own bed. We would be terribly busy the next day scheduling flights, coordinating with one of the out of state hospitals, getting medical records together and nailing down a temporary place to live.

One of the doctors that we met earlier came back into our examination room.

"We've looked over all of your tests and spoken to the doctors that examined you today. Your MELD score is currently twenty-six. But we are all in agreement that you really need to go into the hospital for more testing," he said.

A million times I have heard the old saying "my heart sank." At that moment I could literally feel it happening.

"When?" I asked.

"Right now."

No. I have always trusted my medical professionals and tried to follow their advice to the letter. But I felt that my sagging back was up against the wall and using what little energy I had left I became defiant. I had been hospitalized "to run some tests" more times than I could remember. Each time I was stuck in the hospital for four or five days. Enough testing. I needed to move forward.

"I've been tested up the wazoo. I just want to go home and go to sleep," I pleaded. "Anyway, I can't get a liver here in L.A. with a twenty-six score. Helene and I are going to make plans to go out of state immediately to get the transplant. They can test me in New Orleans."

"You are not well enough to travel. You are also not well enough to go home. You need to be admitted immediately."

It felt like every molecule of oxygen in my body was suddenly sucked out at once. I cannot travel? Even if someone had to throw me over their shoulder and drag me on the plane, I needed to go. If I did not get out of L.A. soon, I would die. Dead. Deceased. All over some testing. I intended to get on a plane and stay conscious until I reached New Orleans, whatever it took.

"I know how this goes," I reasoned with the doctor. "Every time I'm admitted to the hospital for testing I end up staying at least four or five days. I can't afford to do that. We have to make other plans right away."

The doctor sat down, took off his glasses, looked first at Helene to make sure he had her full attention, and then looked me straight in the eyes. "Let me tell you this," he said sternly. "If you were my mother or any other loved one, I would not let you leave this hospital right now under any circumstances."

I knew he was speaking just as much to Helene as he was to me, maybe more so. Helene and I looked at each other. It was a life or death decision.

"I'll go home and get your hospital bag with your stuff," she said. "Back in a few minutes."

* * *

2008

"The polar bears are dying off," Helene declared out of the blue one day while I was studying menu spreadsheets on where to go for dinner.

"I didn't do it and I've got an alibi," I pleaded.

"I'd really like to go see them while we still can."

"Take a warm jacket if you go, Flo." In our private name game world, we would answer to any name as long as it rhymed. My personal favorite was "Let's rock, Spock," but I generally reserved that for special occasions.

Helene adopted her default position, which was to prudently ignore whatever I said. "There's a place in Canada where you can observe the polar bears in their natural habitat," she continued.

"I'll pass. It sounds cold."

"Pleeeaasse?"

* * *

Churchill is located in Manitoba, Canada on the West side of the Hudson Bay. Officially it has eight hundred and ninety-nine human residents, not including those hiding out in a witness protection program. Churchill is so remote that it is accessible only by plane or train. Each year in the late fall, polar bears hold a convention nearby and wait for the water to freeze on Hudson Bay so they can cross and enjoy their favorite snack of ringed seal tartare. Until the freeze occurs, the bears roam the outskirts of Churchill. For a few weeks each year, tourists venture out on tundra buggies and observe the polar bears polishing their cutlery in anticipation.

It is not unusual for rowdy polar bears looking for a good time to venture into the town of Churchill itself. I have no doubt that the polar bears are sadly disappointed when they arrive. I know I was. A general store, a liquor mart, and a handful of small motels that were last updated before I was born. Without even a bowling alley to hang out at, many of the bears become downright surly. Tourists are urged not to go out at night. Residents have learned not to lock their cars, just in case they have to make a quick getaway from an oncoming bear. The town even maintains a polar bear jail where felonious polar bears are sent if they repeatedly wander into town, violate curfew, or get mixed up with rowdy polar bears from the wrong side of the tracks.

I became concerned after we flew into Winnipeg and our tour operator fitted us with boots, glove liners, gloves, scarves, wool hats and hooded jackets lined with the fur of some long dead but very thick animal. Was it going to be chilly in Churchill? In Los Angeles we break out heavy jackets if the temperature dips below sixty degrees Fahrenheit, but I had never seen this much gear.

We dragged all of our new cold weather accoutrements, along with fresh baked cinnamon buns from Winnipeg's Tall Grass Prairie Bread Company, onto the plane to Churchill. A couple of hours later we were herded onto a bus for the short drive to our motel. Each of the motels in Churchill are self-described as offering "basic accommodations." To me, "basic accommodations" means sheets made of pima cotton rather than Egyptian, domestic chocolate mints left on my pillow during evening turndown service instead of Belgian truffles, and having to use a bath towel instead of a proper bath sheet. But I could have used an old stick to carve an igloo more luxurious than our Churchill motel. No bell captain or even a trained team of huskies to assist with our three heavy pieces of luggage. I tried to locate the elevator to take us up to our room. The motel clerk told me that instead of an elevator they have this "new-fangled contraption called stairs." People develop an odd sense of humor when deprived of sunlight for much of the year.

The clerk handed us a metal key to open our room door. Metal key? That is so Sixties chic. I was a bit winded by the time I located our room on the upper floor. Helene seemed even more exhausted when she finally showed up with our luggage. I made a mental note to increase Helene's cardio workouts if we ever got home. I opened the door and surveyed our new accommodations. The sheets were fifty thread count, max. I would have slept on the floor just out of spite but it was a threadbare shag carpet in a color not known to nature. The towels were so slight that if you turned them sideways they disappeared. The brochure for the motel bragged that this establishment featured live music in its lounge. Later that evening I could attest that not only was there live music in the lounge, there was live music in every room whether you liked it or not due to walls that were as thin as the towels. Most frightening of all, the owners of the hotel locked the doors at night. Not the door to your room, mind you. The door to the hotel itself. They claimed this was to keep polar bears out but I have no doubt that it was to keep the guests from trying to escape in the middle of the night. We were trapped like Artic rats.

The next morning after what was quite generously referred to as "breakfast" at the motel coffee shop, Helene and I put on thermal underwear, several layers of shirts, flannel-lined pants, and our newly acquired compliment of gloves, scarfs, wool hats and jackets. Nanook of the North had nothing on us. After a short bus ride we got our first look at our polar bear viewing vehicle, the tundra buggy. The buggy looked like a cross between a school bus on steroids and a World War II tank. If I could have mounted a machine gun turret on top, Helene and I could have staged a coup and taken over of all of Churchill in five minutes. Not that we would want it, of course.

The buggy was perched on six-foot-tall tires to maneuver through the snow. A door in the rear led to an open-air platform for unobstructed picture taking. Each set of seats had a fogged-over window that you could slide open if you pulled hard enough before losing a fingernail. The driver kept the interior of the buggy at a balmy eighty degrees or so, fueled by a powerful heater chugging away in the center aisle. As soon as we sat down we ripped off our hyper-thermal wear as quickly as possible before we sweltered to our deaths. To go out on the exterior platform to view bears unimpeded by the steamy windows, we dressed up again in our top four layers of shirts, glove liners, gloves, hats, scarves and fur lined jackets. I would take a few pictures, shiver my way back inside, and tear off all the extra clothing. Repeat until overcome by exhaustion.

As we got underway we spotted a pair of arctic grouses scouring the ground for mosses and lichens. Except for the tip of their dark beaks, they blended in perfectly with the snow. Our guide told us that the grouses turn brown in the summer months but I had no plans to wait around to find out.

A little further along we followed a set of small tracks to an Arctic fox playing in the snow. It too was completely white except for a black nose and two slanted reddish eyes. Its fur would also turn back to brown in the summer to more easily avoid hungry polar bears and wolves. Slyly, the fox was probably tracking a polar bear from a distance, hoping to dine on any scraps left over from a bear's lunch. But the bears themselves were hungry as well. Whatever fat they had stored up was likely gone by now and they needed desperately for that river to freeze soon and allow access to the nourishing seals.

We saw a polar bear off in the distance curled up in the snow like a dog in front of a warm fire. I was surprised to see that the bear was a yellowish color and easily distinguishable against the whiteness of the snow. I guess when you weigh over a thousand pounds the only land predator you need to worry about arrives on two legs. We spotted a smaller juvenile bear laying against a snowbank for shelter from the wind, its snout tucked in under its paw to keep its nose warm. I might have to give that a try the next time I go outside. A couple of larger bears wandered by, leaving hubcap-sized paw prints in the snow. The bears turned to look at the buggy and we could see them stop to lift their noses in the air to sniff out what we had eaten for breakfast. They probably only smelled gasoline exhaust from our buggy. Come to think of it, that's kind of what our breakfast smelled like as well.

As we turned to spot a family of three bears walking in the distance, a white rainbow appeared over the horizon. Also known as a fog-bow, it consists of small droplets that do not refract light, arching across the sky. Was there a pot of white gold at the end of it? I never got to find out.

One of the more adventuresome bears sauntered right up to the buggy. Satellite television reception is spotty at best in this remote location so the bears use the tourists for their daily entertainment. The windows of the buggy were at least nine or ten feet off the ground. Yet, this bear stood up on his hind legs and stretched all the way up to peer in through the window. The only thing separating us from the polar bear's morning breath was the steamy fingerprint-clustered untempered glass of the buggy. The bear's semi-webbed paws pressed up against the window were enormous, at least twice as big as my hands, with long thick curved claws that were getting a little too close for comfort.

As we drove on it became so hot in the buggy that guests started to slide open their windows six or eight inches to bring the temperature down to something that would support life. As another bear approached, the guide nervously instructed one of the guests to close his window. The guest groused that the window was only cracked open six inches and was far too small for a thousand-plus pound polar bear to climb through. The guide responded that polar bears like to hang out at small openings in the ice where the ringed seals periodically surface to get a gulp of air. When the polar bears spot a seal near an opening, the bears reach in under the water and pull the seal out. The air holes are typically only a few inches in diameter, so this process often involves breaking every bone in the seal's body as it is involuntarily wrenched through the hole. The guest quickly closed both the window and his mouth.

I visited the exterior platform repeatedly throughout the day to take photos. It was tiresome to continually put on all of the outer wear for each visit to the platform only to have to remove the gear when I came back inside. I eventually decided to go out to the platform to take one quick picture before the buggy took us back to our hovel. I went through the rear door and onto the platform without hat, gloves or fur lined jacket. After communing with nature for five seconds or so, I went to press the button on my camera for a photo. My finger stuck to the camera. In fact, as I went to take inventory, I could not even confirm that I still had ten fingers. My entire face was tingling and not in a good way. Another guest opened the door and pulled me back inside. I sat on top of the heater and shivered away ten pounds.

As we started to head back toward town we came upon an old warrior laboriously walking through the snow. His yellow fur was matted in some places, missing in others, and hung loosely on his body. He was frightfully skinny and we could see some of his ribs even through the thick hide. There was a long scar running down his hindquarter and several more scars on his face and snout. He had no doubt stood his ground and battled for survival through a long life. He walked with a bit of a limp, trying to keep moving and ignore the pain of hunger and aching old bones. The old guy was determined to hold on until the big freeze came and allowed for at least one more grand meal. I felt a strange kinship with this combat-tested old timer and was pulling for him to make it. He may not be the fittest, but I had a feeling he would still survive.

The tundra buggy eventually returned us to our motel where we thawed out and enjoyed a welcome rest even on the clumpy mattress. But not for long. It would be a crime to travel to Churchill and not take in the delights of the polar bear jail, which we were told was just outside of town. We bundled up, walked by the stuffed and mounted polar bear in the lobby, and went out into the great white abyss. After slipping and sliding to the edge of town, we could not spot a single structure with guard towers, razor wire and roving search lights. Helene, completely abandoning any sense of honor, asked a local for directions. The friendly stranger pointed us to a simple metal corrugated building down the road.

No motion detectors were planted in the snow because we walked right up to the front door. Not a single automatic weapon brandishing guard came running. I looked at the door. Just a commercial lock. There were not even any barred windows. What do the polar bears rake their metal cups against when they are served tepid left-over seal soup for the third day in a row? I could have led a successful jail break with nothing more than two muskrats and a toothpick.

I banged on the door and requested to see the warden. I expected to be greeted by a monocled guy in a cheap uniform with gaudy epaulettes, obsessively striking a riding crop across the palm of his hand, accompanied by two burly heavily scarred guards with crew cuts and permanent sneers. Instead, out came a smiling bespectacled grandfatherly type wearing a light parka. "Can I help you folks?" he asked.

"We were hoping to visit the polar bears that you have captive," I said.

"We don't have any bears in here right now. We did just let one out yesterday. Anyway, we don't allow visits," he replied.

"What do you mean you let one out?"

"We don't punish the bears. These bears are endangered. If they wander into town and get sent to polar bear jail, we let them sit in there overnight and then take them out in the wild and let them go."

"You've got to be kidding me. You just let them go?"

"That's the policy. Thanks for dropping by."

Great. Rather than force these bears to accept responsibility for their criminal actions, they get a slap on the paw and are set free after a few hours in a comfy "jail" that is undoubtedly better appointed than my motel. They probably even get to keep the soap and shampoo. Crime does pay in Churchill.

We slogged back toward our motel. Past the statue of the howling wolf covered up to its snout in snow. Past the black satellite dish the size of a small house, sitting atop a snow drift that almost covers its polar bear logo. Past the tip top of the stalled snow removal tractor, the rest of which was buried in snow. We walked to what might have once been a path to the front door of our motel and looked up at the cheesy fake icicles dangling all along the edge of the roof. No, those were real icicles.

It was dinnertime, so we got ready to play dining roulette at one of the handful of eateries in town. I selected the one that had the fewest instances of food poisoning reported on Yelp. I asked the server for the polar bear specials. Blank look. By the time we had consumed the most exotic features on the menu, semi-thawed chicken breast and a reheated burger, it was dark outside and we still had to walk back to our motel. We bundled up and went outside.

"You go first, I'll watch your back," I told Helene.

"I've heard that one before."

"Do you know any polar bear mating calls?" I asked.

"There won't be mating of any kind this evening, don't you worry."

*   *   *

In the morning we sat down to the same breakfast as before, except now the restaurant was out of eggs until next week's delivery. I could not decide whether this was good or bad news.

"Let's go to the post office after breakfast," Helene suggested.

"Good idea. We can try to get a message out for somebody to save us."

"No. If you bring them your passport, they'll stamp it with a polar bear stamp."

"The only polar bear stamp I want to see is the Canadian meat inspector's Grade A stamp on a rack of polar bear ribs."

I looked outside. A savage wind was now tearing through town. We spent our usual fifteen minutes putting on our cold weather gear. The post office was three blocks away. After we had walked a block, I heard Helene's faint voice through the biting wind: "I... think...my...lips...are...about...to...freeze...together."

Finally, some good news! "Let's keep going," I replied through chattering teeth. "You don't want to miss out on that stamp."

After two blocks, it was colder than the look I gave the waiter the prior evening when he informed me that the restaurant did not stock Inglenook Rubicon Cabernet but that I could have something called House Red or House White. Churchill is only a few blocks long. Very long, very cold blocks. It was ten degrees below zero but with the wind chill it broke the thermometer. We were told that it routinely gets so cold that Environment Canada had to come up with a lower wind chill warning temperature for Churchill than the rest of Canada, otherwise they would be issuing warnings so often that no one would pay any attention. I do not recall how, but we made it to the post office and the clerk did stamp our passports with an unimpressive outline of a generic polar bear. Lucky us. Then we had to walk back.

Shoot me dead.

After we set ourselves on fire to warm up, we had another outing in the tundra buggy that afternoon. Word must had spread among the polar bears about my visit with the warden. As we drove by they seemed to be mocking me. One looked at me and started laughing so hard that he fell on his back and started to make polar bear snow angels. We fled back to Los Angeles in utter humiliation.

Smart ass polar bear mocking the author.

This bear must have eaten at our motel.

10

ROOTS

November 20, 2016

I spent four days at the hospital being pricked, pummeled, poked and punctured. I fought back valiantly, haranguing every doctor and nurse within earshot that I was feeling well enough to go home. They just nodded and went about their business. I flaunted my good health by forcing myself out of bed each day to casually stand outside the door of my room when the doctors were making their rounds. I forced down all (okay, some) of each meal to demonstrate my voracious appetite. I demanded that the nurses document in my chart the glorious magnificence of each daily bowel movement. I built up a substantial body of evidence that would convince any jury that I should be set free.

I pleaded. I cajoled. I begged. Who could sleep in a hospital? I would be much better off resting at home with my wonderful wife to take care of me. There were all kinds of sick people in the hospital, exposing me daily to ungodly bacteria and viruses. I would be much safer in my own bedroom, which I promised to have hermetically sealed as soon as I returned home. Give my hospital bed away to someone who was truly ill.

Finally, I wore them down. One of the liver doctors relented and said I could go home if I promised to rest. I called Helene to give her the good news and urged her to come pick me up before anyone changed their mind. Relying on recommendations from some of the doctors, Helene and I would shortly be on our way to Ochsner Multi-Organ Transplant Institute in New Orleans and the extended stay hotel directly adjacent to the medical center. If my appetite ever returned, Commander's Palace's Creole Bread Pudding Soufflé was only a few GrubHub minutes away.

I hung up the phone and got up to retrieve my clothes from the hospital room closet so I could get dressed. As I started to return to my bed, a black fog smacked me like a Louisville Slugger and the room looked like fans in Dodger Stadium doing the wave. I dove for the bed and made it, just barely avoiding being splattered on the floor.

I must have gotten up too quickly. I lay still for a few moments and felt a little better. No need to concern anyone, so I said nothing to the doctors or nurses. An attendant pushing a wheelchair arrived to take me to our car and the waiting Helene. I was finally going home!

It was late afternoon when Helene parked in our driveway and stood close as I walked up the steps and through our house to my beloved bed. I caught my breath and walked into my closet to get a change of clothes, but I immediately became so dizzy that I fell to my knees. After a few minutes I got back up and Helene spotted me walking unsteadily back to bed.

"Are you okay?" she asked.

"I just got a bit dizzy," I replied. "I must have gotten up too quickly."

"I'm going to call the doctor."

"I'm fine, really. I just need to lay down."

"Are you sure?"

"Yes, I'm fine. Just a little excited about being home. I'll rest now."

A few hours later I got up to go into the bathroom. Halfway there I passed out on the floor. Helene came running over. "What happened?" she asked.

"I just got dizzy again but it only happens when I stand up."

"I'm going to call an ambulance."

"No, I can make it to the car and you can drive me to the doctor's office. Just help me get onto that rolling desk chair and you can roll me over to the stairs. Then I can pull myself up with the handrail and you can help me crawl to the car."

"I'm calling the ambulance right now. Don't move."

A few minutes later the sound of a siren grew louder. In the hills above Los Angeles where we live, sounds echo and reverberate off the twisting mountain ridges and valleys, making it difficult to determine their origin. But there was no mistaking the two paramedics marching into our bedroom with their medical equipment. One of them strapped a cuff around my arm. I heard him tell Helene: "sixty over thirty." My blood pressure was about the same as that of a turnip.

The rolling gurney was too wide for our stairway so the paramedics strapped me to a backboard and hefted me up the stairs the old-fashioned way. They carried me out in the rain, hoisted me into the ambulance and drove off. Helene tried to follow in her car but soon fell behind at the traffic lights. The wailing siren was the only sound in the lonely night.

* * *

2009

A lone golden trumpet appeared in the window at the top of the ancient church tower. Helene and I stood below in the middle of Krakow, Poland's Rynek Glowny, the largest Medieval square in Europe, as the trumpeter slowly played a stirring anthem through the west window. Then he turned and bugled the same melody through the east window, then the south and lastly the north, bathing the entire square in the lonesome sound. The call of the bugle flew over the fourteenth century Cloth Hall, the statue of poet Adam Mickiewicz, enterprising buskers, outdoor cafes, fresh flower vendors, and horse-drawn carriages until it reverberated off the centuries old brick buildings and palaces that rim the square. Dramatically, the anthem is intentionally cut short in mid-melody to commemorate a trumpeter from Krakow who was shot through the throat with an arrow when the Mongols invaded the city in 1241. A mere 768-year-old tradition.

With my future uncertain and threatening, I found it far easier to look back. I was still seeking connections and I decided to search in Eastern Europe. It was time for Helene and I to get back to our roots and I am not talking about Hakurei turnips gratin. After eating our way through six continents, I was now drawn to sample the neighborhoods, markets and foods of our ancestors. The Ross Family Roots Tour intended to cut through Eastern Europe like a Polish hussar sabre through a fat piece of *ozór wolowy* beef tongue.

Much of Helene's family is of Polish heritage. Her paternal grandfather was born shortly after the turn of the century somewhere near the ever-changing Polish-Russian border. Her paternal grandmother arrived in America from the small village of Siedlce in an area known rather rudely as Lesser Poland. We never researched any further back in her family tree, but if we had I would not have been surprised to find a trail of fake truffle oil peddlers, scoundrels that put ketchup on their hotdogs, and miscreants that sprinkled pre-grated parmesan cheese from a plastic jar onto their seafood.

My paternal grandfather was born in Panad, Romania and my grandmother was from Budapest, Hungary. They arrived in America via La Havre, France in 1921 aboard the good ship La Lorraine, a former World War I French armed merchant cruiser that was scrapped two years later. Their third-class tickets entitled them to single berths six feet long and two feet wide, one berth two and a half feet above the other. Their luggage had to remain on top of their own berths for the duration of the almost week-long voyage. Washrooms used cold saltwater. No soap. No towels. My grandmother was in her eighth month of pregnancy during the lengthy trip.

I know only too well how difficult such a cross-Atlantic voyage can be. Helene and I had to fly to Eastern Europe on a wide-bodied jet that took off over twenty minutes late, we used up all of our rewards miles for Business Class seats that failed to lie completely flat, the choice of movies on board was abominable (*Taken* with Liam Neeson again? Really?), and when we arrived in Krakow our room overlooking the main square was not even made up yet!

To help soothe the pain of this emotional trauma, Miód Malina Restauracja was a welcome site. Just off a side street from Rynek Glowny, its intimate arched space was packed with fellow diners seeking authentic Polish cuisine. Promptly after we were seated our server brought over a basket of fresh brown bread and a small dish containing a gelatinous mass infused with dark brown specks.

"Eew, what's that?" my spouse yelped, pushing away from the table. She usually had a chance to steel herself from new foods that I ordered, but having our server bring something foreign to our table entirely without warning had caught her unprepared.

"It's freshly baked brown bread. It smells good." I responded, pretending not to know what she was referring to.

"That lumpy stuff where the butter is supposed to be. Did you put the waiter up to this?"

"That, my dear, is the lifeblood of your sturdy Polish peasant stock. That's exactly what your ancestors relied upon to survive winters that were colder than a 'you know what's you know what.' "

"Don't they have any butter?" she replied.

"Forget about butter. You've seen pictures of those very wide Polish grandmas with a babushka wrapped around their hair walking two hundred miles through the snow each day carrying an ox strapped to their back? They have forearms the size of tree trunks. How do you think they got that way?" I asked.

"I don't really want to know."

"It's *smalec*. Lard to dip the bread in."

"Check, please."

"Oh, stop it. Try a little bit."

"No, thank you."

"Try some and I'll let you order the chicken breast."

"Like I need your permission. You enjoy."

I did. Two bowls worth of the salty, garlicky, rich spread. Smothered on the bread, it was so delicious I wanted to take a bath in it. But I had to save just enough room for the pleasure of a round pretzel stuffed with boar meat in a venison sauce, a meat pierogi, and some apple pancakes for dessert.

* * *

To really get back to our roots we had to dig deeper, so we hired a guide to take us on a shtetl tour of rural Poland. In the early twentieth century shtetls were small villages throughout Eastern Europe that had significant Jewish populations. Jews living in the shtetls spoke primarily Yiddish and were under Russian control. When the Russian Pogroms made life difficult and dangerous for the Jews, many like my wife's grandparents emigrated to the United States. Most of those that remained in Poland were later exterminated at the German death camps. While the shtetls and Jews are now long gone, temple ruins, ancient cemeteries and building inscriptions remain to offer a hint of those earlier days.

We visited a number of ruins of old synagogues including the remnants of Nowy Korczyn. Built in 1659, it was once home for nearly 2,500 Jews, but it now slumped in roofless ruin. A caretaker unlocked a haphazard gate and we wandered about the large single room. Rotting roof timbers threatened to collapse from above while weeds and bushes sprouted skyward inside. Bricks and stones that originally coalesced to create stylish arched windows lay crumbled and sagging. This building that once honored and protected a sacred Torah now displayed the work of local graffiti artists. At home in Los Angeles anything built before 1960 is considered ancient. It was wonderous to stand inside this once revered link to our Jewish past, yet depressing to witness the decay resulting from hatred followed by indifference.

In contrast, the even older Stara Synagogue in Pińczów dating back to the beginning of the seventeenth century was partially restored. The simple whitewashed exterior gives way to beautiful interior murals and painted patterns incorporating fragments of Hebrew texts on the walls and ceiling, used by the congregants in the days before individual prayer books were available. Elements of stonework by local artisans can still be found peeking out over doors and archways. But those that prayed here at the commencement of World War II were deported to Auschwitz and never returned.

The most memorable part of our shtetl tour was our visit to Chmielnik, currently a small village of approximately four thousand people. Prior to World War II, over ten thousand Jews lived in Chmielnik. That number swelled even larger beginning in 1940 as the Germans expelled Jews from nearby towns and forced them into the Chmielnik ghetto in 1941 where starvation and epidemics were used as tools to control the population. Anyone trying to escape the ghetto or smuggle food in was shot on sight. Virtually the entire Jewish population was sent to death camps in Treblinka and elsewhere. Shortly after the war not a single Jew remained in Chmielnik.

Yet, a small but important change is taking place in Chmielnik as the village rediscovers its Jewish heritage. The Synagogue has recently been restored from ruin and is now a modern interactive museum dedicated to Jewish history. A book has been published about the town's Jewish history. An annual Jewish cultural festival has become a popular event among locals and tourists. Like most Jewish cemeteries throughout Eastern Europe, during and after the war grave headstones were not only vandalized but taken out and used for paving roads. Now the Chmielnik cemetery has been restored and many of the headstones recovered. Each year the town sends a delegation of students to Israel to meet with Holocaust survivors and hear their stories.

As we completed our walk about Chmielnik, our guide asked me one of the most important questions of the day: "There is a little restaurant in this village that serves Jewish food. Would you like to go?" That is what brought us to the Restauracja Zydowska Cymes, a dining experience that transformed my spouse's "roots" adventure into my own.

Restauracja Zydowska Cymes is a tiny restaurant just off the main square in Chmielnik, sporting a bright blue awning outside and a handful of tables inside. Once inside we were presented with menus in Polish. Helene started searching desperately through the menu for a picture of a chicken or at least a drawing of something with feathers. Alas, there were no pictures in the menu.

I read the Polish words out loud to myself hoping that something would sound familiar. Then I saw the menu listing for "*czulent*." Trying not to get too excited, I pointed at the menu and cautiously asked our guide: "Is that the same as cholent?"

"Yes," he said, giving me a quizzical look.

I imagine that I had already impressed him greatly during the tour with my self-professed knowledge of Polish food and culture, so he should not have looked so astonished. I smiled and blew out a very deep breath.

* * *

Cholent is a slow simmering bean stew that dates back to at least the twelfth century. Its specific origins are the subject of much debate, but it spread through Spain, France and Germany as it moved throughout Eastern Europe. It is closely associated with the Jewish Sabbath which runs from sundown on Friday until sundown on Saturday during which time observant Jews are not allowed to cook. What to do?

Cholent to the rescue! It could be prepared in a single pot on Friday afternoon and cooked slowly overnight until it became a hearty meal on Saturday night. But in the little shtetls throughout Eastern Europe, what family was rich enough to keep a fire burning overnight?

The shtetl's baker to the rescue! After mama prepared the cholent in a big black pot, one of the children in the family would be tasked with the all-important duty of delivering the pot to the shtetl's baker, who would collect similar pots from all over the village. Each family would tie a unique ribbon onto the handle of their pot before it went into the oven so that they could later identify whose pot belonged to which family. Once all the shtetl's pots were collected and placed into the baker's oven on Friday afternoon, the slow cooking oven was typically sealed with clay, not to be disturbed until the pots were reclaimed the next night for Saturday's supper. Pity the poor child that returned from the baker on Saturday with the wrong pot.

Over the years each country, each shtetl and indeed each family developed their own closely guarded cholent recipes, passing them down through the generations. When my father was a small boy his Hungarian mother regularly made the family cholent for the Sabbath and it became his favorite dish. He described it to me as a bean stew with onions, garlic and other seasonings. His parents were too poor to afford meat for the family of five but if they were particularly prosperous one week they would get a soup bone in their cholent. My grandmother would cook the cholent overnight until the top was dark and crusty—my father's favorite part. It was his older brother's favorite part as well, so my father learned to act quickly once the pot was placed on the table. My Hungarian grandmother died when I was a small child, I never got to sample her cholent, and my memories of her are limited. My father, aunt and uncle are all still with us, although my uncle is in poor health. But none of them have tried to make my grandmother's cholent recipe.

After my grandmother passed away, I remember my mother attempting to replicate the dish based upon my father's descriptions. However, my mother had never tasted cholent before, my father's descriptions from his boyhood recollection were shaky, and my mother's cholent efforts were not entirely successful. I refused to taste my mother's cholent when I was growing up. As it cooked, the smell of death permeated the entire house. It was like coffee left to burn on the bottom of the pot, only substituting kidney beans and barley. Scooped onto a plate for my father, her cholent looked like shriveled and blackened beans surrounded by rock hard dark grains punctuated by chunks of overly blistered vegetables. My father ate it, but it was never quite like his mother's cholent. Eventually my mother gave up.

* * *

"I'll have the *czulent* please," I told our server at Cymes. Notwithstanding years of cholent inspired nightmares as a child, I was now finally determined to try my first cholent.

I wondered what this Jewish restaurant was doing out in the middle of rural Poland where Jews are as rare as, well, as rare as cholent. "Are there enough Jewish people around here to support a Jewish restaurant?" I asked our guide.

"No, there are very, very few Jewish people anywhere near here," he responded. "This restaurant is mostly for the people in the village here. The food is very tasty."

"Why open a Jewish restaurant out here?" I asked.

"The owners wanted to preserve some of the Jewish culture from the time when Chmielnik was primarily Jewish. So they did research and gathered old Jewish recipes that were used in the town before the war. They started the restaurant using those recipes and the restaurant became quite popular."

Our dishes arrived. I expected a burnt stew but was surprised to see that the cholent had been cooked into a solid loaf form and then sliced for serving. Also on my dish was an orange colored side dish. I took a bite. It was sweet and made of shredded carrots.

"Is this tzimmes?" I asked our guide.

"Yes, it is," he answered, no longer looking surprised at my encyclopedic storehouse of epicurean knowledge.

My maternal great-grandmother taught my mother how to make tzimmes and I enjoyed it as a child. I had not tried it again until my visit to Cymes. Taking another bite, I also finally realized as I slapped my forehead that the restaurant's name "Cymes" was the Polish spelling for the Yiddish word "tzimmes."

I took my first bite of cholent. Neither burnt nor crusty, the loaf was made of beans, onions, potatoes, meat and various seasonings. It made me think of Helene's grandparents living in a shtetl, of my Russian great-grandmother shredding carrots, of my father sneaking a spoonful off the crusty top of his mother's cholent, and of a small child struggling under the weight of a big black pot with a ribbon tied to the handle.

*   *   *

The Ross Family Roots Tour continued south to my grandmother's old turf in Budapest, Hungary. We visited the synagogue where she prayed as a girl, the Jewish district where she lived that later became a ghetto, Klauzál Square and park where she no doubt played, and the Klauzál Square Market where she shopped for food. Speaking of food, it was time to focus on our first Hungarian dinner.

I remember reading a story as a small boy about a band of roving gypsies that stole away women from their villages. A restaurant in Budapest featured a live gypsy band performing nightly. "Honey, get dressed. We're going out for a romantic dinner," I exclaimed.

"Is this a trick?" she asked.

I will never understand that woman.

Mátyás Pince Restaurant was founded in 1904. It features beautiful Renaissance murals, arched doorways, and a seven-piece gypsy band complete with strolling violinist, a cimbalom player, and double bass. Most importantly, I expressly selected this restaurant because the menu includes "Grilled Chicken Breast with Spiced Applesauce and Wild Rice." I knew that would make one member of our party extremely happy. We were seated in a comfortable booth with a pleasant linen clad table. We looked over the menus and our server came to take our order.

"I'll have the beef stroganoff, please," said my wife.

I think she occasionally orders things like that just to screw with me. In retaliation I ordered the Transylvanian Meat Platter so that the aroma of certain coarse sausages of unknown lineage would waft her way.

Speaking of wafting her way, right on cue the strolling gypsy violinist and his band came to our table looking for a tip. He was dressed in the obligatory gypsy outfit of a bright admiral blue vest embroidered with bold gold stitching. He crouched near Helene and supported by the rest of the band started to play slowly as he romantically gazed into her eyes. He began to pick up speed as he ultimately played himself into a frenzy, his dark hair falling into his eyes, his bow flying across the strings like strikes of lightning. When he finally concluded and bowed in recognition of a round of applause from the diners present, he insisted on posing with Helene for a picture. I gave him a tip on the condition that he go away.

The following evening, we dined at Rosenstein Restaurant which serves Hungarian Jewish food. I wrote to the owner in advance to advise him that my grandmother had grown up in Budapest and her family name was also Rosenstein. Perhaps we were related. Related enough to at least get a free appetizer.

Upon our arrival we were warmly greeted by the owner and shown to a well-situated table. He explained that virtually all of his family members were exterminated at death camps during the war. Sadly, he was unable to trace any of his family's history before the war and thus could not determine if he was any relation to my grandmother.

We turned to the menu. Matzo ball soup, lamb shanks with potato latkes, roast leg of goose, and *shalet*—the word used in certain Eastern European countries for cholent. This turned out to be a cholent that my father as a child could only imagine in his dreams. It featured smoked brisket, goose legs, whole roasted eggs, goose fat, beans, barley, onion and a thick helping of paprika. This single serving contained more protein than my father had eaten during his entire childhood. It was delicious.

After the meal, the owner checked in with us once again and presented us with a gift book containing the history of the restaurant and many of its recipes including for cholent. We were leaving Hungary with full stomachs, but I was not ready to let go of my cholent adventure just yet.

* * *

When I was growing up my mother was clearly in command of the kitchen. She was a wonderful cook and baker, having learned at the feet of my great-grandmother. She planned and cooked three meals a day, while baking layer cakes and chocolate chip cookies in between. She loved to experiment with new recipes and insisted that my sister and I always taste at least one bite of everything. But on Saturdays around lunchtime my father would temporarily take residence in our kitchen where he proudly introduced me to foods he loved as a youth and later as a young man, each of which betrayed his Eastern European roots. Scrambled eggs mixed with fried salami, pastrami sandwiches slathered with mustard, sliced beef tongue with roasted potatoes, and fat knockwurst that snapped with each bite. My mother steered clear on these occasions as these culinary masterpieces did not suit her taste. It was just my dad and I, the strong smell of smoked meats, and a mess in the sink.

When Helene and I returned home from our Eastern Europe trip, I was determined to repay the favor. I was going to make a cholent for my father.

I started to research and collect cholent recipes, quickly learning of the countless variations that exist depending upon the country and indeed village of origination. I told my father about my cholent adventures in Poland and Hungary. I knew that the loaf-like example filled with potatoes that I ate in Poland did not match his description of a stew. He also told me that his Hungarian mother would have chopped off her hand before she used potatoes in a cholent. My father chuckled at the Rosenstein Restaurant's inclusion of brisket and goose legs, meats that were nowhere near within the finances of his single mother who was raising three kids.

Combining what I thought were the highlights from several recipes, I gave it a try. The result was a watery mess that went straight into the trash.

A few days later a package arrived in the mail containing a book and a note from my father. Somehow he had located my grandmother's cookbook and it was enclosed. He further reported that he did not know how she used it, because it was in English and she could not read English. The book was entitled "Jewish Cookery In Accordance with the Jewish Dietary Laws" by Leah Leonard and was dated 1949. My grandmother's copy was well used, frayed at the edges, stained, and its covers were almost coming off. I excitedly but gently went directly to the index and saw the listing for cholent. Ms. Leonard even included a cholent poem attributed to Heinrich Heine entitled Princess Sabbath:

"Dearest, smoking is forbidden,
For today it is the Sabbath.
But at noon, as compensation,
There shall steam for thee a dish
That in very truth divine is—
Thou shalt eat today of Shalet!"

Shakespeare it ain't, but I suspect that Heine may have cornered the market on cholent poems. I turned the page and finally got to the recipe. The book lay flat because it had been opened to this page many times before. Most wonderful of all, the worn recipe page was covered in stains—the sole remnants of long ago cholents that had leaped out of the pot while my grandmother stirred in the barley. It was all I could do not to lick the page.

I followed the recipe and the result was a significant improvement over my earlier effort but it still did not have the crusty top. Back to the cutting board. Several more efforts were attempted, each with new tweaks. I added brisket and flanken, something that my grandmother could never afford but which I knew my father would enjoy. I started cooking it overnight and then in the morning transferring the cholent to an uncovered baking pan for further cooking to achieve a nice crusty top.

The cholent was still warm when I rang the doorbell to my father's house. As always, he moved slowly and it took him some time to get to the door. My mother had been diagnosed with Alzheimer's disease a few years earlier and my stubborn father insisted that he would be her primary and only caregiver twenty-four hours a day, seven days a week. He refused help from any source and it had taken its toll on him, along with countless aches and pains. He and my mother recently reached their fifty-fifth wedding anniversary, a bittersweet event due to my mother's lack of awareness.

He looked quizzically at the wrapped baking dish as I carried it to the old kitchen table while he gingerly folded himself into the chair. Before I could even uncover the baking pan, I watched him taking in the distinctive scent as he tried to stir some long hibernating sensory memory to life. When he saw what was in the pan and inspected the crispy cook on top, he nodded approvingly along with a slow smile. But I could see he was holding back just a bit, trying not to get too excited before the all-important first taste. I took a serving spoon and dished out ample portions onto two plates, making sure to include fat pieces of brisket and flanken atop a mound of beans and barley for each of us. He dug in, carefully carving a large spoonful off the crusty top. He paused, looked me in the eye, and tearfully said: "It's just like my mother used to make!"

* * *

I now bring a cholent to family gatherings so my father can enjoy it regularly. As it bakes, the familiar smell of tradition fills our house and I feel a connection to my Hungarian grandmother and to her grandmother. Of course, Helene will not eat it and Jessica is horrified by the mere thought of it. But I am delighted to watch as Matthew always takes a second helping.

Had a new tradition been kickstarted? Had an old tradition been revived? Who knows? But just in case, Matthew, here is the recipe:

Grandma Bertha's Cholent, Final Version 5.1

2 lbs. brisket, cubed

2 slices flanken, cut between bones

8 cloves garlic

1 large onion

1/3 cup schmaltz (rendered chicken or duck fat)

1/2 cup white northern beans

1/2 cup red kidney beans

1 1/2 cups pearl barley

3-4 tablespoons paprika

1 marrow bone cut into four pieces

4 celery stalks cut into 1" pieces salt and pepper

1. Soak beans overnight in water until they confess. Rinse and drain.

2. Get wife to cut up the onion. Sauté garlic and onion in schmaltz over medium heat until tender. Add paprika, salt and black pepper until wife complains about the amount of pepper. Add more pepper. Add brisket and brown in the same pan.

3. Combine sautéed ingredients with beans, barley, celery, flanken and marrow bones in a large Dutch oven (at least 8 quarts size) borrowed from a family in the Netherlands. Add water to cover the ingredients and cover pot with tight top. Cook overnight at 225 degrees for at least 14 hours or until oven door falls off, whichever occurs first.

4. Remove from oven, skim off surface fat, remove marrow bones (be sure to leave the marrow itself in the cholent), remove the flanken bones (but not the flanken meat), and transfer the remaining ingredients to a 13" x 10" aluminum roasting pan. Bake uncovered in oven at 350 degrees for at least one hour or until you can bounce a quarter off the crispy top.

5. Serve with heart defibrillator within easy reach. Do not take cholesterol test for at least three weeks after eating.

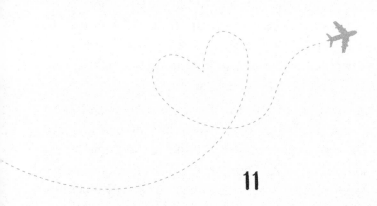

11

A NIGHT AT THE OPERA

November 21, 2016

After the doctor that originally discharged me in the morning finished shaking her head and wagging her finger during my evening readmittance, and the head nurse gave me an "I told you so" look that she must have borrowed from Helene, the hospital medical team got my blood pressure under control and sternly ordered me to rest. I was shamed into compliance and remained in bed. At around ten o'clock the following night I got ready to go to sleep, the lights were dimmed in the hallway and all was quiet on the floor. Until the opera commenced.

I imagined I was hearing Puccini's *Nessun Dorma* being belted out from the patient's room next door. The doctors must have given me the top-of-the-line pain medication normally reserved for celebrities. With drugs like these, this was turning out to be my all-time favorite hospital. The singing sounded loud enough to wake the dead, and what better place than a hospital to do so? I am not even a big opera fan, but this was pretty cool.

I looked up to check the label on the drip bag leading to my IV. I was only receiving fluids, no narcotics. The booming tenor's voice continued to roll down the hallways and bound off the nurses' station like a sonic boom. The hospital architects had done a surprisingly good job on the acoustics for the floor. There was just the appropriate amount of early reflected sound without too much reverberation. It was somewhat reminiscent of the warm but crisp sound one enjoys at the opera house in Vienna.

I waited for a nurse to go into the tenor's room and close his door or to at least ask him to quiet down, but the performance continued. As *Nessun Dorma* concluded the tenor immediately launched into something from *The Barber of Seville*, once again reaching a decibel level that would drown out any MRI machine. After a strong finish to this aria, a brief intermission ensued. It may have been the first time in opera history that a recital was interrupted to change a bedpan. But the singing patient soon started up again to close his performance with *Ave Maria*. From a hospital room across the hall I heard someone yell, "Bravo!" Then suddenly, it was once again as quiet as a hospital.

When a nurse came by later to wake me up from a sound sleep to take my blood pressure, I asked him about the performance. He explained that the patient next door was a retired opera singer who was beginning to suffer from dementia. Each night before the patient went to sleep he sang various operatic songs, which the nurses found greatly entertaining during the slow night shift.

While I appreciate a pop-up operatic performance as much as the next person, at times I found his voice to be not as tightly controlled as I generally prefer and the timbre of his instrument was a bit unsecure at the top end. I also detected an uneven transition into the upper passaggio. Perhaps I just caught him on an off night. He may have been put off his game by the mystery meatloaf in gray gravy that had been served for dinner. I know that I was.

* * *

November 22, 2016

I did not really need a reminder because this had weighed upon me every day for years, but the dementia afflicted opera singer reminded me of my similarly afflicted mother, which reminded me of my father and pushed me to finally call him to tell him what was going on. With so much uncertainty over what might happen to me next, I just could not put it off anymore. The nurse raised my hospital bed a bit and I was both weak and apprehensive as my shaking finger finally hit the correct buttons on the phone.

"Hi Dad," I said with forced energy.

"Hi, how are you?" he said with his usual reply.

"I'm in the hospital."

"What's the matter?" I could hear the immediate panic in his raised voice.

"I went to the doctor a few weeks ago and they discovered some irregularity with my liver." I stretched the truth a bit but only by twenty-three years. "They are doing some tests," I added. Yeah, just a couple.

"Are you going to be alright?" He coughed and choked from emotion, his voice shooting up a full octave.

"Yes, of course. If necessary, they will do a liver transplant." There, it was out.

"Oh my God," he wailed. "My wife is dying, my brother is dying, and now my son is dying!" He started to weep.

Not what I wanted to hear. "The doctors say everything will be fine. I'm at Cedars, it's a great hospital."

No response. Just sobs. "I'll talk to you later, okay?" I continued.

"Okay. I love you," he said quietly.

"I love you," I responded. We always ended our calls that way. Hopefully we could continue to do so for a long time. I hung up the phone.

There are episodes in your life when the spiraling dread of a looming event becomes almost overwhelming, but when you finally are forced to confront it head on, a rush of relief washes in a feeling of serenity. Unfortunately, this was not one of those times.

I lay back against my pillow and let out a heavy sigh as I stared at the monitor that measured my vital signs. My blood pressure was elevated. I returned to focusing all my meager energy on recalling vacations past. I closed my eyes tight and imagined myself elsewhere. Our plane cruising in for a landing in a bustling city, below a ferry boat arriving in the harbor, the morning sunlight reflecting off the water, and then that familiar voice.

*   *   *

2011

"Look, there's the opera house!" exclaimed Helene as we strained to peer out the airplane window on our approach to Sydney Airport. "I want to take a tour of it tomorrow. Oh, and I want to go to the zoo," Helene added with even more enthusiasm.

When it comes to animals, Helene always wants to pet what I want to rotisserie. "Why do we have to go to yet another zoo?" I groaned.

"Featherdale Wildlife Park is not far from Sydney and they let you pet and get your picture taken with a koala. To be very clear, I expect you to be on your best behavior," she warned.

"Sounds tasty, I mean, sounds good."

Having satisfied my husbandly duty of giving Helene a hard time, off we went. On our way to the wildlife park we turned off the highway to visit The Three Sisters, a massive tri-part sandstone formation in the Blue Mountains of New South Wales. But upon arrival we learned that one of the Three Sisters had recently suffered a slide. It was about to drop dead like a stone and collapse into a mound of rubble, leaving just two sisters that were on life support after standing without a break for millions of years. The locals still refer to them as The Three Sisters.

Off the coast of Victoria in Southern Australia is yet another stack of rocks known as The Three Sisters. Of course, there are only two rock formations there. Later during our Australian excursion we drove the Great Ocean Road and visited another series of rock pillars called the Twelve Apostles. Naturally, there are only eight of them. Really. While driving I heard a news report that math scores of Australian students have been slipping. I cannot imagine why.

But the only counting that I wanted to do was a countdown to my next meal. It was time to conduct some Australian delicacies reconnaissance at the wildlife park. I knew that it would show poor etiquette to bring along a portable grill and throw a koala on the barbie in front of a busload of school children enjoying an outing to the wildlife park. However, lean protein-rich kangaroo meat is quite popular in Australia and if a kangaroo somehow happened to hop into the trunk of my car on its own, then all bets were off.

I found to my dismay that the kangaroo enclosure was well secured. But while I continued searching for a breach in the kangaroo pen fencing, I came upon a creature that stopped me in my tracks. There are a few animals in the world that are so mind-numbingly repulsive that even I would have to think twice about eating them. I referred earlier to what I not so lovingly call The African Mistake—the odious wildebeest. While at the Featherdale Wildlife Park we came upon a grotesque creature that has easily earned at least a Second-Place Ribbon in the Butt-Ugliest Animal On The Planet Contest. The Tasmanian Devil.

The Tasmanian Devil is a carnivorous marsupial about the size of a small dog, that is if your dog looks like a salivating overgrown rat. Course black hair with asymmetrical splotches of white, a pink and grey muzzle with thatches of uncontrolled long whiskers shooting out in every direction, and bright red ears that make it look as if it consumed one too many six-packs of Australia's Feral War Hog IPA beer. Its beady vacant eyes peered out at me in a deranged trance. This was a face that even a Tasmanian Devil's mother could not love. Long sharp claws were just waiting to eviscerate some unsuspecting defenseless animal. With a bit of spittle hanging from its menacing mouth, this Devil had carved a circular rut in its pen as it trotted counterclockwise in a psychopathic circle, pausing occasionally to aggressively bare its razor-sharp teeth and screech maniacally while hoping that some small child would reach through the fence and offer up a finger. To top it off, the Tasmanian Devil is one of the foulest smelling creatures on earth, giving off a stench that so reeks of death that any creature with even a semblance of a nose will beat a hasty retreat.

I beat a hasty retreat as we headed over to the Birds Pumped Up on Steroids section of the park. There was a mostly black Australian Cassowary bird with a long neck that looked like a blue color palette for a Sherwin-Williams paint catalog. This guy was only a few feet high but well on his way to almost six feet tall. For some adventuresome Australian locals, these may be the buffalo wings of their dreams. However, the Cassowary has a six-inch claw at the end of each foot that can eviscerate a human's entrails quicker than Paul Hogan with an Outback Eclipse carbon steel knife. Across the way was the notably less colorful emu, a shaggy-looking foul fowl that gave rise to the word "birdbrained." Emus are known to run toward their predators, poke other animals for no apparent reason, and are not even smart enough to fly. They may not be very bright but they can run up to forty miles per hour. The one at the park had a razor-sharp claw that could slice off my ear and launch it into Tasmania with no effort at all.

I followed Helene as she made a beeline to the koala habitat where she could finally have her photo taken with a koala. The sad-looking creature was perched on a fake eucalyptus tree with a train of tourists lined up to torture it and have their pictures taken. The dreary koala was clearly embarrassed about how its life had turned out. It must have had high hopes as a young koala, dreaming of looking out over the beach from a perch high atop a real eucalyptus tree, gearing up to having kinky koala sex with the slutty koala two trees over. Then the next thing he knows he is stuck on a small plastic tree in front of a painted kangaroo logo being cooed over by some camera-toting tourist, earning a few stale eucalyptus leaves if he cooperates and does not bite the tourist's nose off. This particular koala was either drugged up or coming down from a eucalyptus high, its eyes glazed over as it subjected itself to this humiliating scene day after day. Even I was taken by its plight.

Helene got her picture, her nose was still intact, and my stomach cried out for lunch. We exited the wildlife park and pulled into a little roadside cafe. We were seated at a plain wooden table that held salt and pepper shakers, a glass container of sugar, and plastic packets of every Australian's favorite sandwich spread, Vegemite.

"Would you like a taste of Vegemite on your toast?" I asked Helene.

"No, thank you," she replied

Stunner. Who could have anticipated that response? I spread some of the brown, sewer-like substance on my toast and gave it a try. Vegemite turns out to be Australian slang for "yeast experiment gone very wrong."

My Australian culinary adventure had yet to gain any traction, so later in the afternoon we headed out to Harry's Cafe de Wheels for a snack of Australia's iconic meat pie. Although Harry's now has many locations, only the original location in Woolloomooloo would do. I tried to get Helene to say the name three times quickly but she wisely ignored me.

Harry's is no longer owned by Harry. It is not really a cafe as it has no seating. It is not on wheels but rather is permanently affixed to the pavement. The specialty of the house is Tiger Pie but unfortunately the pie has not a speck of tiger in it. I chose to overlook these otherwise serious breaches of gastronomic etiquette because Harry's makes one hell of a good meat pie.

"What is a meat pie again?" queried a reluctant Helene.

"Trust me on this one," I said encouragingly as Helene simultaneously rolled her eyes. "You've got your mystery meat soaked in a mystery brown sauce baked in a crust with mashed potatoes, mushy peas, and a mystery brown gravy, all in a single cup. You even get a plastic fork to use until the fork breaks in half. But wait there's more! If you act today you get to sit on an exposed cold bench in the biting wind with avian pox-infected Crested Pigeons circling in case either you or the meat pie fall to the ground. You'll love it!"

"Sounds great. No, thank you."

I was not giving up easily on this one. "You like chicken pot pie, right?"

"I do."

"Well, with the gravy you can pretend that the beef is chicken. Mashed potatoes are good, right?"

"I suppose."

"Peas aren't going to hurt you, are they?"

"Mushy peas. Who came up with that name?"

"Peas are peas. As a bonus, I promise that there will be no visible insect parts." Thank god for the thick and goopy brown sauce.

We sat down on the cold bench, each cradling the paper plates that held our Tiger Pies and marveled at the distinctive layers to this feat of culinary engineering. A flaky crust set a firm foundation for the lean beefy stew nestled within. A homey layer of mashed potatoes sat above like slightly lumpy clouds. The pie masters next set in a thick layer of florescent green mushy peas, while building a crater in the middle to hold the very brown gravy. Helene and I each agreed we should dig in from the center rather than the side, so as not to spring a leak in the mushy pea dike and send gravy overflowing onto our pants. The trick was to get as many layers as possible onto the flimsy plastic fork, allowing the various ingredients to coalesce in a single bite. The pies were warm and filling, beefy and starchy. The colors of the brown gravy and the green mushy peas were so strikingly vibrant that my nascent artistic side tried to mix the two together to see what color would emerge, but they stubbornly held on to their own unique hues. Helene conceded that her pie tasted surprisingly good, and to the dismay of the circling pigeons she finished it all. For once this loving husband and wife had a romantic meal together enjoying the exact same dish. Thank you, Harry, wherever you are.

* * *

Getting to Heron Island is not easy. The island is a coral cay located directly on the Great Barrier Reef that can only be reached by boat, seaplane or helicopter. Helene gets extremely seasick on a boat, she is petrified of small planes, and her fear of heights had prevented her from ever taking a helicopter ride. She would rather listen to Men At Work's "Down Under" on a repeating loop for twenty-four hours than select one of these modes of transportation.

"Sweetie, we should go to Heron Island. It is right on the Great Barrier Reef and has terrific snorkeling with a shipwreck only a few feet from shore. It's got lots of birds and is also a sea turtle sanctuary," I said excitedly, trying to sweeten the deal.

"Sounds great," she cautiously replied. "And?"

"And what?"

"You know and what. Keep going."

"Nothing else. Except because you are my one and only all-time favorite wife, you get to decide how we get there."

"This isn't going to be pleasant, is it?"

"Would you prefer to take a boat trip for two and a half hours over rough pounding seas, an aged seaplane that often successfully performs a water landing on a pair of thin but brittle skis, or a deafeningly noisy helicopter that will be buffeted by hurricane level winds for a half hour ride?"

I truly was not quite sure what the correct answer was going to be. There was a long, long pause.

"Helicopter," she said very, very softly.

"Helicopter it is."

A couple of days later we checked in for the flight at the airport in Gladstone, Australia and met the helicopter pilot out on the tarmac. "G-day folks," he said cheerily as he assisted a visibly shaking Helene into the back seat. "Mr. Ross, you can sit right up here in the co-pilot's seat." He handed us each a set of headphones so we could communicate over the noise of the copter. I took in all of the dials and switches in the cockpit.

"Let me know if you get tired and want to take a nap. I can take over for a while," I offered with a smile.

"Oh, are you a pilot, mate?" he asked.

"Not exactly, but I did successfully pilot an attack helicopter in the Call of Duty videogame series."

He laughed. "Well mate, I'll keep that in mind if I run into any trouble."

We took off and were almost immediately over the ocean. The pilot seemed to know what he was doing so I relaxed and observed the scenery. I never realized there were that many shades of blue. And that was just Helene's complexion as she held her breath in the back seat. The sea below looked like a broken mosaic of greens and blues interrupted by dots and dashes of brown reef. But almost before you could say "aquamarine," stunning Heron Island came into view, growing larger and larger until our pilot performed a flawless unassisted landing.

Based upon our Australian experiences during the prior week, Helene and I nodded knowingly when the hotel desk clerk told us that there were no herons on Heron Island. There was however bird poop. Oodles of bird poop. Mounds and piles and loads and heaps of bird poop. Heron Island is the Bird Poop Capital of the World. The island consists of only about forty acres but is home to over one hundred thousand bowel-blasting black noddy terns. They make their nests in every tree on the island with dozens and dozens of birds in each tree. The locals boast that the guano from these birds is quite prized for the nutrients it adds to soil. I had quite a prized specimen myself after breakfast, but I was not about to get into some bragging contest with a stupid tern.

Promptly upon arrival at Heron Island the hotel staff instructed us in the three unbreakable rules while visiting: 1) Do not go outdoors without wearing a hat; 2) Do not go outdoors without wearing old shoes that can be abandoned when you leave the island; and most importantly, 3) Never, ever look up.

The ubiquitous terns have no natural enemies on the island and are in a protected habitat, so they propagate with wild abandon. After a few days of sliding on bird poop on every sidewalk, running away while under any tree, and listening to their incessant harsh cawing, shrieking and chittering (which is so bad the hotel provides ear plugs for the guests in every room), I would have given anything for just one ravenous tree-climbing Tasmanian Devil.

We considered setting our soiled shoes on fire and letting them burn for several days, but instead Helene and I broke out our snorkeling gear and headed for some underwater adventure where the terns could not follow. The tropical fish were plentiful as we swam our way out to the wreck of the HMAS Protector, a nineteenth century gunboat sticking out of the water not far from shore. I tried to find the galley and hopefully some leftover salt pork and biscuits, but some hungry sailor from decades earlier had grabbed the last ones. We left the ship empty-handed and swam around a bit, but it was too late for turtle season and we trekked back to our room where the endlessly cawing terns sat outside, still pooping like it was New Year's Day. It was time to move on and find a rack of kangaroo with koala gravy.

* * *

I was shocked to arrive on Kangaroo Island off the coast of Southern Australia and learn that they actually have kangaroos there. Lots of kangaroos. The place was downright lousy with kangaroos. At the rental car agency we had to sign a contract agreeing not to drive the car after dusk because every night kangaroos with a death wish jump in front of cars driving on the roads. Sure enough, as we drove to see the sights the next morning, road-kill kangaroos littered both sides of the highway. I made a note to find a kangaroo road-kill recipe when we got back to the hotel but our culinary adventure on Kangaroo Island was just beginning.

As a warm-up I had to track down a King George whiting burger. Part of the smelt family, King George whiting is found along the bays of Southern Australia and the finest preparation in the land can be found only at the Vivonne Bay General Store and Bottle Shop. We pulled up to the small store decorated with painted surfboards and two rusting but still operative gasoline pumps out front. Once inside, we made our way past the fishing tackle, sunglasses display, and handful of mismatched wooden tables until we reached the order counter in the back where Helene and I started our usual dance. She led.

"Okay, let's get it over with," she said. "Go ahead, ask me."

"Would you like to taste a famous King George whiting burger?" I obliged.

"What's whiting?" Helene was ready for me today.

"It's kind of like a fish."

"I'm guessing that kind of like a fish means it's a fish. No, thank you."

"Fish and chips"

"Really?"

"They also have shark burgers."

Exasperated look.

Sufficiently pleased with myself, I ordered my King George whiting burger. Helene ordered a bag of crisps and we sat down at one of the tables.

My whiting burger came deep-fried on a toasted sesame seed bun with cucumbers and all the toppings. It tasted fresh, clean and with just the right crunch. Helene enjoyed her crisps. But we could not dawdle. We were off to see the Pelican Man of Kangaroo Island and he keeps a strict schedule. Each afternoon for over twenty years at Kingscote Wharf he has appeared with nasty-smelling fish offal that he throws to an adoring crowd of close to one hundred wild pelicans, creating a flying feeding frenzy. I did not care who or what was involved, I was not going to miss a feeding frenzy.

We arrived at the small wharf only to be immediately warned not to get too close to the staging area so as not to get pooped upon and/or sideswiped by a dive-bombing pelican. I started having Heron Island flashbacks as we climbed up a few rows toward the back of the small tiered seating platform. The pelicans swooped in one by one, not daring to be late. The Pelican Man swooped in as well, tastefully wearing wading boots, a crusty set of overalls, and an old poop-covered floppy hat that gave shade to his scraggly white beard. He reached into a plastic tub and cast a handful of delectable fish guts out onto the water as dozens of pelicans dove and fought each other for the same morsel. The pelican that got to the morsel first would then openly mock the other pelicans. It reminded me of dinners with Helene.

The Pelican Man asked the few dozen people in attendance if they had any questions. I asked the Pelican Man what the local pelicans tasted like. He became agitated and started ranting about protected species and other such nonsense. However, he did mention something about internal parasites. I decided just to watch the show and he did not invite any further questions from the crowd. About halfway through the spectacle the Pelican Man announced that he was charging everyone in attendance five dollars apiece. Some observers got up to leave without paying and were promptly berated and verbally abused by the Pelican Man until they paid up. These Australians are not nearly as friendly as they appear to be on television. The Pelican Man soon ran out of offal and the pelicans moved on to the second act of the show, which was pooping on the tourists. We hustled over to our car.

I had taken Helene to dodge pooping terns, swim with tropical fish, nestle with a koala at the wildlife park and commune with dozens of gluttonous pelicans. My husbandly duties should have been fully satisfied, but I was wrong. Helene now politely informed me that she wished to see fairy penguins in the wild.

We drove all the way out to Penneshaw on the east side of the island where the little creatures allegedly emerge from the surf at dusk. There was a tiny wooden observation platform above the rocks overlooking the small crescent beach and we climbed up. No penguins yet. We waited. Dusk arrived. Not a single stinking penguin. We waited some more. Darkness arrived. There were no lights anywhere and posted warning signs stated that flashlights were forbidden because they scare the poor delicate penguins. I wanted to leave. Helene wanted to wait. We waited even longer. I could not see my hand in front of my face. I was not sure I could have seen a penguin if it was sitting on my shoe. Then suddenly I heard Helene trying to contain a squeal.

"There they are!" she half-whispered with unrestrained glee. I squinted and turned my head at just the right angle so that out of the corner of my eye I could see slight movement on the beach. Several creatures less than a foot tall were moving about. Were they penguins? Rats that had been taught to walk upright? Australian elves? My spouse was happy. Life was good. I think.

But the bucket on my list was still empty. Where was my dry-aged kangaroo steak? We had spotted plenty of the creatures, both dead and alive, as we made our way about the island. Now I needed one on a plate and Zest and Thyme restaurant in Willoughby on Kangaroo Island was calling my name. Just drive to the end of the earth and make a sharp left. They have a lighthouse. They have a patio. They have ocean for as far as one could see. They have Kangaroo Pot Pie. Helene loves chicken pot pie. However, after the long drive I was not in the mood for our usual clever repartee. I just wanted to eat, and I did. The kangaroo tasted quite nice, particularly in the gravy. Mildly gamey, very lean meat. After finishing every morsel of my kangaroo pot pie, I drove back to our lodge and hopped into bed.

* * *

Bucket list checked, the next morning we boarded our plane back to Los Angeles. I pulled the card out from the seat back to check the movies. *Taken* starring Liam Neeson. Again. Unbelievable. I would have to look into getting a restraining order against Liam Neeson to keep him from stalking me. I tried unsuccessfully to sleep. A mere fourteen hours later the plane bounced twice and skidded to a stop on the tarmac of LAX.

"Don't forget to call your father and let him know we're back," Helene reminded. "You know how he worries."

Hungry pelican show-off

Pre-pot pie

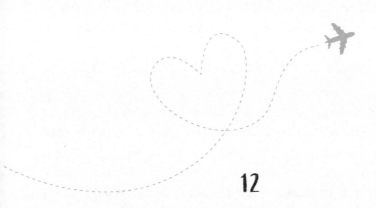

12

THE HOLY GRAIL OF RUGELACH

November 23, 2016

The metal meal cart rolled up to my hospital door three times a day, announced first by the clickety-clack of the wheels on the tiled floor and then by whiffs of food hidden under boiled plastic domes. The chemical smell of the disinfected domes always rushed through my nostrils as on a thrill ride, abruptly plunging into that portion of my brain that screamed "unpleasant."

The nurses commented that my appetite had waned. I did not argue with them. My daily blood tests showed that my liver was getting worse, but I could have told them myself without the blood draw. I was extremely fatigued and no longer able to get out of bed. Moving any part of my body was an energy consuming exertion that left me limp. I also found it a labor just to breath. My MELD score had inched up to 28, not that it did me any good laying in a Los Angeles hospital. I started to wonder whether the hospital room would be the last thing that I ever saw.

At least lunch had arrived. I knew it did not make much sense to get excited about a hospital meal but in some Pavlovian way the sound of the food cart rolling toward my room always elevated my blood pressure a few beats. It not only broke the monotony and boredom of just lying in bed but it introduced a sense of intrigue into the day. No matter what I ordered, often some type of surprise was uncovered beneath the dome.

A nurse helped me lift the plastic dome from the food tray and I noticed that something seemed amiss. Yes, both the thinly sliced unsalted turkey and the well-cooked carrots were resting in their regular spots on the plate next to the plastic-wrapped salad and small cup of apple juice. No matter what I ordered, most days the hospital cook sent over either a snack-sized cup of vanilla pudding or one of the least popular flavors of Jell-O for dessert. But on this grand occasion my still functioning nose detected a new scent gently wafting up from the tray, the ever so slightly sweet aroma of something baked.

In place of the Jell-O cup was a small paper wrapper with a shortbread cookie poking out of it. I tried to remember but it was neither my birthday nor a National holiday. I squeezed out the contents of the small plastic packet of ranch dressing onto my salad as if I was going to eat it, cut up the turkey meat into bite-sized pieces and skid them around in the gravy so the nurse on duty would note in my chart that some actual dining activity had taken place, and declared myself ready for dessert. It was a cookie!

I finished off the simple shortbread cookie in a couple of bites. It was not only a minute-long celebration of the culmination of a meal but a sugary reminder of the simple sweet prizes in life. At home I would not have given the cookie a second thought, but in my hospital bed it reminded me of a time when being handed a cookie was an amazing adventure.

A short while later one of the doctors came in. The doctors always introduced themselves but I could never remember most of their names. He explained that they were going to intubate me by sticking a tube connected to a ventilator down my throat to help me breath. Going forward I would have to be fed intravenously. For how long? Until I did not need it anymore. This was just awesome. After traveling the world in search of exotic bites, that plain bit of cookie might have been my last meal.

If I could just return to the simple but life-changing cookies of my youth. My maternal grandmother certainly appreciated the power of the cookie. She lived nearby and my parents would take me to see her every week. Youthful and energetic despite her gray hair, Grandma was always smartly dressed and favored a long strand of pearls around her neck. I very much looked forward to these visits, which almost always included her holding my hand as we walked the couple of blocks to the local bakery to stock up on just-baked bread and a sweet honey cake. Her pearls would make a click-clack sound as we walked, keeping time with the tinkling charms on her bracelet in a melodious percussion ensemble. When she opened the glass door to the bakery, a jingling bell atop the door joined in the symphony.

My first thrill upon entering the shop was the yeasty scent of freshly baked breads and pastries. The second thrill was when one of the ladies behind the counter would hold out a sprinkle-covered butter cookie wrapped in tissue paper for me to sample while my grandmother fussed over which bread had the best golden coloring. Finally, my grandmother would hold me up over the counter so I could watch the blades of the miraculous bread slicing machine work their magic in an ear-splitting machine gun staccato. Grandma would always tell me, "That machine is the greatest thing since sliced bread." I believed her.

I never lingered over the sprinkled butter cookie, which disappeared in two bites and only increased my craving. My nose quickly created a smudge on the glass counter as I inspected the splendid majesty of the double lines of black and white cookies that were so tantalizingly near but sensibly protected by glass. These ingenious round shortbread treats were each nearly the size of my head, divided precisely in half by a white vanilla frosting on one side and its dark chocolate counterpart on the other side. How did they do that?

It was in that bakery that I first heard a heated debate about the correct way to eat a black and white cookie: "You eat the chocolate side first, then the white side," insisted another grandma who was waiting in line.

"What are you, meshuga?" demanded a woman from her canasta group. "You eat the white side first and save the chocolate for last because chocolate is best."

"I always take one bite from one side and then a bite from the other side," a man further down the line offered.

"Butt out!" the first two said in unison.

It was at that bakery when I first realized that cookies were a serious business. It was also at that bakery that I tried my first chocolate rugelach.

* * *

2012

There exist certain heretics who claim in whispered tones that the specialty at Humus Said is the finest in the world. Others give thanks to God every day for the hummus at Abu Hassan. Which was better? Helene and I were in a bar near Jerusalem enjoying a few sips of Dancing Camel Golem beer when I casually asked some of the locals which hummus establishment they preferred. There seemed to be some rather strong opinions on this topic, as the various camps quickly started heatedly arguing with each other. For a moment, it looked like an old-fashioned chair-breaking, eye-gouging, *payot*-pulling fight was about to break out.

Helene and I snuck out the back door and drove off in our hideously pot-marked rented Lancer with over two hundred and fifty thousand kilometers on it. I believe, but could not swear to the fact, that there was a small area near the front-left fender that had not already been dented by those famously fearless Israeli drivers.

At a stop light we spotted a camel laying down in a sandy lot. "Oh, look!" Helene exclaimed as she pointed at the camel. "That camel is Preston."

"How do you know that?" I asked.

"He's right there," she said, pointing again.

"How can you possibly know that camel's name?"

"What are you talking about?"

"You called that camel Preston?"

"No, I didn't."

"Yes, you did."

"I said the camel was resting, not Preston," she laughed.

If you stay married long enough, you too can have these types of scintillating conversations.

We were headed to the coast and eventually on our way to the ancient city of Akko, one of the oldest continuously inhabited cities in the world. But Preston's owner had spotted us and was now enthusiastically summoning us from across the street. We pulled over and could now see two camels lolling around in the sun. From the smell of those camels, I believe they were two of the oldest continuously unbathed dromedaries in the world. Preston remained aloof upon our arrival, as did I, but Helene excitedly ran over to pet him and Preston's owner greeted us warmly with an offer of a camel ride. I would much prefer to eat a camel than to ride one, but the next thing I knew my wife was hoisted up on Preston and I was aloft on his testy cousin. The jovial owner led us on a plodding trip around the block. No power steering, worn out shock absorbers, and my camel was in desperate need of a pine-scented air freshener.

According to Greek myth, it was at Akko that Hercules discovered curative herbs to heal his battle wounds. There is no doubt that it would take Herculean miracle herbs to cure the camel sores that I was developing. I was also in desperate need of some world-class hummus to give me the strength to continue our journey. At home, hummus is most commonly served as an appetizer or side dish for dipping. The combination of mashed chickpeas, tahini, garlic, olive oil and lemon is irresistible when accompanied by fresh, fluffy pita. However, in Israel a great bowl of soft and creamy hummus is a sacred main meal to be savored in the morning or early afternoon to carry one through the day.

Akko was hours away and I just could not wait. An emergency detour was in order so we headed to the ancient port city of Jaffa south of Tel Aviv and the home of the Shuk Hapishpishim flea market. You can buy anything there. Persian rugs, phony Persian rugs, ancient artifacts, phony ancient artifacts, a kidney, a phony kidney. Much more importantly, Jaffa is the home of Abu Hassan, one of the oldest and finest hummus establishments in Israel. As Lonely Planet describes Abu Hassan: "If hummus is a religion, then this could be its Mecca." Amen.

There was nothing phony about the hummus served at Abu Hassan. The line was twenty deep under Abu Hassan's green awning and we thought we would have a long wait for one of the precious shared tables. But the gods were with us on this particular morning because the line moved quickly, we were served quickly, and Mr. Hassan expected us to get our butts back out the door quickly. No printed menus. We could order hummus or we could order hummus. We decided to order hummus. A huge bowl of creamy hummus with whole bean *ful*, a mountain and a half of pita, a peck of pickles, a stack of napkins, and stay out of my way. It was hummus heaven and I could pray there every day.

Onward up the coast to Akko and its magnificent excavated ruins. Akko boasts Crusader vaults and halls that date back to 1100, an ancient Turkish bathhouse, the El-Jazzar Mosque built in the seventeenth century by Ahmed "the Butcher" el-Jazzar (who did *not* earn his nickname by his skill at carving schnitzel) and a harbor with views to forever. But we were on a hummus crusade. We were told it was secreted deep inside the underground *souq*, or old marketplace. We wandered around the ancient stone steps where others had walked for a thousand years. Perhaps not that much had changed. Vendors sat behind mounds of exotic spices in reds, greens, yellows and every color in-between, hand-woven tapestries hung from above our heads, enormous bins contained too many varieties of olives to count, fish were stacked neatly in rows, unrefrigerated meat sent an invitation to the local flies, gold jewelry glistened, elaborate tea sets were neatly stacked on tables, all was set out and ready for bargaining. Everything but hummus. We found ourselves lost in a labyrinth of former goat trails. Hadn't anyone in the Middle East ever heard of a grid pattern? As it was, we would need a miracle to find our way. Then a miracle occurred. Indeed, three miracles.

First, my not only culinary challenged but navigationally hopeless wife was the first to spot the sign for Humus Said. This was unprecedented. A second miracle closely followed: there was no wait for a table. Third and perhaps most startling, the waiter wiped off our table when we sat down!

All-you-can-eat warm hummus mixed with whole chick-peas, fresh baked pitas, and heaping plates of olives, tomatoes, and onions. Yes, I think I will. Indeed, I did. The hummus was outstanding, the pitas were plentiful, and after a while I thought we might need the Israeli equivalent of the Jaws of Life to extract us from our seats. We did manage to successfully waddle out the door, where I was immediately rendered woozy by a blaze of florescent orange light emanating from across the path. If not for the fact that we were in an underground *souq*, the glow might very well have been visible from outer space.

As my eyes adjusted I could see the outline of a gray-bearded man dressed in a flowing white robe and sandals. He was standing guard over an old creaking wooden cart that struggled to remain upright under the weight of the mother source of the neon radiance. I glided ever closer to the cart as if under a spell, until directly before me stood a *knafeh* peddler. As I reverently gazed at him, the peddler carved out onto a paper plate a generous serving of a bright orange, soft goat cheese-infused pastry that he generously bathed in a sweet syrup. He nodded to me knowingly as he held it out to me with both hands and I silently accepted his offering. I thought that I could detect just a bit of envy in the man's wise eyes as I cut off a piece of *knafeh* with a plastic fork. Perhaps he was longingly thinking back to his first time. Without using any protection, I took a bite.

KNAFEH! I became lightheaded and my knees started to buckle. Where had this been all my life? I wanted to embrace the man and inquire whether he had an eligible daughter or even much younger sister if necessary that would like to join me in opening a chain of *knafeh* franchises throughout America. McKnafeh? Knafeh Hut? I was flexible on the name. I turned and called out to Helene, who was reapplying her lip gloss for the eighteenth time since we left the hotel: "Honey, you've got to try this!"

"Yes dear, what is it this time?"

"Knafeh, look," as I held up my plate.

"I don't like foods that are neon orange," came the reply. "It looks radioactive. If we go out tonight you're going to light up like a skeleton x-ray."

More for me. I turned back to the man to plead for a second helping but he had vanished. I called out to him but only my own voice echoed back through the ancient walls of the *souq*. He was gone, but I willed the magic of that *knafeh* to linger on my tongue for quite some time.

* * *

The legend, which may or may not have been started by a drunken shawarma carver in a dive bar in central Tel Aviv, told of the mysterious Falafel Hazkenim where one could dine upon the finest falafel in the land. It was rumored to exist on a particularly unfashionable corner deep in the bowels of Old Haifa, protected by a warren of nearly impassable one-way streets so narrow that you could stretch out your arms and touch the crumbling ancient buildings on both sides at once, assuming that you were up-to-date on all of your vaccinations. We ventured over to a dark and mostly forgotten corner of the local flea market where we purchased a "rare" map of the area. The vendor told us that the map may have once been smuggled out of ancient Persia by a marauding tribe of irritable Bedouins, but I am fairly certain that the map had been downloaded that very morning from Google Maps.

Armed only with our precious treasure map and a fistful of newly printed shekel notes from the ATM, we set out. After a few kilometers the Lancer gave a sad little cough and decided on its own to rest for a while. It had pragmatically surrendered to the blistering sun and interminable maze of streets. We got out, left the key in the ignition hoping that someone would take what was left of the car, and continued on foot.

Well past the point where any sane person would have given up, and with our Evian supply exhausted, we finally found ourselves at the door of the desert oasis that was Falafel Hazkenim. How was the falafel, you ask? I do not know. It was Sunday and Falafel Hazkenim was closed, its doors shuttered up tighter than Preston's butt in a sandstorm. There was no falafel high for me that day. However, that was not the worst of my heartache. As we retraced our steps, the Lancer was still where we had left it.

* * *

Rather than attend driving school, I believe that prospective drivers in Israel are trained by the Israeli Armored Corps using Merkava battle tanks. Even the shortest drive in Tel Aviv is a life-and-death game of bumper cars. It would be easier to find Noah's Ark than to find a car on the road in Israel that is not covered in dents and scrapes. Stop signs, traffic lights, and painted lanes on the road are taken as mere suggestions. Drive fast, because if the drivers behind you cannot swerve around you, they will go right through you. Even more fun, once you start driving you can never stop to park because there are no words in Hebrew that translate to "empty parking space."

For a change of pace we decided to get lost in the countryside rather than in the city. This fortuitous turn of events led me to discover my all-time favorite city name in the entire world, as we delightfully came upon Horshat, Israel. Helene declined to get out and investigate the food specialty of this charmingly named hamlet, so instead we continued in our quest for world-class falafel.

The Lancer made it as far as the city of Tzfat in the Northern Galilee. We dodged Hassidic Jews dressed in full-length black coats and fur-lined round hats as they talked on cell phones while sticking out their thumbs to hitchhike, eventually finding our way to

Falafel Hakikar in the Old Jewish Section of the city. The garru-lous Hakikar himself was out in front of the bright blue doors of his falafel stand, furiously beckoning us as if we were old backgam-mon buddies. He gave us samples of his signature dish and I was immediately smitten. I raced a Talmudic scholar and was able to snatch the last available table and wicker chairs under an outdoor blue awning. You snooze, you lose.

Tourists, soldiers, Orthodox Jews, everyone was here, chow-ing down in the baking sun on some of the finest falafel around. They were hot, covered lightly in oil, slightly crusty on the outside, tender on the inside, a bit spicy, and dripping with hummus. So were the falafel.

I could have sat under Hakikar's awning all day nibbling away, but Helene and I still hoped to see some of the beautiful countryside before being struck dead in a crosswalk, so we searched online and hired a private tour guide to show us around the next day.

We arrived a bit early outside of a local cafe where we were to meet our guide Rafi for a full day of exploring historic towns and ruins in the Galilea. Having picked up a few driving tips from observing the locals, I triple-parked in the middle of the road. An eruption of bleating grew louder and louder, confirming that our car was blocking the migratory pattern of a herd of ill-mannered goats. Helene got out of the car to try to find our guide while I kept the Lancer warm in case we needed to make a hasty getaway. A few minutes later Helene returned, vigorously scraping something from the bottom of her shoe. She reported that our guide had not arrived yet, as the only person out front of the cafe was a little old man with a long beard and a short cane.

We waited some more but no one showed up. Once the goats moved on to where the meager grass was greener, Helene played goat dung hopscotch back to the cafe to make further inquiries. Yes indeed, the old man was our guide.

Rafi was old, but boy could he talk. And talk. And talk. This man could outtalk my wife, which is a feat of biblical proportions. We learned that not only did Rafi personally know everyone in the entire State of Israel but his son had invented everything in sight. We drove by an irrigation system that turned the desert into a garden—brought to Israel by his son to feed the people. We passed a roller coaster ride—introduced to Israel by his son to make children smile. His son discovered a coin in a ditch that helped to establish the date of the town. I half expected Rafi to tell us that his son provided Moses with tidal research to assist in the parting of the Red Sea.

After hours in the car listening to Rafi's son's never-ending resume, I considered giving Rafi a little push right off the Golan Heights. Three bounces and he is in Syria. Lucky for him, I still needed his help to keep us from accidentally crossing the border into Lebanon on one side or a field posted with landmine warnings on the other side.

Rafi knew everyone and knew the location of every rock for a thousand kilometers around. However, he was somehow completely incapable of guiding us to a bakery for an afternoon treat of crispy cheese filled *bourekas* topped with toasted sesame seeds. We said our good-byes and dropped him off back by the cafe.

*   *   *

Our circle tour of Israel brought us to the Harmony Hotel in the Nahalat Shiv'a neighborhood of Jerusalem to drop off our cursed vehicle in the carpark and continue our journey on foot. Helene foolishly suggested that we visit the Western Wall, the Church of the Holy Sepulcher, and the Dome of the Rock. *Feh!* I had selected our hotel for its close proximity to the most holy site in Jerusalem and there was no time to waste. We were only a few blocks away from Marzipan Bakery and its famous warm chocolate rugelach. What kind of disturbed individual plans a trip to Jerusalem around rugelach? You have your answer.

Rugelach. Is it a cookie? Is it a pastry? Yes and yes. No, it was not invented by Julia Child, although she introduced it to many Americans in her 1960's television show. Rugelach go back a bit further, perhaps hundreds of years to Central Europe where the crescent-shaped rolled treats were filled with cinnamon and raisons, raspberries, or dare I say, chocolate. As if they do not contain enough calories already, Americans tend to mix the dough with cream cheese, making the rugelach firm and often crunchy after baking. But in Israel, I heard that only a yeast-based dough is used yielding a softer result. A taste test was in order, indeed demanded.

So commenced our trek to the Marzipan Bakery for the Holy Grail of rugelach. The unrelenting sun blazed down upon us and I was forced to borrow Helene's only hat for shade so that I could continue to lead us on our mission. A cruel sandstorm kicked up, biting our uncovered faces with grit from the time of Moses. I became fatigued, a not so subtle reminder from my liver to take it easy, but we forged ahead. The wind howled like a baying dog, swirling around us as if propelled by a Vitamix 1363 blender. I was lost.

An old babushka with a cane in hand and a *shmata* on her head came walking toward us on the sidewalk. I stopped her to ask for directions and she pointed us down the block with a crooked wrinkled finger. We trudged on until I saw red. A red awning covering a red floor with red trimmed counters hiding behind a red sign in Hebrew and English that screamed "Marzipan." Below it, row upon row of warm chocolate rugelach right out of the oven. I sprinted toward the pans of rugelach, ordered a full bag, and gleefully handed over my shekels. Long ago I had been taught in school that the three states of matter were gas, solid, and liquid. I now know that the fourth state is Marzipan's rugelach. I could barely hold the bag because the rugelach were hot and steaming. I delicately but firmly removed one from the now-gooey bag and held it in an upright position, balanced carefully so the molten chocolate center did not cause the pillowy dough to fold over on itself or worse yet, onto my relatively clean khaki pants. I took a bite. On my tongue the rugelach quivered slightly as it slowly began to stream an ethereal bath of decadent chocolate over my taste buds, and then without further warning, the rugelach exploded in a warm chocolate big-bang nirvana! Marzipan Bakery's fresh from the oven warm chocolate rugelach remain the single greatest thing that ever passed my lips.

Hummus Heaven

The Holy Grail of Rugelach

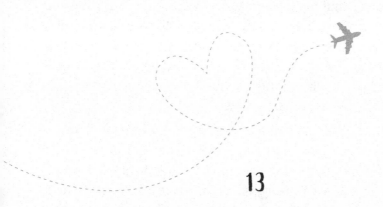

13

COOL IN THE CENTER

November 24, 2016

I was cold. Really cold.

Once the liver stops removing toxins, everything else turns to shit. My blood could no longer filter properly through the liver and I was bleeding internally. The intubation tube was shoving oxygen down my throat because I was too weak to breath on my own. Fluids built-up internally causing my stomach to protrude. I was actually quite relieved to hear this because the only other explanation was that I was nine months pregnant. My hands and feet swelled with fluid to three times their normal size, causing them to look like rough-hewn wooden clubs. My brave little kidneys tried to pick up the slack and remove some of the toxins but after a while they tired of the extra work and went on strike.

I apparently did not have enough tubes, lines, ports, and catheters already poking out of my body, because the doctors dug a new hole and placed a chronic dialysis catheter in my chest so I could receive dialysis twenty-four hours a day. The nurses wheeled a dialysis machine into my room to extract my blood, remove excess fluid and toxins, and pump the cleansed blood back into my pathetic body.

It turned out that my blood was really filthy. I could not even remember the last time I cleaned it, so I guess it was my own fault. Whatever was mucking around in my vessels and arteries caused the filter on the machine to clog with great regularity. This would set off the shrillest of alarms and the nurses would come running. But I barely even noticed because I was freezing.

My skin had thinned considerably from my disease. Muscle and fat both fled my body and I lost twenty percent of my body weight. My internal thermostat went on the blink. Who knew what kind of nasty infections were running rampant inside me? Then the dialysis machine started sucking my sweet ninety-eight degree blood out of my body and pumped it into a seventy-degree hospital room as it worked its way through tubing, the dialysis machine, filters, and yet more tubes until it returned gasping and wheezing back into my body. My blood cooled during its path outside my body and because the dialysis was going every minute of the day, my precious life fluid never had a chance to fully warm back up.

I was freezing from the inside out. Teeth chattering, limbs shaking cold, all day and all night. The nurses tried to help with warm blankets but the outside of my skin was not the problem, it was the blood inside. They put me in an airtight plastic warming suit with a heater that blew warm air in one side and out the other. It was like being in the center of a hot air balloon. I remembered that it was Thanksgiving Day. If I were not so sick, I would have entered myself in the Macy's Thanksgiving Day Parade to float over the crowd. I was seared on the outside but still cool inside. I had become a human version of *Bistecca alla Fiorentina*.

Thankfully, one of the doctors making the rounds came in with good news. My condition had grown worse.

"Now that you are on dialysis 24/7, your MELD score automatically goes up. Your score is now thirty-two," he said.

I could not talk with the intubation tube down my throat so I motioned for the doctor to give me a paper and pen from the table. My toxin-scrambled brain wanted to write "FUCK DARWIN" but instead I managed to scrawl "whatever you do, don't take me off of that thing," as I nodded toward the dialysis machine. I had become an official resident of Bizzaro World. I could not leave the hospital, so all I could do each day was hope to become sicker so I could qualify for a liver. Most importantly, I had to get sicker quickly. The longer I lingered the more organs would fail. At some point, even if I received a liver transplant, some of my damaged organs would never recover. Or worse yet, irreparable organ failure could cause me to be too sick to qualify for a liver. I needed to hit the precise sickness sweet spot, fast.

I thought about past Thanksgiving dinners. About setting up the tables and chairs in preparation for the guests. About climbing up on the stepladder to get the serving platters down from the cupboard, along with the two turkey decorations made out of pinecones that Helene insists on using to adorn the tables. About turkey with gravy and cornbread stuffing and green bean casserole topped by crispy onions and two kinds of cranberry sauce and buttery mashed potatoes and my mother's sweet noodle *kugel* and pumpkin pie with lots of whipped cream.

I tried not to think about how shivering cold I felt, but I was really cold.

* * *

2013

I was hot. Really hot.

Our wooden dugout canoe glided silently through the swollen waters of the Amazon River, the tranquility occasionally punctured by the piercing howl of an unseen tree monkey warning us to turn back. The humidity was as thick as the forest and the ruthless sun bore down upon Helene and I without mercy. I paddled effortlessly for the first three minutes or so but an old shoulder injury from an almost forgotten fight with a short-tempered racoon hiding in our garbage bin back home eventually caused me to slow the pace. Helene was behind me in the canoe using her paddle mostly as a fashion accessory. The river bided its time, its murky depths waiting to swallow us without a trace.

The impenetrable forest looked the same on both sides for as far as I could see. Trees sprouted out of the river, obscuring any actual shoreline. My brand-new starched and pressed L.L. Bean safari outfit was soaked through with sweat under the bulky life jacket. How would we ever find our way back to civilization? I pulled my paddle in and considered using it as kindling to start a signal fire. But instead of slowing, our canoe was actually picking up speed. Indeed, now that I had stopped paddling the canoe was breezing forward as if propelled by the pair of Amazon River pink dolphins that had teased us further back up the river.

I looked up to see the third person in our vessel, a barefoot eleven-year-old local girl wearing cut-off jeans and a pink T-shirt, who supplemented her river family's income by taking tourists out for canoe rides. The girl, who must have weighed all of seventy pounds sopping wet while holding her pet sloth, was at the head of the canoe. With Helene and I no longer interfering, our youthful guide quietly paddled straight and true without missing a stroke. Fifteen minutes later we arrived back at our small cruise ship. We paid the girl for the ride and gave her a bright pink plastic hoop bracelet, one of many small items we had brought along from home to give out to local kids. The girl rewarded us with a huge bright smile.

It was the height of the annual rainy season. The river flooded for miles inland, inducing river families to move everything they owned including pigs, chickens, and if there was room left over their in-laws, to the second floor of their open-air thatched homes where they could bicker with each other for months until the river receded. Then they would spread out back down to the first floor where they would not have to spoon with the livestock at night. But travel now was strictly by canoe or small boat and our new young friend had been happy to oblige us with a brief tour.

It was still a few hours until dinner would be served on the ship. Through the jungle grapevine, which was hanging within easy reach, I heard about a nearby animal-rescue shelter that allowed tourists to visit for a fee. This would give Helene and I a chance to get up close and personal with some of the local fauna. If one of the tastier animals happened to make a break for it and land in our skiff, I would be delighted to assist the shelter with any overcrowding problem that it might have.

We set off in the small skiff with a few other cruise passengers. Before our group had even fully docked at the shelter, a gang of squirrel monkeys that had never received proper parenting leaped from nearby trees directly into our skiff. They jumped on our heads, grabbed water bottles out of our hands, and engaged in entirely uncivilized behavior that could only be described as monkeying around. I had the feeling at least one of them had been professionally trained as a pickpocket and was using the others to create a diversion. With one hand on my wallet, I climbed onto the small dock and entered the shelter.

The shelter was a small one-room open-air thatched hut supported by cut logs, similar to the homes we had seen in the villages along the river. Two parrots, one bright blue with marigold markings, the other orange with shining cobalt wings, were perched next to each other on a wooden railing while a toucan with a beak almost as long as he was tall strutted along the floor as if he owned the place. The orange parrot squawked incessantly while the blue parrot gazed silently into the jungle, presumably trying to spot some fatty grubs for lunch. It reminded me that through some tragic booking mistake, the cruise line had placed Helene and I at the same table for meals.

On the other side of the small room clinging upside down from the thatching was a sloth. It had thick coarse hair that stopped abruptly on its forehead, causing it to bear a striking resemblance to Moe from The Three Stooges. Sloths rarely move except to eat and defecate, and this particular sloth looked like it was glued to the roof.

Where were all the other animals? Did I really have to fight off a gang of renegade monkeys just to see a couple of birds and a sloth that may or may not have been stuffed? But a few minutes later two handlers employed by the shelter began to bring out animals one by one from some unseen containers. Helene gladly accepted a tiny baby monkey that she held in the palm of her hand. She gave the monkey to me and it promptly nestled into the crook of my arm. Cute, in a monkey sort of way. The bitsy beast became restless, so I handed it back to the handler only to discover that the little pisher had relieved itself on the sleeve of my last clean shirt. These Millennials just do not show much respect.

I looked down at the wooden floor planks and noticed a pile of leaves crawling toward me. This struck me as odd. It turned out to be a mata mata turtle with a camouflaged bumpy shell that looked like an inverted egg carton and a flat triangular head topped by a horn. It was moving very deliberately but to the sloth it must have seemed like a blur.

It took both handlers to bring out the next resident of the shelter, a massive ten-foot-long anaconda snake. This monster could feed a family of four for several days and still leave some leftover anaconda casserole in the fridge. The handlers held up the giant snake waist high and offered it up for a photo opportunity. Everyone else in the crowd took three giant steps back but I held my ground. Surely standing next to the creature for a quick photo was perfectly safe, as the shelter would not let tourists near a dangerous snake. I assumed that the reptile must have had its teeth removed and suffered from gout. Natural-born leader that I am, I stepped forward to show the others that there was nothing to fear.

One of the handlers grasped the slithering serpent directly behind its head. The other handler braced himself like a Bulgarian weightlifter and with some effort hoisted the balance of the snake to shoulder height. Once he had stabilized himself, he told me to place my hands in a similar position under the snake. The snake was so thick that I barely got my hands beneath it. Then the handler passed the body of the snake off to me and walked away! Excuse me? I could see the head of the beast being held by one handler only inches from my face. The tail end was now undulating somewhere behind me, probably trying to knock the sloth off the wall just for fun. In between was a beefy ration of reptile. Helene used my camera to take the obligatory picture with my head cut off. After several attempts she ultimately snapped an acceptable photo of me, the hefty reptile, and my new hernia.

The handlers took back the snake before I crumpled to the ground and laid the serpent on the floor in preparation for returning it to its cage. A moment later I heard a hiss that to this day remains the single most evil sound I have ever heard. The great serpent opened its mouth wide enough to swallow a medium-sized two-legged mammal and lunged four feet through the air, fangs first, in an effort to strike the first handler in the neck as a prelude to squeezing the life out of him. The experienced handler had cautiously positioned himself four and a half feet away. By the time the snake lunged a second time, I was trying to use the sloth as a step-stool to scramble up to the roof.

Safe? My butt cheeks clinched up as tight as...well, as an anaconda smothering a tourist, Tilley hat and all. I grabbed Helene and raced back to the skiff. I think the other visitors were somewhere behind me. I kept telling myself that I did not have to be really fast. I just had to be faster than they were.

As our guide headed our skiff back to the ship, he asked if anyone wanted to take a quick cooling dip in a calm portion of the Amazon River before dinner. Given that the forest's humidity felt like the inside of a howler monkey with a bad case of gastritis, several passengers gladly jumped in to cool off while the guide remained in the skiff. One fellow belatedly yelled up to the guide from the water, "Should we be concerned about piranhas in this section of the river?"

"No," the guide said dismissively, "piranhas rarely eat humans."

After a calculated pause for effect the guide continued: "If I were you, *Señor*, I would be more afraid of the *candiru*." The guide now had everyone's complete attention.

My fellow traveler quickly and prudently followed up, "What's a *candiru*?"

"*Candiru*? It is tiny fish in the river," the guide calmly responded. "With whiskers on its face and sharp spines on its back. How you say...it is *parásito* that swims up a man's *pene*, you know...," he said, motioning to his groin area. "Those spines make it an *hijo de puta* to pull out."

Like an Olympic synchronized swimming team, every male in the river simultaneously catapulted out of the water as if shot out of a water cannon back into the skiff. For the duration of the trip back to the ship, several of them were seen to have their legs crossed just in case.

Everyone's spirits brightened considerably when we saw that the cruise chef had set out a magnificent spread comprised mostly of local ingredients for our final dinner on the cruise. Pisco sours put everyone in the mood for the highlight of the evening—grilled paiche. Paiche is one of the largest freshwater fish in the world, growing up to fifteen feet in length and weighing up to four hundred pounds. This prehistoric-looking taste treat has been around essentially unchanged for five million years since the Miocene era. It looks like an overstuffed torpedo with a wide mouth trying unsuccessfully to conceal a nasty underbite. While a paiche is unlikely to win any Creatures of the Deep beauty contest, even in the rapidly diminishing Miocene category, what it lacks in aesthetics it more than makes up for in taste.

"Would you like to nibble on an ancient sea monster with poor dental hygiene?" I asked while holding out a forkful to Helene.

She ignored me.

The paiche turned out to be a firm, mild-tasting whitefish. It is considered a delicacy by the river people, but it became too popular and was overfished. Now farm-raised paiche has made it a low-cost favorite once again. Perfectly grilled, it tasted fantastic after a hard day of fending off defecating monkeys, anaconda wrestling, and penis protecting.

The next morning I gorged on a variety of fresh baked pastries and bid a tearful farewell to the cruise chef. With breakfast out of the way it was time to get serious about planning for lunch. We heard of a celebration at one of the villages upriver, so Helene and I found a guide, hopped in a skiff and were on our way. The village consisted of a grassy area about the size of a football field, ringed by thatched huts. Near some of the huts we could see male villagers wearing traditional grass skirts with grass headpieces that started at the forehead and ran straight down the back past the shoulders like an award winning 1980's mullet. The women were topless and wore scarlet wraparound skirts. With no Petco store within canoeing distance, many of the children walked around cradling pet sloths and monkeys.

I expected that any Amazonian celebration would include an ample feast of exotic specialties. Perhaps some sautéed loin of llama over a bed of smashed purple potatoes. Yet, not a soul came by to take my *chicha* drink order or offer passed empanadas. After a careful exploratory survey of the grounds, I thought I had finally located the buffet table and excitedly moved in. It contained local delicacies alright—handmade necklaces for sale featuring deceased pieces of Peruvian roadkill. Hairy howler monkey hands. Snake heads with fangs poised to attack. Piranha skeletons with threatening razor-sharp teeth. Long clawed caiman feet. I swear I saw one item with a distinct likeness to one of Helene's great-aunts, but it might have just been the way the sun was striking the display. I could not imagine wearing any of these local fashion accessories out to dinner in Beverly Hills. Besides, none of the necklaces went well with my shoes. In fact, some of them should have been made into shoes.

The rhythmic beat of a drum on a hollowed log signaled that the entertainment portion of the program was about to begin as the village chief strutted into the center of the grassy area. A stout fellow, the chief showed a flair for color by using red dye from an achiote plant to decorate his face, mated with a slimming ankle-length grass skirt and fully accessorized headdress. Using both hands, he carried a hand-carved tapered blow gun that was at least twice his height. Attached to a strap over his shoulder was a woven pouch with wooden darts poking out of the top. We all looked downfield as the chief confidently pointed at two wooden stakes that had been driven into the ground over fifty feet away. With the villagers and guests gathered along the sides of the field, a hush fell as the chief took aim, gathered in a mighty breath, and blasted a wooden dart right into the heart of one of the stakes. Just to show that it was not a fluke, he did it a second time, placing the second dart only a few inches away from the first. The crowd gasped and then raised a well-deserved hearty cheer.

Now holding the blowgun with outstretched arms toward the crowd, the chief offered it up to any blowhard who wanted to give it a try. Of course, I immediately stepped forward. This caused a near riot as both villagers and visitors alike trampled over each other trying to get well behind me, if not away to the safety of a different village entirely. My prior blowgun experience was limited to shooting spit wads through a straw at Helene and I had not practiced that for several months. Undeterred, I loaded a dart and hefted the blowgun to take aim as I looked downfield trying to locate the second stake. It was so far away that I could barely see it. I could not have hit that stake with a hand grenade, so my main objective was to not shoot myself in the foot. Literally.

The entire village was staring at me and the pressure was on. I hefted up the blowgun to my lips, took a mighty breath, and pretended that I was trying to extinguish candles on the world's largest birthday cake as I blew out. The dart sputtered out of the blowgun like an Amazon Kingfisher trying to fly with one wing tied behind its back and landed about twenty feet short of the stake. The chief looked relieved and I received polite applause from the crowd for not having killed or maimed anyone. However, the chief got two tries and so should I. I reloaded with a new dart and started to take aim, when I heard that voice again yelling at me from the sidelines. I looked over to see Helene frantically waving at me and shouting, "Stop! There's a chicken behind the stake!"

I squinted for a look. Indeed, the scrawny village chicken had strolled a few feet behind my stake. The smart-ass chicken had intentionally walked over there to taunt me, no doubt assuming that the safest spot in the village was near the stake that I was aiming to hit. Never one to shy away from being challenged by a chicken, I took in a breath until I turned blue, blasted it out so hard my eyeballs started to roll back in my head, and watched the dart take flight. As I belatedly wondered what the local penalty was for killing the village chicken, the dart arced and landed only a couple of feet to the left of the stake. Not a bad shot, and the chicken was safe to taunt visitors for another day.

The chief grabbed his blowgun back before I could try again. I briefly returned to thinking about *tequeños* appetizers, when the sound of wooden *tarka* flutes caused the villagers to erupt into dance. Having shown off my considerable blowgun skills, I was not surprised when one of the village women immediately snatched me up and hauled me over to the dancing throng. When later asked by friends at home about my trip, I dutifully reported that I danced with a topless woman who was not my wife.

All this gaiety was delightful but after busting a move on the dance field I was hungrier than ever. A brave leader needed to emerge and lead an expedition into the unforgiving jungle to save the day. With Helene and a couple of other guests in tow, I hopped into a small skiff along with a local guide so that I could go *mano a aleta* with the local red-bellied piranha. Thirty minutes later the guide delivered us to a shady spot that he insisted was prime piranha territory. I suggested that Helene jump into the shallow water and yell, "*Aqui, piranha! Aqui, piranha!*" but she exhibited a decided lack of enthusiasm for this plan, so instead we used roughly cut wooden poles and line to dangle hooked cubes of beef bait in the water.

We had either stumbled upon the equivalent of a piranha Mensa meeting under the shadowy water or one of my excessively hungry co-travelers was really talented at holding his breath underwater, because something (or someone) was repeatedly eating the beef off the hooks while eschewing capture. I had almost gone through an entire standing rib roast when a piranha that had been held back twice in third grade was finally foolish enough to latch onto the hook. I proudly hauled that low-IQ carnivore into the boat and went back to try and entice his inbred cousins to follow suit. By the end of the afternoon the score read: Daring Culinary Raconteur

3, Piranha 0. As this book goes to print, my beloved is still trying to bait her hook.

I released one fish back into the water as a warning to the other piranhas not to mess with me. I named the other two "Hors d'oeuvre" and "Amuse-Bouche" and brought them back to the lodge where we were staying the night. While delivering my two new fishy pals to the lodge chef, our guide helped translate my request. I asked to have the piranhas added to my dinner menu for the evening and I wanted to bring home the skeletal remains of one piranha head, similar to the ones I had seen in the village "boutique." For years Helene had adamantly barred me from buying a massive moose head to place over the mantle at home, but she could not possibly object to a cute little piranha head above the fireplace.

"No problem," assured our smiling guide.

While the chef was in the kitchen performing his magic on the piranhas, Helene and I strolled over to the dinner buffet. My wife was excited to see chicken as one of the two main entrees. She was less excited after she took a bite. I made the near fatal decision to try the beef. Perhaps I would have enjoyed it more if it had been pre-chewed. But I was downright giddy when the chef sent out my specialty plate. There lying before me were my two beautiful piranhas. Only one had its head attached. The chef and our guide were obviously working together as a finely tuned machine back in the kitchen. But before I could even take a bite, our guide returned bearing an unconvincing smile. "The chef is having a little trouble getting all the meat off the head. He's going to keep boiling it for a while."

"Okay. No hurry," I lied.

Our guide went back to the kitchen to oversee the delicate operation. I returned to my plate for an equally delicate but far more delicious operation. Why did those piranhas taste so spectacular? Was it because I had risked life and limb to capture them, because they had been swimming in the Amazon only two hours earlier, because I had been unjustly denied substance for several hours, or some combination of the three? I can unequivocally state that my piranhas were the tastiest fish I had ever eaten. White flesh, moist and delicate, it was *pescado* paradise. My only quibble was that the fish were 95% bones with very little meat. I could eat a dozen or more for a quick snack and still have room left over for an alpaca or two. But the return of the now unsmiling guide swiftly jolted me out of my piscatorial euphoria. "The chef says that the head is giving him a big problem. He can probably only save the jaws."

"Okay, have him do the best he can," I muttered magnanimously. I could live with the set of threatening open jaws lined by machete-sharp teeth gleaming as if to move in for a kill.

Speaking of moving in for the kill, I turned my attention to the traditional *mazamorra morada* dessert. It was a chilled purple-corn pudding with a gooey texture. Lurking inside the pudding was the occasional stone-hard fruit seed, possibly hidden there by the village dentist. This sweet was in no danger of being added to my top ten favorite purple dessert list.

Here he came again, our now very chagrined-looking guide with his head down. "I'm afraid I have some bad news. The chef worked hard but he was only able to save the lower jawbone."

Our guide then opened a white cloth napkin and held it before me for examination. I looked once, twice, and on the third try was able to spot a small jawbone with a few gaps where teeth were missing. Out of an entire piranha, a few loosely connected bottom teeth were all that remained.

* * *

Things were looking up. The previous day we had explored the dark depths of the muddy and merciless Amazon River by trolling for unsuspecting piranha. Today we took to the sky, ready to explore above the trees on the Amazon Rainforest Canopy Walkway. The walkway consists of a series of netted suspension bridges hoisted up over ten stories high and stretching out over a third of a mile between fourteen platforms. According to the brochure, the walkway "provides a view of the rainforest from the treetops, the best vantage point for observing wildlife." This would be our optimal opportunity to observe the unique and colorful birds that call the Amazon home.

"You know very well that I'm afraid of heights," my favorite spouse reminded me.

"It's perfectly safe. The walkway has been around for almost twenty years and they perform a safety inspection every decade," I replied in my most comforting tone.

"And you know I dislike suspension bridges. All that swaying back and forth makes me queasy and unsteady."

"I'll be right there to catch you in my muscular arms. What's more romantic than that?"

"I can't imagine," she said with a tone of exasperation. "Are you sure it's safe?"

"Absolutely." I almost added that maybe I could catch a bird or two for lunch but I decided to save that as a surprise.

For just this one time I should had listened to my wife. When we arrived at the entrance to the walkway I performed a reconnaissance maneuver to locate the closest elevator. No elevator. No escalator. Not even a hot air balloon. We were expected to climb ten stories of makeshift stairs to get to the top of the first walkway, in weather so hot and humid it was like being in the middle of a jungle. In fact, we were in the middle of a jungle.

We started the ascent. Helene took the lead so I could keep an eye on her and prevent her from escaping. Oxygen became scarce. Like a 2008 bottle of Tacama Don Manuel Tannat waiting to be decanted, I was desperate for air. My legs started to wobble. My liver screamed for mercy. Our water supply evaporated in the heat. I would have given anything for a Sherpa or two. Just then a couple of eight-year-old kids pushed past us as they ran up the stairs. The kids were laughing as if racing to the top of the walkway was some sort of fun game. Just as disorientation was starting to kick in, Helene and I finally reached the first platform. The side netting of the narrow walkway strung out from the platform like a delicate spider's web between the trees. It appeared to be just as sturdy as a spider's web.

"You go first," I told my loving spouse.

"You got me into this. You go first," she responded. Helene's face bore her now common look of advanced trepidation.

I delicately stepped onto the walkway. It started to sway. I held the netting in a death grip as I took a few steps forward. My head went east. My stomach went west. Then they traded. There are over two hundred species of termites in the Amazon. I wondered how many made their home on the wooden planks of the walkway. Close behind me Helene tentatively stepped forward, briefly lost her balance, and careened from one side of the netting to the other. This just made the walkway sway all the more.

"I want to go back down," she pleaded.

"But we haven't even seen any birds yet," I pointed out.

"I don't care."

"Keep going, I promise it will get better." Fabrication was one of my specialties. "Let's get to the next platform so we can stop and look for birds."

She begrudgingly lurched her way with me to the second stationary platform. We stopped to give our stomachs time to catch up with the rest of our bodies and looked around. No birds. Not a single tweet.

"I guess we have to keep going to the next platform to see the birds," I offered.

"I'm going back," she responded.

"You can't go back now. All that climbing will have been for nothing. I think the next platform is just up ahead."

I repeated those words a dozen times during the next two hours as we staggered over the constantly shifting walkway to reach the fourteen different platforms. In the Amazon rainforest, bright scarlet macaws with yellow- and blue-tipped wings rest on branches and squawk out the latest jungle gossip to their rumor-starved cousins a mile away. Blue-headed parrot refugees from a Jimmy Buffett concert sway in the trees while screeching out the latest tunes, as their friends the cream-colored woodpeckers keep time by tapping against the trunks of *lupuna* trees. Toucan Sam, with his enormous rainbow beak and bright blue body, soars over the lush canopy searching the trees for Froot Loops but settles for wild cherries.

But not on the Amazon Rainforest Canopy Walkway. In over two hours of caroming back and forth over the top of the rainforest we spotted exactly zero birds. Not even a feather. I can drive down the freeway in smog-choked downtown Los Angeles during rush hour and spot more birds than we saw on the Amazon Rainforest Canopy Walkway. On tottering legs, we eventually made it to the last platform and then back down to ground level. The ticket booth attendant had some explaining to do.

"Oh, we used to have lots of birds here but no more," he belatedly informed me. "There is much logging and cattle ranching around the protected walkway area now and the birds have left."

Great. I can report that from the height of the suspended walkway the top of the leaves on the Amazonian trees look strikingly similar to the bottom of the leaves as seen from the ground.

* * *

Before leaving on our trip to Peru, I bragged to friends that I intended to sample the popular Peruvian delicacy known as *cuy*. "What's a *cuy*?" they would ask. "Guinea pig," I would smugly reply as I watched them shudder in disgust. It never ceased to amuse me. When I read during my trip planning that *cuy* was described as a "guinea pig," I assumed that rather than referring to the cute little pets that children play with at home, the Peruvians had a different style of porcine creature that they referred to as a guinea pig. Something with a large snout, curly tail, and tender baby back ribs.

I was wrong, yet again.

My quest for *cuy* brought us to the Peruvian town of Cusco, the former historic capital of the Inca empire. At a height of almost eleven thousand feet, Cusco presented us with our first real altitude challenge in the Andes. Naturally, Helene was stricken by altitude sickness fourteen seconds after our plane landed. We could hardly begin a quest for *cuy* under such difficult circumstances. I left her tucked in the fetal position in our hotel room and walked through town in search of a *farmacia* where I might pick up a remedy for her illness. I passed stores selling every color of scarves allegedly made from the wool of baby alpacas (referred to with distain by the locals as "maybe alpaca" due to the doubtful origin of the wool), braided women in bowler hats sitting on cobblestone streets selling local vegetables and herbs while cuddling baby llamas in their laps, and vendors on almost every corner selling coca candies. Yes, that coca, the same one used for manufacturing cocaine. For centuries the locals have chewed coca leaves or drank coca tea as an altitude-sickness remedy. The raw leaves deliver a far milder effect than refined cocaine. Now coca had found its way into candy form, which must be very convenient for prospective cocaine-addicted toddlers.

I refused to settle for some wimpy candy or sips of watered-down tea. My beloved spouse deserved nothing but the full-strength best. I returned to our hotel and notified our hotel concierge of my poor wife's perilous condition. A few minutes later an artfully arranged plate of unadulterated coca leaves was delivered to our room and I offered them to Helene. Who could have guessed that she would refuse to try them, preferring instead to suffer from altitude sickness rather than experience a potential new taste sensation?

Although I was not feeling any adverse effects from the altitude, there was no reason to wait until the last minute. I looked around for some written instructions but saw only a plate topped with leaves. I placed a few of the leaves in my cheek like chewing tobacco, only to discover the hard way that one must first remove the stems. After my mouth stopped bleeding I tried again. I quickly learned why coca was being offered on the street in a sweet candy form. The leaves tasted like the bottom of my boots after a particularly muddy trek up the Inca trail behind a herd of slow-moving vicunas. It was only later I learned that when chewing coca leaves most locals add some *ilucta*, made from the ash of the quinoa plant, to counter the coca's highly astringent taste. Now they tell me. I felt great before I tried the coca leaves. Afterward, my cheek was numb and punctured, I had a headache, and I was no longer on speaking terms with my taste buds. The coca leaves did not even pack enough punch to provide a mild high.

Bravely and without any further chemical inducement, Helene and I rallied later that afternoon and commenced our search for *cuy*. Like most great adventures, this one started in a bakery. Yes, it was on the cobblestone streets of Cusco where I followed my nose off the main plaza into a local *pasteleria*. A welcoming aroma and pans of freshly baked empanadas greeted us. Dominating the room was a massive wood-fired clay oven. Dominating the oven was the massive baker. I thought it was a woman. Helene thought it was a man. He/she was covered from neck to toes in a stained indigo apron and despite the scorching heat from the oven, wore an orange, green, and yellow alpaca fur chullo on his/her head. In a woven basket resting on top of the massive slate hearth were whole roasted potatoes and some type of steaming brown mass. Upon closer inspection, the brown mass revealed itself to be a pyramid of grilled and blackened *cuyes*.

I quickly averted my eyes to the opposite side of the room, only to spy a series of metal cages stacked from floor to ceiling. Yes, each cage contained a bright-eyed, pink-nose-twitching, adorable guinea pig praying for a phone call from the governor or at least a lock pick hidden in an empanada. What kind of sick pastry shop was this? Chocolate cake with *cuy* frosting? *Cuy* sprinkled cupcakes? With the altitude still giving Helene some difficulties and the disturbing thought of *cuy* chip cookies in my head, I suspended our search. We would try to pick up the porky scent again later that evening with dinner at Pacha Papa Restaurant.

Pacha Papa is at the top of a very tall hill. We climbed and climbed. Air was scarcer than my spouse at a fishmonger's convention. My lungs screamed for me to turn around. Yet, we forged ahead, following the subtle scent of roasting *cuy* that had been wafting down the hill. We finally stumbled into Pacha Papa to find a welcoming open-air courtyard, a huge wood-fired clay oven, a local musician doing a surprisingly strong medley of Tom Jones' greatest Peruvian hits, and the promise of one of the preeminent *cuyes* in town.

It took a while for me to catch my breath so I slowly worked my way up to the main dish. I started with a fine quinoa soup with purple potatoes. There are over four thousand varieties of potatoes grown in the Peruvian Andes. They come in all kinds of shapes and colors. Yet, every dish I ordered in Peru was accompanied by purple potatoes. They were cute the first meal or so but were the other colored potatoes on strike? As I caught myself thinking about a brown Idaho spud under a fat dollop of fresh sour cream and hand-cut sprinkled chives, my *cuy* arrived. It was served whole, adorned with colorful peppers and a side dish of more purple potatoes. The *cuy's* previously whiskered face was frozen in a snarl. Sharp teeth protruded from its mouth as if to attack. Little *cuy* feet ended in little *cuy* claws. Its now hairless skin was blistered and bubbling. It did not look like it was having a pleasant day.

The blackened beast looked like a giant scorched rat, which it was. *Cuyes* are rodents, sharing much of their DNA with mice.

"You've got to be kidding me," my bride coughed out while trying to cover her eyes from the dish of honor. "They serve it whole on a plate?"

"Of course," I replied. "You want to make sure you're getting the real thing, don't you? You don't want to be served some cheap *cuy* substitute, do you?"

"I don't even want to think about that."

"There you go."

The *cuy* stared at me through vacant charred eyes, seemingly daring me to make a move. Did its one remaining whisker just twitch or was the altitude playing tricks on me? I tightened my grip on my knife and fork. I was not sure about the local custom of how to consume a *cuy*. What end do you start from? I decided to start on one of the back legs. No, it did not taste like chicken. But it did taste like a cross between the dark meat of a game bird and a rabbit. Here at Pacha Papa it was basted in a red pepper sauce that gave it a kick (which was good because after I ate its leg, it was not kicking much on its own). I moved to the meatier areas in its mid-section and on up toward the tender cheeks. I put the tail in my pocket to use as a toothpick later. If there is one thing I hate, it's when people converse with *cuy* stuck in their teeth.

After dinner, it was all downhill from there as we strolled back to our hotel.

* * *

Of course, no proper trip to Peru would be complete without a traditional treatment from a local Amazonian shaman. The next day we found ourselves trudging uphill on a narrow dirt path that wound deep into the jungle. Chivalrous husband that I am, I followed closely behind my wife in case our path was blocked by a Peruvian Goliath birdeater spider and I needed to run for help. After an hour's torturous climb we finally reached the shaman's three-sided, thatched hut. We were sopping wet from the humidity, our legs were cramping, and our tongues were hanging out. Other than that, we were quite comfortable.

But the shaman was nowhere to be seen. As the excitement of his anticipated big entrance grew, I pictured a grass skirt-wearing, garishly painted, wrinkled old man with a bone through his nose and hair as untamed as my spouse in a Peruvian chocolate factory. Instead we were eventually greeted by a well-groomed gentleman in his thirties wearing Western-style clothes. What a letdown.

I started to ask to see his shaman diploma and evidence of his class ranking in shaman school but he cut me off and offered us a "relaxation" treatment. Before I could nudge my wife in front of him to volunteer, the shaman led me to a small wooden bench where he smeared some evil-smelling concoction on my forehead and placed over it an entirely unhygienic woven headband that was held together mostly by the remnants of evil-smelling concoctions from countless earlier treatments. The shaman then put an even more elaborately decorated cloth headband on his own head, topped with two large brilliant blue parrot feathers. At least that was more like it, although for what I was paying I would not have minded having a feather or two of my own.

The shaman stood behind me and started to chant in an Amazonian dialect that was not in my guidebook. While hovering over me from behind, our shaman lit what might have been the world's largest Amazonian blunt and blew smoke into my hair as he commenced smacking my head with large, leafy branches, all the while continuing to chant. He stopped just short of beating me senseless, no doubt because he wanted to be paid before I slipped into a coma. I must admit I felt more relaxed after he stopped thrashing me.

Following this relaxation treatment the shaman explained to us the contents of numerous glass containers that were resting on a makeshift wooden bar, each filled with medicinal herbs and potions. The last container held a murky, decidedly threatening liquid with pieces of moldy leaves floating about. Amazonians drink the hallucinogenic ayahuasca as a means of spiritual awakening and as a portal to communicate with extradimensional beings who can offer spiritual guidance. Having been rendered almost senseless from the relaxation treatment, I was hoping that an extradimensional being would appear and beam me back to our lodge, even if I first had to submit to some alien medical experimentation. My second choice would have been an Uber ride but the nearest LUX car was forty-seven villages away.

The shaman offered me a sip from his jug, one dose of which typically causes a person to black out and experience a vision. I took a whiff. It smelled like the socks I was wearing following that long sweaty hike up to the shaman's hut. Acrid, oily, rotting bark. My nose was highly offended. We paid the shaman and crawled back down the hill toward our lodge at sloth-like speed.

* * *

After dinner each night the lodge director usually had a few announcements to report to the diners. These typically included the weather report for the next day, information on organized hiking trips that would be going out in the morning, and a short memorial service for lodgers that had stepped on a poison dart frog or were swallowed whole by an anaconda. On our final night he added a plea for prescription drugs:

"As each of you have seen up close, the Amazon is a wonderous and beautiful place. It can also be quite dangerous, particularly among the river people who have limited access to medicines and health care. Almost twenty-five percent of all drugs used in Western modern medicine were derived from rainforest plants, yet the people living on the river of the Amazon have access to very few of them and scant access to hospitals or traditional doctors. You all know that there are dangerous animals and insects in the Amazon region. But for the river people, merely falling and breaking a leg while out in the jungle can prove fatal. If you have brought with you any medicines that you can spare, please let us know and we will distribute them where they will greatly impact the lives of the warm and friendly people that you have met during your journey. Thank you for coming to experience our river home and we hope you will return soon."

I was taking a number of drugs to deal with my illness. I had no idea whether any of them had been developed based upon Amazonian plants, but I took out my two bottles of pain pills and deposited them in the collection box.

Headless piranha

Head on *cuy*

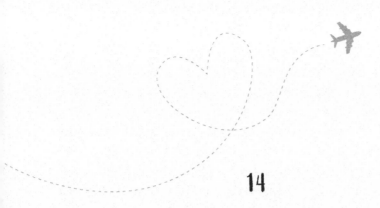

14

OCTOPUS BALLS

November 25, 2016

No visitors, no telephone calls.

When I entered the hospital those were my adamant instructions to Helene. She was to be the gatekeeper and bar anyone from visiting me at the hospital. Also, all telephone calls were to end with her.

It is almost impossible to rest in a hospital. Blood pressure sleeves and leg compression pumps rev up every few minutes, codes of all colors are blasted through the central speaker system, doctors pop in throughout the day to thump your chest, nurses come in to take your temperature, maintenance personnel empty trash and mop the floor, meals are dropped off, trays are picked up, supplies are replenished, sponge baths are administered, 3:00 a.m. chest x-rays occur each night. It is difficult to close your eyes and rest for even half an hour.

Then visitors show up. The visitors would rather be just about anywhere else but have taken time from their already exhausting day to drive to the hospital, fight for a parking space, check in among the hacking, sneezing, moaning throng, stumble their way down a maze of long hallways while dodging gurneys, and then battle for the lone hard chair in each room to stare at the patient who is having the worst hair day of his or her life. The least the patient can do is stay awake and converse during the visit.

I did not have the strength to do that. I did not have the strength to talk on the phone. I did not have the strength to even hold my phone or to push the buttons. I could not control my fingers sufficiently to send a text. My cognitive functioning was slightly above that of a kumquat. Everything was fuzzy. I could not concentrate on anything for more than a few seconds. I knew that I needed to do everything possible to conserve what little strength and focus that I had left, and that meant to do absolutely as little as possible.

So, Helene fielded daily calls and texts from my friends, colleagues from my office, her friends, my family, her family, pharmacists and seemingly a cast of thousands. This was of course, in addition to visiting me every day, paying the bills, buying the groceries, taking care of Snoring Dog, battling the insurance companies, assisting in the care of her parents, watering the plants, doing the laundry, and juggling countless other workings of the household. She also had to steel herself for the frequent sound of a ringing telephone and the voice of a doctor alerting her to the latest bad news

Additionally, Helene had to mentally prepare for what would happens next. If I was lucky enough to receive a liver transplant, she needed to ready the house for an invalid husband, prepare a rigorous daily course of medications, learn how to administer injections, take my blood pressure, check my blood sugar levels, oversee physical therapy, chauffer me to doctor appointments and continue to serve as "Communications Central." If I was not so fortunate, there was other planning to do.

Helene continued to just place one foot in front of the other, refusing to falter as she forged forward. There was no time to worry. She did not have the luxury to lay in bed and have a good cry. Helene alone was in charge and there was much to do.

Everything changed the day Helene dialed 911. After I blacked out a third time and Helene called for the ambulance, overruling my crackpot scheme to roll me into our car and drive ourselves to the doctor, Helene realized that like it or not she must now take on the sole burden of responsibility for increasingly important decisions and that I wasn't going to be able to help. Yes, that Helene, the one who despises having to make even the simplest decision.

Suddenly, life and death issues assaulted Helene in relentless surges. I was not aware of much of it until Helene came for her midday visit. The doctors had just removed my intubation tube and I was able to speak for the first time in several days. Helene plopped into the hard chair, as always smiling despite the obvious strain, and spoke first.

"How are you feeling today?" she asked.

"Never better," I said, not out of positivity but rather from whatever sarcasm I could still muster. I discovered that my throat was sore from the intubation tube. "At least they took that tube out for a while and I can talk a bit."

"I know. One of the doctors called a couple days ago to say that you were having trouble breathing. I had to authorize the intubation."

"So you're to blame."

"Yep, it was me. Add that to the list of my many other offenses."

"Do you know if there is any change in my MELD score?"

"Still thirty-two."

"Wonderful," I sighed with derision. "On a positive note, I guess my kidneys are still failing. It looks like I'm still hooked up to that dialysis machine but with all these wires and tubes it's hard to see"

"Yes, I had to approve that as well. The doctor said there is a good chance that once you get a transplant, your kidneys will improve."

"*If* I get a transplant. What's this new thing sticking out of my neck?"

"It's a central line. It makes it easier for the nurses to draw blood or administer fluids."

"I don't remember them telling me about that."

"I was here with the doctor when he explained it to you."

"News to me."

"You were a bit out of it. I told him to go ahead."

"Sure, why not. I need that like I need another hole in my head. Oh wait, it is a hole in my head."

"Glad you still have your sense of humor."

"I'm losing body parts by the minute. My sense of humor is all I have left."

"You gained some blood this morning. Dr. Parker called early to say that you were bleeding internally. I approved a blood transfusion."

"This is like a never-ending Whack-A-Mole arcade game."

"I know, but I get to pick out a giant stuffed panda if I can win ten more award tickets."

"If I ever get out of here, you can have a real panda. Now that I can talk a little, why don't you bring the kids by later."

"I will. They've been waiting to see you."

* * *

Jessica, who was now twenty-nine years old, took a deep breath, looked straight ahead, and tried her hardest not to see anything as she walked with Helene and Matthew down the hospital's intensive care corridors to my room. As they came in, I was in my usual position flat on my back and shivering under three blankets. What was left of my body was wilted and yellow. I had more tubes coming out of me than an old Philco radio. My family crowded in among the dialysis machine, blood pressure monitor, ventilator, IV stand, EEG machine, bedside monitor, Hemedex monitor, compression boot pack, and half a dozen other contraptions I could not pronounce even when I was lucid.

Helene looked tired but of course wore a smile. Matthew had just rushed over from the college English class he was teaching and still had his messenger bag full of papers slung over his shoulder. Jessica, who had never gotten over her fear of all thing medical, looked like she just swallowed a live squid. I hid my grotesque stump hands under the covers so as not to further scare anyone.

"Hi guys," I said as loud and as upbeat as I could muster.

"Hi Dad!" they both replied in unison.

"I'm very happy to see you guys."

"How are you feeling?" Jessica asked.

"Good. I've got a pudding left over from lunch if anybody is hungry."

There were no takers for the pudding. Smart family.

"I see that you didn't open your box of apple juice," Matthew said.

"Yeah, those boxes with the plastic tops are impossible to open," I replied.

"I'd loan you my Greek pocketknife but you'd probably slice off your finger. Do you want some help with the juice box?"

"No, I'm good, thanks. What did you guys do this morning?" I asked.

"I taught my class and I've got British Lit papers to grade this afternoon," Matthew said.

"I just slept in and looked after my kitten," Jessica offered.

A nurse came in and interrupted, politely telling us that a doctor had ordered a test for me and everyone would need to clear out in a minute. It was time for me to get down to business.

"Matthew, I want you to know that I am very proud of you." It was something I should have said far more often to both kids. "I'm always bragging to people about how you got your Ph.D. and are teaching."

Matthew looked down at his shoes.

"And Jessica," I said as she moved closer. "I am so proud of you..."

"Don't say that," Jessica interrupted softly as she choked up. The whole scene had finally gotten the best of her. It sounded too much like a final good-bye.

The nurse started to shoo everyone out of the room.

"Love you!" I croaked out to the group, my voice a raspy whisper.

"Love you Dad!" Matthew and Jessica called back as the nurse ushered Helene and the kids out.

I listened as long as I could to their footsteps echoing on the tile floor hallway until the sound faded away and all that remained was the whir of the dialysis machine and the whoosh of the compression pumps on my legs.

* * *

2014

At home in Los Angeles, Helene snuggled up in her puppy dog-themed flannel pajamas, baby blue terrycloth bathrobe and frayed fuzzy slippers. She was enjoying a peaceful moment at the breakfast table reading the newspaper and sipping chamomile tea from an oversized Tinkerbell mug. Too peaceful. It was my husbandly obligation to liven things up.

"I've been reading the brochure about our cruise. Our first stop is Tokyo. How about we go out for a nice sushi dinner?" I suggested, just to get her adrenaline going. "You know I've always dreamed about having a world-class sushi experience."

"Are you talking to me?" she asked incredulously.

"Yes, De Niro, I'm talking to you."

"You know very well that I don't eat fish. How often do we need to go over this?"

"But Tokyo has the greatest sushi in the world."

"It still tastes fishy."

"How many times have you had sushi?" I asked, knowing the answer was never.

She returned to reading the newspaper. Years of experience had taught her to wisely ignore me at the early stages of most conversations. However, I had to be persistent if I was going to keep her on her toes. "I'm told that fugu is not fishy-tasting at all," I suggested.

"I assume that's the one that's poisonous," she wisely guessed. This was one of the main reasons I married her. She was exceedingly smart and difficult to fool, so I always had to be on top of my game. "You can have my portion," she continued, with a smile just short of gracious.

"It tastes just like chicken," I lied.

"No, thank you."

Impetuously, I had already purchased both of us nonrefundable plane tickets to Tokyo, so I had to find a way to make this work. I commenced a search to locate a world-class sushi restaurant in Tokyo that also served some kind of tasteless chicken. I consulted websites, purchased guidebooks, studied blogs, and scrutinized menus, but this particular search had me stymied. I even posted an inquiry on a popular foodie website, introducing my dear wife to the readers and explaining my plight. Fifty-seven percent of those who replied confirmed that no self-respecting master sushi chef would also serve cooked chicken dishes. The other forty-three percent strongly suggested that I dump my wife.

I remained determined to indulge in a world-class sushi meal during this trip, but there was no bribe large enough to convince Helene to try raw or even cooked fish. By this point in our marriage she was on to all of my tricks, but I refused to give up on my sushi dreams. I was older and wiser, and it was time to draw a line in the rice. The sashimi had hit the fan and I had to play my final card.

I approached her a few days later at the breakfast table. "Look, about that sushi dinner in Tokyo. You don't want a repeat of The Bouillabaisse Incident do you?" I said, more as a plea than a question.

"No, I certainly do not," Helene replied instantly, "and I also have no intention whatsoever of eating raw fish."

"Well, what do you want to do?"

"You go on without me."

"Are you sure?"

"Positive. You go, have a good time, I'll find something to eat at the hotel."

Dine without my wife at a world-class sushi restaurant while on vacation in Tokyo? Absolutely! After assuring Helene that there was a McDonald's waiting for her near our Tokyo hotel, I resumed my search. I learned that certain of the top sushi restaurants in Tokyo will not serve foreigners. Others will not accept a reservation unless the caller speaks Japanese. Ultimately, I decided upon the foreigner-friendly, three-Michelin-star Sushi Yoshitake in the Ginza district, only to learn that it did not accept overseas reservations. I considered shifting my research to the proper way to commit seppuku.

However, I was not to be denied. I contacted my soon-to-be hotel concierge in Tokyo. He confirmed that I had made an excellent choice and explained that Sushi Yoshitake only accepted reservations thirty days in advance. He promised to personally call the restaurant early on the first possible day and try to reserve one of the seven coveted seats. My friendly concierge also explained that I must present my credit card now to place a $250 nonrefundable deposit. Well, in for a yen, in for a dollar. A few weeks later an email arrived notifying me that I had hit the sushi lottery and a reservation for one had been confirmed in my name.

Although Helene would not be accompanying me on my great sushi adventure, I did not want her to miss out entirely on the Tokyo fish experience, so on the first morning of our trip we visited the world-famous Tokyo Tsukiji Fish Market. In anticipation I had studied up on various "fun facts" regarding the market and amassed a significant quantity of fishy puns that would come in handy during a tour of the largest wholesale fish-and-seafood market in the world. Close to one thousand vendors are crammed together shoulder-to-shoulder among sky-high stacked pallets and an ocean of seafood under a single roof. Wearing fish gut-proof floor-length aprons and wielding massive knives, workers chop away at breakneck speed as they clean and cut over four hundred varieties of fish to be shipped all around the world. Motorized carts towing stacked fish cartons the height of a modest tsunami zip by without warning from every direction. Many of the workers still have ten fingers and only the sprightliest of picture-snapping tourists survive.

Helene would not want this to be made public but she adores the 1960's television show *Flipper* about a Harvard-educated dolphin that speaks several languages, can perform complex trigonometry, and catches criminals single-finned. Plied with enough alcohol, Helene has been known to perform a weak Flipper imitation: "Eh eh eh eh, eh eh eh eh." Remarkably, Helene believes this to be high entertainment. I figured that a visit to the Tokyo fish market would give her an opportunity to see what happens to dolphin television stars after their careers are over.

We dodged dozens of kamikaze forklifts as we worked our way through the maze of vendors. "Why, there's Flipper now!" I pointed out. Atop a massive cutting board, a large fish was splayed neatly into three huge pieces. Its tail fin was limp, its mouth gaping in the humiliation of no longer receiving residuals.

"Stop that," my spouse pleaded.

Not quite yet. "Look over there, its Flipper's TV friend Oswald The Octopus!" I shouted above the din. A huge bright crimson octopus was displayed on a bed of ice, his tentacles glistening under the overhead lights. "His Nielsen ratings went down too and now he's off to the sushi bar."

"Just stop," she begged again.

We moved on to a different part of the market, every few steps shaking fish guts off my new Saucony running shoes. I pointed down a long aisle of fish vendors.

"That's the less desirable section of the market," I pointed out.

"Why is that?" she asked, taking the bait once again.

"Look around," I replied. "It's squid row."

In another section Helene and I stopped to watch a knife-wielding vendor in a blue apron expertly shucking shellfish at a rapid pace that no machine could match. "Maybe you should inquire about getting a job as his assistant," Helene kiddingly suggested.

"No thanks," I replied without missing a beat. "I don't want to pull a mussel."

From the look on Helene's face it appeared that pun appreciation time had now expired and she was ready to depart. But I was not about to leave before getting some snacks from the intriguing variety of food stalls ringing the market. We stopped in front of one with a large sign that I just could not pass by.

"How about some octopus balls?" I asked, trying to get a rise out of her.

"No, thank you."

"Some poor octopus is singing soprano at this very moment and you won't even try one?"

"I don't like octopus balls."

"Name the last time that you had octopus balls in your mouth."

"There's no way that I'm going to dignify that one."

As always, more for me. I tried an order of the octopus balls, or *takoyaki*, which consisted of round pieces of octopus (I did not ask which pieces) fried in a flour batter. Aside from inducing third-degree burns when I popped one into my mouth fresh out of the fryer, they were a tad chewy but quite tasty.

But for the help of a local friend and his crudely scribbled map, I might still be searching for Sushi Yoshitake. Who knew that not all the street signs in Tokyo were in English? I had been told that Sushi Yoshitake, like most other shops and restaurants in the city, was on the upper floor of an office building. It felt like I had walked half the sidewalks of Tokyo with my head thrust back as if I was trying to gargle, before I finally stumbled upon a forbidding back street and the exterior sign high up above for Sushi Yoshitake. It sat upon another sign that had a large heart on it. Wedding chapel? Bondage shop? Love motel? Rubbing the mother of all cricks out of my neck, I took an elevator up and made my way to a plain wooden door that I prayed was the entrance to a sushi restaurant.

Luck was with me that evening, at least at the beginning. A host promptly greeted and escorted me to my single seat at the end of a blond wood sushi bar that spanned just far enough to comfortably seat seven people inside the elegantly minimalist interior. Wooden chopsticks were meticulously placed in perfect symmetry on holders in front of each seat, along with smooth wooden bowls, precision rolled towels and polished plates. Four other diners soon trickled into the intimate room for a magical evening of sushi at its finest. The two seats to my left remained vacant as a server came to take my drink order. Two assistants on the other side of the counter worked to have the great chef's knives, bowls, and towels lined up perfectly. I have had surgery in operating rooms that were not this clean and orderly. The two assistants now stood at stoic attention. Additional workers were visible scurrying around behind a side curtain in the small kitchen off to the side. Clearly the restaurant workers had the diners outnumbered.

It became still and quiet, a calm meditative moment before the sushi show was to begin. We waited. The two assistants remained fixed in place, staring straight ahead as if on guard duty at the Imperial Palace. We waited some more.

There was a commotion at the front door. The diners all turned as one toward the source of the noise. Even one of the assistants could not help but peak over with a raised eyebrow. Bursting through the door was a twentysomething skinny-pants man bun talking loudly on his cellphone in a Brooklynese accent, accompanied by what appeared to be his half-blond girlfriend wearing chunky jewelry and strategically sliced faded jeans. She was texting on her cellphone while simultaneously trying to balance several large shopping bags.

Saying "gotta go" to his caller, he put the phone in his pocket and sat next to me with his girlfriend sitting in the third chair. A server came to take their drink orders. He tried to order a Budweiser but settled for a Japanese beer. The girlfriend ordered a diet coke, then called the server back: "Do we get free refills?" she asked.

It was going to be a long night.

My new dining buddy, whose Asian dining expertise was apparently restricted to ordering orange chicken at Panda Express back home in Flatbush, decided to show off to his girlfriend and began directing her in the proper use of chopsticks: "The very first thing you have to do is to rub them together like this, so that you don't get any splinters," he announced. He picked up the already meticulously polished chopsticks and rubbed them together like he was trying to start a fire. I said a silent prayer that he would spontaneously combust.

With all seven diners finally present the white-clad Chef Yoshitake strode out from the kitchen and the two assistants assumed their positions at his sides. A respectful hush settled over the small room as all eyes focused on the great chef. The sushi symphony was about to begin. Chef Yoshitake politely bowed and stood. Nothing happened. I pretended to closely examine the workmanship on my chopsticks while slyly glancing at my neighbor to watch his first move. He pretended to closely examine the workmanship on his chopsticks while slyly glancing at me to watch my first move. Someone had to take charge of our side of the sushi bar. I picked up the moist towel that lay in front of me and washed my hands for the big event. I looked over to my left, fearful that I would catch him giving his armpits the once over, but thankfully he was now following my lead. I folded the used towel neatly and placed it back on the wooden holder in front of me. My neighbor left his in a crumpled mess.

I looked up. Chef Yoshitake did not appear to be impressed with either of us.

But the great feast commenced. Chef Yoshitake took command in the center of the bar behind a pristine cutting board, several wooden bowls containing mysterious sauces, and a small mountain of wasabi. With the skill of a concert pianist, the chef's finely tuned hands delicately placed a precise portion of sweet crab on seven plates, topped each with a dollop of orange roe, and personally delivered one to each diner. The cutting board was wiped clean, the knives shined and returned to their position of attention at the great chef's side, our used plates quickly removed, and a bright red tentacle appeared on the cutting board. Almost faster than the eye could follow, the tentacle was sliced into seven identical portions of the sweetest and most tender octopus on the planet. I continued to watch in awe as Chef Yoshitake expertly trimmed the finest fish and seafood in the world, fastidiously molded rice around fresh wasabi, and masterfully positioned each morsel on our plates with the precision of a Japanese Credor watchmaker. As Chef Yoshitake demonstrated knife skills that would have made Jack the Ripper wasabi green with jealousy, I realized that the trimmings he was throwing away were far better sushi than I had ever eaten in my life. Bonito, squid, snapper, fatty tuna, sardine, mackerel, clam, fugu and many more came in scrupulous succession. As he delivered each plate, Chef Yoshitake stated the name of the fish in heavily accented English.

After each course, his two assistants were tasked with immediately cleaning and realigning the chef's knives and towels. One of the assistants must have stayed up too late at the karaoke bar the previous night because following a serving of spectacular fatty tuna, he placed one of the chef's knives a few degrees off-center. Chef Yoshitake barked loud enough at the assistant to rattle our chopsticks in their holders. The assistant recoiled in fear and bowed his apology, while I sat up a little straighter in my chair.

The highlight of the evening was the chef's specialty—steamed abalone with abalone liver sauce. The sauce was precisely the color of the green projectile vomit used in The Exorcist. I used my chopsticks to gently lift a single piece of abalone from the sauce and placed the treat in my mouth, allowing that magic morsel to linger on my tongue for an extra moment before chewing. It tasted like tiny Japanese *yōsei* ocean fairies were delicately dancing in my mouth. It was mesmerizing and I savored that mouthful for as long as possible before finally swallowing. For just that fleeting moment, the freshness of the entire ocean swept over my taste buds and then receded once more. But my exhilaration was tempered by the fact that the magical effect of the sauce was already dissipating. Before I could reach a state of despair, Chef Yoshitake came over and placed a few grains of rice in my sauce bowl so that I could sop up the remainder of the sauce and not miss a single drop. Genius.

Just when Chef Yoshitake and I had fallen into an easy rhythm and were meshing well together as a team, disaster struck. It was time for the highly anticipated *uni* course. *Uni* is the gonads of sea urchins and I was very much looking forward to sampling the different kinds of *uni* available only in Japan. Chef Yoshitake scrupulously placed several types of the highest quality *uni* in a seaweed nori wrapper and delicately positioned it on my plate. The result was a rather substantial piece of sushi. I decided to enjoy it for as long as possible by eating it in two bites. That plan, however, was foiled. The monument of *uni* had been craftily spring-loaded because as soon as I took the first bite the entire creation exploded. It was an *uni* meteor shower with *uni* flying everywhere. On the table. On my lap. Even on Mr. Brooklyn's embarrassing polyester-blend shirt. Time came to a halt as the entire room looked on in disbelief. I tried to remain calm as if I had planned this all along. As six diners, two assistants and one unhappy chef stared incredulously, I used my fingers to peel golden *uni* off of the table. As a courtesy, like a monkey at the zoo picking bugs off his companion, I picked fifty dollars' worth of *uni* off of Man Bun's shirt.

Chef Yoshitake was not amused. He stomped over to me with his gleaming knife still in hand, bent down and leaned over until his face was only inches from mine. He raised his hand in front of my nose, extended his forefinger skyward, and in a fierce growl that still rings in my ears to this day, snarled: "ONE BITE!"

Heavy accent or not, I heard him loud and clear. I nodded sheepishly, grateful that Chef Yoshitake had generously spared my life.

After taking a few moments to compose himself, the chef graciously continued on to the next course. However, his grave concerns about me had not been completely placated because as he next placed a delicate piece of sea eel on my plate, he once again positioned himself inches from my face, extended his forefinger, and for a second time sent those humiliating words resounding through the room: "ONE BITE!"

"*Hai* chef, one bite." Message received.

After the meal, Chef Yoshitake came around from his side of the bar, bowed respectfully, and showed me the way out. I think he wanted to personally ensure that I promptly departed the premises.

Helene greeted me when I arrived back at the hotel. "How was your big sushi adventure?" she asked.

"Stunning. The sushi was unbelievably good and I think Chef Yoshitake and I really bonded. We may go out for some karaoke and sake later," I replied. "And how was your McDonald's adventure?"

"It was perfect. They even had free coke refills," she beamed.

Before

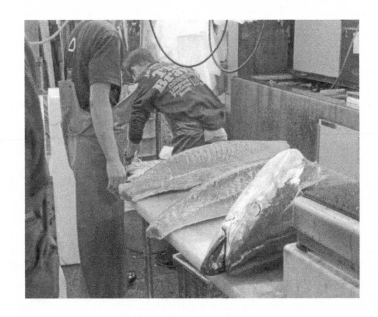

After

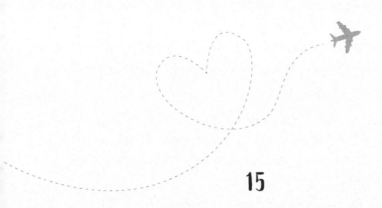

15

CRY ME A LIVER

November 26, 2016

I cry at everything.

When I was a little kid my father made it clear to me that crying was for babies. He grew up in the hardened steel town of Bethlehem, Pennsylvania. Even in the winter snow, he sold newspapers on the street corner for two cents apiece and then walked home each night to turn over the profits to his mother and to his often physically abusive father. The other youths in the neighborhood looked for any opening to prey on the weak, whether to steal lunch money or simply to beat someone up for sport. When my father was fourteen his mother fled to California with the three kids where she took a job in a sewing sweatshop to support the family. Life was tough. There was no room for sissies. I learned the lesson well and had not cried since I was nine years old.

I only saw Helene cry a couple of times during our relationship, both times during an extreme family crisis. But she demonstrated remarkable strength and never shed a single tear in front of me during the years of my illness. She was about to be tested again because I insisted that we discuss plans for my possible funeral. As soon as I brought it up, her once permanent smile disappeared. She raised the head of my bed a few degrees so that we could see each other clearly and pulled up the hard chair as close to my bed as possible as she slumped into it.

"Okay, so it will be at Mount Sinai cemetery," I confirmed.

"Yes," she said solemnly.

I could see her struggling to deal with this in a matter-of-fact manner without breaking down but I knew she would succeed. I could also see that she wanted to conclude this conversation as quickly as possible.

"We'll buy two plots side by side," she continued. "That way I can haunt you for eternity." Finally, a hint of a smile again.

"I was afraid of that. What about music at the funeral? How about Born to Run?"

"I know it's your favorite song but it's not really very funereal. 'It's a death trap, it's a suicide rap.' Really?"

"Alright, Hallelujah then, but only the original version sung by Leonard Cohen. Not some lame American Idol version."

"Are we finished?"

"Not until we agree on the headstone inscription. I don't want any of that boring 'Beloved Husband and Father' stuff."

"Let me guess. You have something else in mind?"

"I've given this a lot of thought. What do you think of 'Get Off My Lawn!'?"

"It's a bit harsh, don't you think?" The full smile had returned.

"You're right. Let's go with that old 1970's deejay sign-off, 'Too Hip, Gotta Go.'"

"If that's what you want, but I'm still going to sneak in some 'Beloved' stuff."

"Deal."

To Helene's great relief a nurse interrupted to bring in my breakfast tray. Helene helped me lift off the plastic dome and revealed a surprise. Along with scrambled eggs, I ordered a fruit cup.

I expected to find reconstituted cubes of long-ago frozen fruit in a cloyingly sweet syrup, but instead before me was a cup of freshly cut watermelon and cantaloupe squares. With some help from Helene, I speared a piece of cantaloupe and maneuvered it into my mouth. I took one bite of that sweet melon and before I could even swallow, I started crying. Deep, body-rocking, uncontrollable crying. The cantaloupe was delicious!

I spent much of the day crying, usually out of happiness. I cried when the new nurse came on shift. I cried watching a Property Brothers rerun on television. I cried when the medical assistant fluffed my pillow. When my liver surgeon Dr. Lee came to see me on her rounds, I cried because I was crying.

"I've been crying all day," I told her as the tears ran down my cheeks. "I never cry but now I can't control it. I am emotional over everything. It's not like me."

Dr. Lee knelt by the side of my bed and took my hand. "It's completely normal. We have you on a very high dosage of prednisone. It's a steroid that often causes dramatic mood swings from euphoria to anxiety. Don't worry. It's only temporary."

"Are you sure?"

"Positive. And remember, we're going to get you a new liver."

"Okay."

I cried myself through two entire boxes of tissues by the time early evening came around and the nurse finally turned out the light. But I was still awake hours later. When a nurse came in to take my temperature, I asked her to help me use my phone to call Helene. My club hands were too weak and shaky to do it on my own.

"Are you okay?" Helene asked. It was unusual for me to call her in the evening.

"You know how sometimes you get a song in your head and you can't stop humming it?" I asked her.

"Sure."

"Well, I've had a song in my head for hours and I can't shake it. It's keeping me awake."

"What song?"

"I don't want to say."

"What do you mean you don't want to say?"

"It's embarrassing."

"You called me. What song is it?"

"Don't tell anyone but it's that ABBA song Fernando."

I heard Helene trying to muffle a snicker on the other end of the line. "You don't even like ABBA," she finally said.

"I'm well aware of that. I'm going to die and the only thing people will remember is that I died humming an ABBA song." I was serious. I was also out of my mind.

"You've got all your own songs right there on your iPhone. Why don't you ask the nurse to help you plug in your earbuds and listen to some Dylan or John Fogerty. Or you can listen to Fred."

A brilliant idea! Why hadn't I thought of that? In a fleeting moment of unexpected clarity, I knew exactly what I wanted to hear. I said good-bye to Helene and asked the nurse to hook me up and play a particular song on repeat. Before the first line of the song had even ended, I began to cry. Tears flooded onto my pillow. I was too weak to wipe them away and I really did not care. But ABBA mercifully disappeared from my brain as I cried myself to sleep.

Ship

By Fred Eaglesmith

Seems like I've been out here in stormy seas
About as long as I can stand
And it's like you send me another wave
Every time I catch my breath
And I've trimmed my sails
And set my course
Again, Lord, and again
Lord, if you could find me a place to land
My ship needs to come in
And there's dark clouds to my left, Lord

And dark clouds to my right
There's thunderin' and there's lightnin'
And I keep sending out my signals of distress
With no one there to see them
And the waves crash up over the bow
And soak me to my skin
Lord, if you could find me a place to land
My ship needs to come in
If you could clear the skies Lord, for just one minute
And I could see the stars
I could find my points and head on out
And try Lord just once more
But Lord I'm beat up and I'm broken

And my light is getting weak
Lord, if you could find me a place to land
My ship needs to come in

* * *

2014

Our ship cruised into the port at Shanghai on a sun-splashed Tuesday. We were anxious to disembark, but the Captain's booming voice came over the loudspeaker to announce a minor delay due to some customs mishap. His chance of being invited to my table for dinner was sinking faster than the Titanic. Meanwhile, the line at Yang's Fry Dumpling was not getting any shorter.

Of course, while Yang's now has several locations, only the original Old City location will suffice. The fry oil, unchanged since the last Mongol invasion, adds just the correct amount of tang to the dumplings. When Helene and I finally arrived the line was breathtakingly long. I looked around at the few benches in the area but they were all fully occupied by several Chinese families that had not moved from those same spots since the end of World War II. I asked Helene to be on the alert and grab any space that might become available while I went to wait in line.

The end of the line seemed to be two *hutongs* removed from the take-out window. Twenty minutes later the line still had not moved. Neither had Helene, who was way too polite to ever survive on her own in China. Waiting to get on a bus or train? Courteous to a fault Helene will step out of the way and let three million people board in front of her. Jockeying for position to grab a spot on a crowded bench? The enormous bronze statue on the Bund of former Shanghai mayor Chen Yi moves quicker than my soulmate.

It felt like three Chinese dynasties had come and gone by the time I closed in on the ordering window. The excitement built when I could finally observe through the side window the expert dumpling artistes dressed in white surgical suits meticulously stuffing dough with pork, pinching the top of the dough into perfectly even pleats and then placing the dumplings in circular bamboo containers to await frying. The Chinese family of five in front of me finally made it to the ordering window. Notwithstanding having spent the prime years of their lives waiting in this line, they still had not yet decided whether to order the crab dumplings or the pork dumplings and commenced debating the matter amongst themselves while my stomach gurgled. Arrgh.

Meanwhile, dozens of dumplings cozied up in a giant cast iron pan were receiving a sizzling bronze tan as the scent of their greasy goodness snaked its way out of the take-out window opening. While the fry master flipped the latest batch of dumplings, the Chinese family finally decided upon both pork and crab dumplings and shuffled over to wait in another line at the pickup window. I watched with envy as each person that came away with a paper carton of steaming dumplings grinned widely as if they had just won the China Sports Lottery. When it was finally my turn at bat, without delay I placed my order for eight pork dumplings. I moved into the pickup line and a few minutes later snatched up my treasure at the window. It was the first and only time a pickup line worked for me.

I took a moment to conduct an exploratory inspection. The dumplings were perfectly cooked, with sesames sprinkled on top and a golden crunchy bottom from the frying. Yang was on his game that day.

Carefully balancing the hissing hot carton of dumplings, I jogged back to where Helene was still waiting for a space on a bench. It looked like we would be enjoying our dumplings standing up. I pierced the top of a dumpling with a chopstick to allow some of the scalding steam to escape, then popped the entire dumpling into my mouth. Just a mere nudge from my teeth caused the delicate thin dough to quickly release the molten soup surrounding the rich pork filling inside.

"How is it?" Helene asked, sensibly waiting to see if I survived prior to her trying a dumpling.

"Aaayyyyyeee," I squealed.

"What?"

"Haaaagh, haaaagh."

"Huh?"

"Hot!" I cried.

"Well, blow on it," she offered helpfully.

"Great idea. I'll do that as soon as this third degree burn on my tongue settles down and I regain some feeling in my lips."

But my wife was not the only helpful person in the vicinity. A withered old Chinese woman sitting on the bench motioned me over. She had her hair pulled back in a bun and was lounging comfortably in her dark puffy jacket and worn sandals. Was she finally going to get her butt up and let me have her seat? No. Although she was not wearing a badge, the old lady had assumed the self-appointed position of Yang's Chief Inspector of Dumpling Eating. She mimed me poking a hole in the top of the dumpling, shook her head in disgust, and then motioned that I should plop the whole dumpling in my mouth at once without letting the steam out. I vigorously waved my hand in front of my open mouth, indicating to her that my mouth already felt like an erupting volcano. She laughed and dismissed me with a wave of her hand.

Now it was time for Helene to interrupt. "I'm ready, Freddie," she said.

"Steady, Betty. Ready for what?" I replied. Feigning ignorance had become second nature.

"I'm ready to try my dumpling."

"*Your* dumpling? I'm the one that stood in line."

She just stood there waiting, polite, smiling, and silent.

"Sweetie, why don't you try one of these dumplings?" I offered. "Please be sure to blow on it first."

* * *

The original Old Jesse location in the Xuhui neighborhood of Shanghai serves up home-style Shanghainese dishes in a slender but bustling two-story restaurant marked by an arched sign in English and Chinese. Bentwood chairs line up along the exterior of the restaurant to comfort the crowds waiting outside. Those lucky diners invited inside are shown to modest wooden chairs that snuggle up to tables sheathed in dark blue tablecloths. Helene and I were awarded the very last available table near a busy dark wood-paneled staircase where the waitstaff bound up and down a hundred times a night with overflowing platters of food. As a result the servers each weighed about ninety pounds, fifty pounds of which appeared to be thighs and calves. This night Jesse's was hopping as usual.

Our server was a harried young woman fighting to keep her long dark hair from falling in her eyes as she repeatedly ran the stairs obstacle course. She brusquely dropped off our menus and hustled away. We were on our own. The familiar look of panic set in as Helene began to scan the menu. Deep-fried stinky tofu. Jellyfish in scallion oil. Crab roe in tofu powder. Meanwhile, I sat across from her with a smug look on my face, having knowingly pre-ordered Jesse's signature fish head with scallions dish the day before.

I caught our server's attention as she was about to breeze by us again. With Helene on the verge of apoplexy I ordered a hairy crab dish appetizer to buy time so she could try to calm her trembling hands and read through the menu a third time. A few minutes later a whole fire orange crab was dropped off at our table. Two immense Bette Davis eyes on steroids bugged out of its body, something akin to fur ran down its claws, and its antennae pointed accusingly at Helene. I just hoped it had already been steamed.

Brave Helene tried to rally with gallows humor. "I didn't realize we would be a party of three. Ask it if it would like a pot sticker as a starter?" she quipped, although I could tell that her heart wasn't really in it. With Helene still on the precipice of collapse, I dug right in without going through our usual ritual. My crustacean buddy tasted sweet and fresh. Helene did her best not to look in its direction and rifled through the menu pages for the fourth time.

"You've got to order something," I said. "How about..."

"I certainly don't want *your* help."

"Fine but please pick something."

Our server arrived along with the moment of truth. I ordered Jesse's famous braised pork appetizer and alerted the server about my pre-ordered fish head. What was left of the crab, the server and I were now all staring at Helene. My spouse bravely ordered a beef dish. When it arrived she refused to touch it.

The braised pork was dark and forbidding. Quite chewy with a thick sauce that was way too syrupy sweet for my taste and I stopped eating after a few bites. However, a few minutes later I spotted the Big Show making its way down the stairs with our server. I had been looking forward to sampling Jesse's legendary fish head for months. The dish placed before me was completely shrouded in a thick blanket of scallions. Helene leaned over to observe exactly how I intended to tackle this. I have no doubt that she was greatly repulsed by even the thought of a gaping fish head but she just could not look away. I parted the scallions with my chopsticks and found myself staring into the maw of a huge bodyless cod head. It stared back. I conducted an exploratory probe of the head with my chopsticks, causing the cod's right eye to pop out of its socket. Helene jumped back. It was entirely possible that I did this on purpose.

The eyes are considered a great delicacy in China and eating one is considered good luck. I did not have a whole lot of luck picking the eye up with my chopsticks but I was finally able to corral it after several attempts. I held it up. "I'm keeping an eye out for you," I said to Helene proudly, having saved that line just for this occasion.

"I've got something for you too," she said, holding a single chopstick in an unnatural position for dining.

Once again, more for me. Parts of the head had great caramelization. I zeroed in on the tastiest part of any animal or fish, the cheeks. Delicate, buttery, fatty goodness. The head had a surprising amount of meat and I did not mind fighting through a forest of scallions to get at it. As with most great meals it was over way too soon. I just could not bring myself to pull the trigger on the eye, so I left it on the table as a tip for the staff, thanked our server, and hailed a taxi.

* * *

The looming mountain was formidable. Craggy outcroppings, precariously perched boulders, near vertical walls with no discernible trails. It was hard to imagine how Helene and I were going to tackle this. Especially because she was wearing her new pointy toe pumps and carrying her latest Kate Spade handbag. As if this challenge could not get any worse, it began to snow. At first just on the top of the mountain but then all over. Great. Neither of us had even brought an overcoat. It was not just a coincidence that the butte was known to the locals as Snowy Mountain. Flakes of snow continued to fall on my clothing and drifted onto my face. I stuck out my tongue and captured a snowflake. It was sweet as candy. I looked up at our server. "Enough with the snow," I indicated by holding up my hands. She stopped, bowed and departed.

Snowy Mountain Spare Ribs is one of the appetizer specialties at the famous DaDong Roast Duck Restaurant in Beijing, the second port on our cruise. The bite-sized ribs are stacked into the shape of a mountain. Once delivered to the table, the server sprinkles powdered sugar "snow" over the mountain of ribs. I tried one of the DaDong ribs. Cloyingly sweet. No bark or pink smoke ring. Back home in the United States, if you ask the smoke-soaked pit master at Joe's Kansas City Bar-B-Que to sprinkle powdered sugar on top of the ribs, expect to be hit with a carving knife right between the eyes.

However, I was not in Beijing to toy with spareribs. I was waiting for the main event, Beijing Roast Duck. This crispy-skinned Ming Dynasty dish is prepared in the traditional way using specially raised force-fed ducks that after abruptly departing this world due to a well-aimed cleaver are cleaned and left to rest standing before reaching their final destination, a sharp hook in a fiery hung oven. Setting aside the oven part, being force-fed, cleaned and left to rest sounds like my fantasy vacation.

From our now snow-dusted table at DaDong we had an unob-structed view of the open central kitchen where a dozen or so chefs hung and fussed over the famous ducks crackling over open fires. A toque-crowned carving master decked out in chef whites came rolling down the aisle with a fowl-topped metal cart and stopped at our table. Showing off skills that would compare favorably to any transplant surgeon, he expertly dissected our lean and crispy duck tableside. The duck was accompanied by thin pancakes, pickled radishes, slender strips of cucumber and small plates of other veg-etables, sugar, garlic and hoisin sauce. Our helpful server returned to give Helene and I a quick lesson on how to use chopsticks to fold the pancakes around slices of duck and condiments to form a small wrap.

My dexterity with chopsticks is unlikely to win me a trophy, particularly in the top-ranked Asia Division, but I was already on my third pancake treat while Helene was still trying to figure out how to pick up a delicate pancake using one chopstick in each hand. More duck for me! The skin was particularly crispy with the per-fect amount of smokiness. DaDong boasts about the leanness of its ducks and indeed the fat layer under the skin was thinner than oth-ers, yet the meat remained juicy and flavorful. I could see where some would enjoy the condiments as a compliment to the duck, but after trying a few flavor combinations I found that I preferred the pure taste of the duck on its own.

The last course was delivered to us on a large mound of dry ice, causing a cloud of fog to slowly creep over our table. Settled in the dry ice were hard round objects the size of plums. They turned out to be jujubes, similar to apples. The frozen balls were quite difficult to pick up and balance with chopsticks. I actually saw an icy jujube slip off of someone's chopsticks, bounce onto the floor and careen down the restaurant aisle past several diners. I pretended that it was not mine.

Time to leave.

*　*　*

A quick search on the internet for Chinese restaurants in the United States named "The Great Wall" generates tens of millions of hits. It seems as if every city in the USA is required by law to have a Great Wall Chinese restaurant. But I had come to doubt the authenticity of the food being served in such establishments. For example, one of our local Great Wall Chinese restaurants in Los Angeles offers Strawberry-Banana Smoothies on its menu. Was it really a nightly Strawberry-Banana Smoothie that made Confucius so wise?

When our guide in China told us that he would be taking us to visit The Great Wall near Beijing, I hoped that we would finally be dining at a genuine Chinese restaurant worthy of the name. Following a considerable drive out of town our Chinese guide announced that we had finally arrived at The Great Wall, but alas we were at that other one. All I saw was a very steep hill. Why is it that at least once during every vacation we have to become sopping wet from climbing at a ninety-degree angle to a remote location where air is almost nonexistent? Had China run out of amusing attractions that lay upon flat ground thick with sweet oxygen? Our guide just smiled at us and motioned for us to start climbing.

We plodded skyward to a high ridge near what looked to be a massive stone wall that, as far as I could tell, circled the globe. Now that we had climbed the hill, significant stair climbing ensued on endless worn stones, until we finally emerged panting onto a long narrow raised area at the top of the monument. For as far as we could see in both directions, ancient carved stone walls hugged the top of the ridge, punctuated only by imposing guard stations of chiseled rock. Peering out over the wall revealed an endless vista of craggy peaks and stark terrain. I envisioned a spectacular patio area for alfresco dining with a fire pit and perhaps a kitschy tiki bar. Better yet, with a killer designer and a bottomless pocketbook, this could be turned into an awesome prison-themed restaurant. It certainly was not hurting for foot traffic. Hundreds of unsightly camera-carrying tourists in shorts, just like us, were traipsing about, probably in search of a restroom. It was hot and I was still panting from the climb. I needed some food. In fact, at that point I would have been pleased with a glass of relatively benzene-free water.

"Let's go," I said to Helene. "We've looked around and I'm starved."

"I'm tired too, but at least take my picture before we go," she pleaded. "The scenery is spectacular."

"Okay, stand over there," I instructed.

"Is this okay?"

"Take a few steps back," I said, pretending that my camera could not envelope the entire majesty of the scene.

She moved back. "Is this better?" she asked.

"A few more steps back."

She moved to the very edge of the wall. "How about now?"

"Just another couple of steps back," I said.

"If I move any further back I'll be flying down the hill and end up in Mongolia."

I gave her a knowing look but prudently remained silent before taking the picture.

We hiked back down the stairs and stumbled down the hill. Helene was instantly reinvigorated when she spotted a single dining establishment at the very base of the mountain—a Subway franchise. Grinning ear to ear as if she had just received winning Gee Joon tiles in a *pai gow* game, Helene bounded inside. I refused to follow her, choosing instead to try my luck with some of the nearby street food vendors. Perhaps one of them would be selling Strawberry-Banana Smoothies.

When we finally made it back to town we headed over to Guan Yuan Hua Niao Yu Chong Shi Chang. No, that is not the name of the latest Canto Hip-Hop release by MC Jin. It is Beijing's Flower, Bird, Fish and Bug Market, selling quite inexplicably, flowers, birds, fish and bugs. The market originally specialized in items that were traditionally considered to be good luck. However, what may be good luck for the purchaser of a tasty blowfish may not be such good luck for the blowfish. It depends entirely upon which side of the chopsticks you are seated at. In any event, if I could not pick up some good eats here, something was rotten in Beijing besides the meat used at McDonalds.

I do not want to eat flowers nor do I ever want to see them on my plate, so we cruised quickly through the narrow aisles of the flower section. Just as quickly we saw hundreds of live birds of every color and plumage hung in hand-woven bamboo cages. Many of the birds were wild caught and may have been tasty depending upon whether they were able to munch on prime grade Chinese red-headed centipedes. But they were mostly pet-sized tiny finches and other diminutive species that would barely be enough to put on a cracker. I also was not sure whether these birds had received their flu shots.

The swimming occupants of the fish section were small and colorful but also appeared to be for the benefit of hobbyists. I looked around but found no rice, chopsticks or plates. The fish were safe for at least the moment.

A faint siren's song compelled us to plunge deeper into the warren of caged vermin and flea-bitten fauna. Past the salmonella-laden tiny turtles. Past the parasitic nematodes hitching a ride on the Chinese Water Dragons. The irresistible song grew louder and our will grew weaker. Helene and I drifted deeper into the womb of the market. Was that dinner calling? Not exactly. We had been summoned by chirping crickets. From tiny clear-top boxes holding crickets smaller than the tip of my pinky to meaty crickets almost the size of my fist trapped in large colorful glass jars, thousands of crickets that had never been trained to chirp in harmony sang out to us. I could see from the labels on the containers that some of the crickets were selling for hundreds of dollars each. More expensive than Shanghainese hairy crab roe with a braised abalone chaser.

The crickets were not alone. Intense looking men stood around poking the crickets with small sticks, scrutinizing the crickets as if they were diamonds. What makes a good cricket? Are crickets rated as to color, clarity, carat and cut? And what kind of a grown man tortures a tiny cricket with a stick? Someone should arm these crickets with their own sticks so at least it would be a fairer fight.

But it turned out these were fighting crickets, which is a big business that dates back over one thousand years in China. Crickets have hard mandibles near their mouths which they use to inter-lock with other crickets during fighting, much like Helene and I during our second date. They push each other in a demonstration of strength and power until one cricket retreats and there is a clear winner. Like prized thoroughbreds, crickets are selectively bred and their pedigrees dramatically impact their value. Although techni-cally illegal, I have heard whispers that betting occasionally occurs during such matches. At the cricket market, prospective cricket purchasers rub a cricket's mandibles with a sharp stick to deter-mine whether a particular cricket is aggressive and strong. I did not intend to lock mandibles with a cricket. It was time to move on.

* * *

In the historical Chinese city of Dongyang, enterprising street vendors are known to hawk "virgin boy eggs." These culinary clas-sics are indeed eggs soaked in the urine of young boys. Such eggs are believed to possess healthy properties and closely guarded fam-ily recipes are passed down through the generations. I was able to secure the secret to one such recipe on the condition that I did not share it with anyone.

First you get your urine. Not just any urine, of course. It must be taken from a boy under the age of ten who is a virgin and who does not possess any copies of the Chinese Playboy Magazine. The urine is collected in buckets strategically placed in primary school toilet areas. I am not making this up! Once you have selected your extra-virgin urine, boil and soak the eggs in a large pot filled with the urine. Preferably this is not the same pot used to serve hot pot dinners at family meals. After a proper boiling, dig the eggs out of the vat, peel off the hard-boiled shells, and return the eggs to the urine for more soaking. Discard the shells. Eating the shells would be gauche. It takes an experienced virgin boy egg master to keep the eggs from overcooking yet ensure that the fresh urine taste permeates each egg. As you can imagine, the streets of Dongyang are quite fragrant with simmering pots in abundance and street vendors calling out: "Get your hot virgin boy eggs here!"

I checked and Dongyang was about a day's travel from where we were in Beijing. Uh, no.

Much closer and far more tempting was the Beijing Donghuamen Night Market. Brightly lit outdoor food stalls come alive at night to present a wide variety of unusual Chinese delicacies. Aggressive vendors in red caps and aprons offer up the most extensive selection of fried insects in China. I knew Helene would have a difficult time containing her excitement, so we had to go visit.

Some of my cricket friends from the Flower, Bird, Fish and Bug Market must have escaped, albeit briefly, because they were being fried and offered up on a stick. Have a craving for scorpions? Need a quick fix of fried sea horse? Mental images of virgin boy eggs had unexpectedly put a slight damper on my appetite. I just needed something light to tide me over, and then I saw it. A new tempting taste treat that my spouse refuses to cook at home—fried tarantula on a stick.

Selecting just the right tarantula was more difficult than I would have imagined. Should I go with one that had hairier legs than the others? Big fatty body or one that was more muscular? The tarantula fry master was not much help, particularly when I asked him if these were free-range tarantulas. What exactly was that frying oil made from? Scorpion juice? Essence of cricket? All I could see was a big nasty vat of boiling something and neat rows of impaled tarantulas of dubious ancestry. I pointed out a friendly looking specimen with extra hairy legs and asked the tarantula wrangler to prepare him medium rare. Moments later I had my tarantula on a stick. I gallantly handed it over to my wife.

"How much would someone have to pay you to eat that tarantula?" I inquired, just to prolong this intimate marital moment.

"You know I hate to play this stupid game," she protested.

"Just tell me a number."

"No, you ask me this every time you see some weird new food. We've been through this a thousand times."

"I just want to know. How much?"

"Whatever I say you're just going to ridicule me."

"I won't, I promise."

"You always say that, right before you ridicule me."

"No ridiculing. I mean it. Just tell me the absolute minimum amount someone would have to pay you to eat our hairy friend here on the stick."

"Ten million dollars."

"Are you kidding me?"

"You asked me. Ten million dollars is the answer."

"So, you wouldn't take nine million dollars to eat that tarantula?"

"No."

"Are you insane?" I bellowed. "You wouldn't eat that for nine million dollars? Let me tell you, for nine million dollars I assure you that tarantula would be down your throat before you could say Mao Tse-Tung."

"Well, thanks so much for not ridiculing me," she declared.

"No problem."

It was now or never. I had laid out twenty bucks for a fried tarantula and I sure was not going to let it go to waste. The legs were crunchy. Really crunchy. Really, really crunchy. Little crunchy tarantula particles stuck in my teeth and refused to dislodge. I worked my way up to the body of what was quickly becoming my least favorite hairy arachnid. Ever so gently, my teeth pierced the hirsute bulbous abdomen. Juicy spider innards spewed out and ran down my chin. All too late, I realized that I should have ordered it medium well.

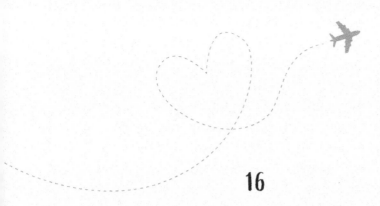

16

A FUNGUS AMONG US

November 28, 2016

I rotted away in the intensive care ward of the hospital, progressively decaying from the inside out. During the early days of intubation, I scribbled notes to the nurses and doctors as I tried to get updates on my blood test scores and my MELD number, but I was so weak that after a while even I could not recognize what I had written. Later I could talk a bit to ask questions, but whatever information they told me would float out of my head a few minutes later anyway. At the office I negotiated deals on behalf of Fortune 500 companies. Now I negotiated with the nurses for just one more ice chip. When I remembered.

Everything I once knew about the world was wrong. When my fever broke and the nurse informed me that my temperature had returned to normal, I was devastated. My condition had to get worse if I was going to have any chance at a liver. Part of me was hot, part was cold, all at the same time. Long ago my organs just chugged away doing whatever it is they did, I never gave them any thought. In the hospital each morning I took inventory to see which ones still worked, whether I would be able to breathe on my own, whether I could move my arms and legs a few inches in the bed.

There was nothing to cling to, no real constant. I could not count on any part of my body anymore. My one-time optimism about being released one day with a new liver was deflating faster than a shaken soufflé. Deep in my abdomen I could feel my liver rehearsing its death rattle. The amuse-bouche and appetizers had been excellent, the main course roundly enjoyed, I had sampled amply from the cheese cart, gorged on more than my share of desserts, but it was finally time to pay the bill of life.

I smiled as I thought of someone who was indeed one real constant in my life. But as I drifted in and out of consciousness, my eyes fell decidedly closed, perhaps for the last time.

You can imagine my astonishment when I heard an angel sing out to me. It was a voice as light as a Pierre Hermé macaron, as sweet as a 1989 bottle of Château d'Yquem. My eyes flew open to see the angel hovering directly over me, looking pure and angelic as angels are prone to do. To be perfectly honest, I always assumed that I would end up in that other place, where all the food comes well-seared. Perhaps a bookkeeping error had been made but nonetheless it was a delightful surprise. I always wondered, what would be the first words that I would hear if I ever made it to heaven? Then the angel spoke to me once again in the purest and most perfectly divine voice I have ever heard.

"I brought you a chocolate brownie," Helene said with her enduring smile. She was leaning over my bed holding up a paper bag with a brownie peeking out. She sat down in the hard chair next to my bed and fed me a small bite of brownie at a time. A tear rolled on to my pillow.

Over the course of my life I have given considerable thought as to what I would choose as my last meal. *Magnificencia gastronómica* at El Celler de Can Roca in Spain? A Nordic nosh at Noma in Copenhagen? Antica Corona Reale in Cervere, Italy during the height of truffle season? If I returned to Lockhart, Texas and ate the beef rib at Black's Barbecue, smoked sausage at Kreutz Market and brisket at Smitty's Market all in the same afternoon, would it count as a single meal? I might have to get a ruling from the judges. But it really did not matter. At that moment, I would not have traded that chocolate brownie for any other meal in the world.

* * *

2015

"Helene!" I called out from atop my reclining chair at home.

Helene came in from the other room, hair slightly disheveled and wearing her "The Last Time I Cooked Hardly Anyone Got Sick" apron she puts on while pretending to do housework.

"Yes, sweetheart?" she replied. "Can I bring you anything?"

"How do you feel about truffles?"

"I love chocolate truffles! Don't you remember, you bought me some twelve years ago for my birthday?"

"Well, once again you are one lucky woman. I'm taking you to Croatia for truffles!"

"I'm the luckiest!"

* * *

After multiple airport delays resulting in five separate flights, we trudged half a day late into the airport at Zagreb, Croatia. While waiting in line at the rental car booth, I hoped that our delayed arrival had not caused all of the good truffles to have been eaten already. When I finally made it to the front of the line I decided to rough it and rented an amusingly underpowered Czech-made Skoda diesel automobile fitted with Volkswagen's finest emissions-cheating software. We were already late heading out to the hill towns of rural Istria but before we did there was one thing that I needed to do first.

"How about a *štrukli* before we leave Zagreb?" I asked Helene.

"Geez. We don't even have a motel room yet and there's no way I'm getting in the back seat of that rental car!" she responded indignantly.

"A *štrukli* is a famous Zagreb pastry. And fix your hair."

"What's wrong with my hair? And what horrific part of a dead animal do they use to make *štrukli*?"

"Less talking, more eating," I said as I drove into the city center. Of course, if you want the most elite *štrukli* in Zagreb you go directly to La Štruk. We walked through a maze-like passage until we entered La Štruk's plant-lined patio dining area. "They have truffle *štrukli* today!" I exclaimed after scanning the menu.

"That's the mushroom kind of truffle. I knew you were going to torture me over a simple pastry."

"Okay, if you're going to be grumpy you can have the apple cinnamon *štrukli*. I'm sticking with traditional sweet cheese."

A few minutes later our respective *štrukli* arrived in their square baking dishes, piping hot and delicious.

"I've got to admit, this is really good," Helene conceded after a few bites.

"See, you've got to start trusting me. And fix your hair."

"What's wrong with my hair?"

* * *

Satiated for at least the next ten minutes, I turned the Skoda toward the gastronomically delightful hill village of Motovun in Istria. Istria lies a few hours west of Zagreb and includes medieval hilltop villages with nowhere to park, forests thick as the Istrian vegetable soup *maneštra od bobići*, ruins from those Romans who never quite got the hang of using rebar to reinforce their buildings, and my new all-time favorite seaside fishing town Rovinj. Istria also has truffles. In fact, it boasts the world's record setting largest white truffle and is one of the only places in the world where black truffles can be found year-round. Single truffles can be worth hundreds of thousands of dollars. Helene often has a fungus on her feet but to date no one has ever offered her any money for it.

Truffles are so expensive because they can't be cultivated in large quantities. Often found in the roots of oak trees, a highly trained nose is needed to follow the scent and unearth these tantalizing buried treasures. At one time truffle hunters used female pigs to root around and discover the goods because truffles smell like testosterone to female pigs. Imagine the horny pig's disappointment after working hard to track down the scent only to be left standing at the alter with a dirty mushroom. When pigs locate and unearth a truffle rather than a new porcine boyfriend, they often deal with their depression not by consuming a quart of stracciatella gelato but by eating the truffle.

After a pig has eaten a multi-thousand-dollar truffle, truffle hunters tend to get depressed themselves. So most truffle hunters have stopped using pigs and instead turn to man's best friend for truffle hunting. Anyone who has watched a dog eat breakfast in under thirty seconds knows that canines are not very discerning when it comes to food. Dogs can be trained to stupidly drop a fresh truffle in exchange for a bite-sized artificial liver-flavored dog biscuit. This is a win-win for the Istrians as it also frees up more pigs to be transformed into the Istrian prosciutto product *pršut*.

One of the most popular dogs used for truffle hunting is the trusty Labrador Retriever. This is difficult for me to imagine, given that we cannot get Snoring Dog to move off of our bed unless an overstuffed butcher's truck hits a crater-sized pothole and a side of Hereford beef bounces directly in front of her.

As we drove along in the city center I noted a peculiar proliferation of speed limit signs. We saw a sign that read "60 Kilometers." Then a mere hundred feet later another sign read "80 Kilometers" so I sped up a bit. Another hundred feet revealed yet another sign that read "100 Kilometers" so I increased my speed even more, causing the Skoda to wheeze a bit going uphill. Then a hundred feet further a sign read "60 Kilometers." Why do the Croatian traffic engineers have drivers speed up only to have to slow down a few feet later?

Those traffic engineers must have blown their entire speed limit sign budget on those extra signs in the city, because once we were out in the Istrian countryside the speed limit was anyone's guess. After an hour or so of driving and rarely seeing another driver,

I passed a small grove of trees only to be greeted by a Croatian police car hidden in a leafy turnoff on the side of the two-lane country highway along with several other cars. One police officer was inside the police car meticulously consuming the Croatian equivalent of a sugar donut. His uniformed partner, who also appeared to be no stranger at the local Croatian donut store, was standing across the road holding up a Las Vegas style battery-operated sign with a blinking arrow indicating that I should pull over with the other cars. I did so and waited until he had finished his business transactions with the other drivers. Then he ambled over slowly and deliberately to my side of the car, thumbs hooked in his belt, looking like he had watched too many John Wayne movies. That thought quickly vanished when he spoke.

"*Dokumenti!*" he barked.

I did not recall The Duke ever speaking Croatian. I instinctively handed the officer my passport. He seemed a bit peeved.

"*Ne, vozačka dozvola!*" he growled. I was now dealing with the only person in Croatia that did not speak at least some English. I took another guess and handed him my California driver's license. He scrutinized it as if it were made of gold.

"Los Angeles?" he finally read off of my license. "Lakers!" he exclaimed.

We were finally making progress. Those Croatians love their basketball. "Yes, Los Angeles Lakers! I'm very good friends with many of the Laker players," I lied. "In fact, when we get back home I can send you a team photo signed by all the players. Whom should they make it out to, officer?"

The police officer was not as pleased with this offer as I had hoped. Instead, he held up a radar gun and pointed at the display. "Seventy!" he snarled as he showed me the readout from the radar gun. Then he pointed at the road, looked at me gravely and snapped: "Fifty!"

I had exceeded the speed trap speed limit of fifty kilometers per hour or about thirty-one miles per hour. We were on a two-lane country road with few other cars. Any slower and we would have been moving backwards. Race car driver Mario Andretti, whose boyhood home still stands in Motovun, would have been ashamed at how slow I had been going. Then the officer stuck his palm out and demanded: "Five hundred Kuna."

"The Lakers will not be happy about this," I said weakly. The officer was unmoved.

I tried to do the math in my head. Five hundred Croatian Kuna is about $75. I acted like I did not speak Croatian and tried to look confused, neither of which took much effort. My officer did not seem to have a lot of patience. "Five hundred Kuna! *Plati mi!*" he demanded again with his hand out, confirming that I should pay him sooner rather than later.

I fumbled around in my wallet looking for some small bills. I did not want to give him anything too large and have him claim that he did not have any change. I do not know if he was dreaming of California palm trees, feeling sorry for me because I was driving the Skoda, or my confused face worked, because the next thing I heard was the impatient officer saying: "Okay, two hundred and fifty Kuna."

"Wow, he's having an Introductory Fifty Percent Off Sale for tourists," I whispered to Helene who was completely paralyzed in the passenger seat.

"Just pay him," she said, finally managing to speak through a clenched teeth smile.

"I bet I can negotiate him down to one hundred Kuna plus a set of kitchen knives," I told her.

"Just pay him, now!" she said in a tone I had heard only a few times before and did not want to hear again anytime soon.

"Do you think he would let me take his picture with that ridiculous arrow sign? It will look great in our photo album."

"Now!" she said, "Before you end up in a Croatian jail afraid to bend over to pick up the soap in the prison shower." She had my attention.

I peeled off two hundred and fifty Kuna and gave them to the officer who quickly put the money in his pocket. With my driver's license in one hand, he flipped open a weathered leather notebook and scrupulously wrote out an original and copy of a receipt. He handed me the original. He no doubt intended to set fire to his copy as soon as I left. It would certainly never make it back to the police station. Neither would my money. I wonder how much he intended to share with his donut buddy in the police car. He took one more look at my license to confirm that I didn't look too much like any of the pictures hanging in the local Croatian Post Office and handed it back to me while pointing at the road again: "Fifty!" he barked once more.

"*Da*, fifty" I responded meekly as I drove off.

Perhaps I should had asked if he was a Clippers fan.

*   *   *

This trip was on the precipice of a downward death spiral. I needed to do something and fast. The perfect cure was waiting for us in Motovun if we could just find a place to park. Who knew that the medieval hill towns of Istria, like Motovun, sit atop hills? The Istrians will tell you that the hilltop locations afforded natural protection against their enemies. In reality, the lofty locations just gave the local residents a better view of being repeatedly ransacked and pillaged by the Celts, the Romans, the Slavs, the Franks, the Venetians, the Habsburgs, the Turks, the French, the Austrians, the Italians, the Germans, the Yugoslavs, and marauding Boy Scout troops armed with slingshots. The 10th century Motovun village planners were so busy having their asses kicked by everyone within a thousand-mile radius that they completely forgot to provide for adequate parking spaces. To stroll the charming cobblestone streets of Motovun one must park at the bottom of a hill and then climb a long and steep path to reach the town. We had reserved a room in the village at the Villa Marija bed and breakfast featuring made-to-order omelets in the morning on our private balcony overlooking vineyards and nearby towns, a ride with our luggage directly to the property, and most importantly a treasured "locals only" parking spot halfway up the hill. We had arranged to meet the owner halfway up the hill to be directed to our parking spot and then escorted to the property. Between my weakening condition and constant fatigue, there was no way I could walk up the hill and live to complain about it.

The Skoda rattled and squeaked its way into the lower parking area of Motovun at the base of the hill, took one look at the steep climb ahead and started leaking oil and backfiring. I calmed it down, assuring it that it only needed to get us halfway up the hill and then it could take a long nap in its very own parking spot in the shade. In response to my soothing tone it slowly trundled forward toward the former goat path that now served as a road up to the town.

Suddenly, a menacing creature of monstrous proportions blocked out the sun as well as our path. The Skoda whimpered and slumped to a stop. Having studied up on Croatian folklore before our trip, I was all too familiar with the legend of Baba Roga, the ugliest, cruelest, child-eating, wart-covered Croatian witch. If that was not her up ahead, it must have been her even meaner twin sister. The ogress impeding our ascent was big enough to dwarf the entire Croatian women's weightlifting team, the warts on her nose alone could feed a family of four for a week, and she had not trimmed her moustache since she was four years old. The badge on her chest proclaimed that she was the traffic guard of Motovun and the heavy wooden baton that she carried proclaimed that she meant business.

From the driver's seat I motioned to get Baba's attention and pointed to indicate that we wanted to drive up the road. Baba shook her head and pointed with her baton toward the lower parking area. I rolled down my window, politely shook my head and pointed up the hill. Baba pointed again to the lower parking area and gave me a hissing scowl that almost sucked the marrow right out of my bones. I convinced the cowardly Skoda to pull up a little further toward her but Baba refused to budge. There is no doubt that in any collision between Baba and the Skoda, the Skoda would come in second place.

I turned to consult with my wife on our predicament but Helene did not move a hair. I waved my hand in front of her face. She did not blink. Helene was intent on spending a significant portion of this trip in a catatonic state. I got out of the car and walked slowly toward Baba, who glared at me the whole way. "We are staying at Villa Marija and are supposed to drive up this road to meet the owner," I told her with as much courage as I could muster. Baba was unmoved, except for one long hair on her moustache that quivered just a bit. "Here, take a look," I said as I showed her a printed copy of our room confirmation.

Baba squinted at the paper, then at me, and flexed her right bicep for emphasis, but I could see in her bloodshot eyes that she knew she was beaten. She took two steps to her right, leaving just enough room for the Skoda to pass. I got back in the car and willed the Skoda up the hill to where we parked in the beautiful shade of a pine tree and were escorted to our room for a welcome nap.

* * *

The intoxicating delights of Konoba Mondo beckoned. I knew that only a great meal could salvage this trip and Konoba Mondo was more than up to the challenge with a truffle-centric menu of delights. A steep trek down a cobblestone lane brought us to Mondo's colorful seafoam doors and the blackboard menu out front was calling my name. We were seated at one of the worn-smooth wooden tables in the small dining room and knew immediately that we were in the right place when we spotted Anthony Bourdain's picture on the wall from his prior trip to the restaurant. After several near disasters on this vacation, all would soon be made right again. Until I heard that familiar voice.

"What am I going to eat? Every dish has truffles. I don't like truffles."

There she was, with that all too familiar look of terror only partially hidden by the menu. Well, the least I could do was try to help. "How about a cheese with truffles appetizer? Or pate with truffles? Or even carpaccio with truffles? That sounds good. An omelet with truffles? Perhaps poached eggs with truffles? Then you could have risotto with truffles or polenta with truffles. See, there are lots of great things to eat here. How about homemade gnocchi with truffles? Raviolis with truffles?"

As I was helping Helene order, the waiter brought over homemade bread with an olive and truffle tapenade. "I could take a bath in this stuff," I moaned to my spouse as I stuffed the fourth piece of tapenade-mounded bread into my mouth. "Now, where were we? Oh yeah, then there are all kinds of roasted meats with truffles. They've got..."

"Stop! Enough with the truffles. Do you think they can make me a steak without the truffles?" she asked me.

"Only if the chef can stop laughing long enough to grill it," I hooted.

She had her grilled truffle-less steak. I salivated over every bit of my perfect tagliatelle with freshly shaved truffles. For just a few moments, everything was right with the world.

* * *

The next night the Motovun truffle hit parade continued at Pod Napun, another small home-style restaurant where truffles abound.

"You're kidding me! Again?" Helene's voice shot across the table as she took her first glance at the menu.

She needed a peace offering. "Look, they have a traditional Istrian vegetable soup without any truffles," I pointed out. "Really." She brightened a bit. We both ordered and enjoyed the vegetable soup, which I followed up with a veal *peka* dish baked under a dome and then smothered in fresh truffles. The confused chef stopped shaking his head and grilled Helene a truffle-less chicken breast.

"What, no truffles for dessert?" mocked my wife.

"Of course truffles for dessert. I'm ordering the truffle strudel." I was quite glad that I did.

* * *

Vižinada, Grožnjan, Učka, Oprtalj, Završje. No wonder these impossible to spell edges-of-the-keyboard Istrian hill villages now lay in ruins. The remaining crumbling stone houses stand like rows of crooked teeth, with roofs caved in and vegetation sprouting inside what were once medieval living rooms where sixteenth century families would gather around a warm fire to try to figure out why they were not getting their mail. The entire population fled as soon as they discovered that there were no decent restaurants in most of these hill towns. Were it not for a woman with a small cart in Grožnjan selling the Croatian donut ball delicacy *krafne* liberally sprinkled with sugar and strategically mounded in a small paper cone, I may not have had the strength to continue.

But continue we did through the hills and valleys of Istria on our journey to the sea. I did not want to overburden the already tired Skoda as we drove on, but before Helene could start talking to me I turned on the car radio. The power drain from the radio caused the Skoda to slow considerably. After a few minutes of tuning, I determined that the Skoda was capable of receiving three different radio stations. The first was a Croatian station that played nothing but American semi-hits from the 1980's, all by unknown cover bands. Apparently it was too much trouble to play the actual hit records by the original groups. The second station was a combination news and talk radio format from somewhere in Slovenia. Regrettably, I had left my English-Slovene dictionary at home. The third station was intermittent static. The fourth alternative was to engage my spouse in conversation. Did you know that the Slovenian sugar beet crop will be very plentifull this year?

Ah, Rovinj! Where barefoot children laugh and frolic in the fountain just below your open hotel room window as a gentle sea zephyr wafts in. Where fishing boats of every shape and color line up in a finely orchestrated aquatic ballet in the harbor. Where under the protective shadow of Balbi's Arch the braided gypsy girl in the gold and red flowered peasant skirt coaxes popular tunes from her second-hand Crucianelli accordion and then passes her floppy hat among the crowd. Where after a short climb up a serious cobblestone path, Sergio will reward you with the most flavorful wood-fired *salumi* pizza this side of Naples, and where every outdoor cafe of the dozens that ring the harbor serve at least a dozen flavors of soothing gelato.

Ah, the Hotel Adriatic in Rovinj! Where each morning the string quartet serenades you with classical music as you sit *al fresco* sampling croissants in an overstuffed chair while watching the fishermen bring in their fresh catch. Where the carafe of filtered water in your room is replaced several times throughout the day. Where the gentle knock on your door in the late afternoon announces a plate of finally sculptured chocolates to set the mood for dinner (as if I needed a reason). Where the thread count is magnificent.

Ah, the Rio Bar! Where the waitress speaks five languages and explains that she can tell the time of year by the nationality of the tourists that come into the restaurant (English and Germans in the Spring when it is still cold up North, Eastern Europeans in early Summer, and the French and Italians during their typical vacation time in July and August). Where the prawns are sweet, the grilled gilt-head bream taken from the harbor a few hours earlier is flaky and tender and the mussels are muscular. Where the nightly promenade of tourists, locals, families and lovers stroll...where else, on the promenade.

I was so enchanted by Rovinj that following dinner I bought Helene her very own gelato. I never wanted to leave this charming place and there were way too many enticing restaurants to try but not nearly enough time. On our last night in Rovinj I felt compelled to create a lasting memory of this magical village for eternity. Helene and I strolled hand in hand along the promenade as the sun began to set. We stopped at water's edge and I placed my hand on her shoulder.

"Would you please move out of the way," I implored her as I gave her a nudge.

I was trying to line up the perfect photo—a rugged fisherman in screaming yellow waders was standing on his bobbing boat with a cigarette in his mouth as he hauled in his net, dozens of fishing boats in a full palette of colors were docked in the harbor behind him, in the distance the Hotel Adriatic, main plaza and the glorious Rovinj waterfront bathed in an orange sky as the nightly parade of strolling romantics cruised the outdoor cafes and children pleaded with their parents for a chocolate gelato. I held in my breath and snapped the picture—just as the fisherman dropped the net (but not the cigarette) and peed off the side of his boat into the harbor. Luckily, he was a man of modest proportions and he did not become entangled in the net. Not so luckily, my harbor-caught gilt-head bream that I had for dinner earlier that evening did not seem quite so delicious after that.

Tagliatelle with truffles—Konoba Mondo

Fresh grill of the day—Rio Bar

17

ARTISTRY WITH LIVER

November 29, 2016, 9:00 p.m.

"Mr. Ross, Mr. Ross." Dr. Lee is yelling at me and shaking me by both shoulders in an attempt to wake me up. "We have a liver offer for you!" she shouts.

It is dark in my room and I mostly just see her silhouette over my bed. It takes me a moment for my eyeballs to lock into place.

"That's great," I reply, still a bit wobbly.

"The liver is from a fifty-two-year-old woman. It is a bit on the small side but we think it will work for you. It's a good solid liver and the donor has a clean history."

"Okay." I am still dazed and hoping my brain will snap to attention sooner rather than never.

"You understand that you can die from this procedure!" Dr. Lee is still shouting and holding me about the shoulders, making sure that I understand and consent.

"Yes, I understand. Please help me call Helene."

The universe decides that Helene does not already have enough on her plate, so to increase the degree of difficulty, Helene's father is having prostate surgery this very night and Helene is with him at a different hospital on the other side of town. It is 9:00 p.m. when Dr. Lee and I call Helene to give her the news. We all agree that Helene will stay with her father and Dr. Lee will call her when we get closer to the transplant surgery time, which she estimates will be around midnight.

One of the doctors informed me earlier in the day that my MELD score was up to thirty-eight. Without a new liver I might only last a few more weeks, if that long. But now I watch the minutes go by in a transplant count-down. I think back to the woman at the liver clinic who was left at the liver alter multiple times before finally finding success. I hope this liver will turn out to be viable and give me a decent chance.

At 11:30 p.m. I wonder why I have not been wheeled out to be prepped for surgery. I am still in my room at midnight, alone and discouraged.

*   *   *

November 30, 2016, 12:15 a.m.

I lay in my hospital bed watching the clock on the wall, counting as my chance at a new liver ticks away. Nurses come in every so often but no one can give me any news. 1:00 a.m. comes and goes. I know something is very wrong but no one tells me what is happening. Finally, Dr. Lee comes in to see me around 2:00 a.m.

"Mr. Ross, we think we may have a better liver for you. It is from a thirty-year-old man and it's a perfect size for you. But the liver is in Arizona. We have to fly a team out to inspect it and see if it is a good match for you. We won't know until we see it in person. You need to decide right now whether you want to wait a few hours for us to check out the liver in Arizona."

My brain begs to explode. All of a sudden I have two liver offers. If I agree to wait for the man's liver in Arizona, I could lose out on the women's liver that is ready to go. But if the man's liver turns out to be unsuitable, I could end up empty-livered. In any event, can I even last several more hours? Helene is not here and I have to decide.

"What happened to the donor in Arizona?" I rasp.

"He died of a trauma. Due to privacy laws, I can't tell you any more than that."

"Let's go for the one in Arizona. If the perfect liver is out there, I want to give it my best shot."

"We'll get a team ready as soon as possible."

"Thank you. And please let Helene know."

"Of course. Now rest."

After Dr. Lee leaves, the only bit of light in my room leaks out in greens and yellows from the various medical monitors that crowd around me. I watch my heartbeat on the monitor, pleased to see that I have not flatlined. It is quiet on the floor and I imagine that I can hear the wall clock ticking, even though I know it is silent. I stare at the clock, trying to will the hands to move faster, but my effort only seems to slow it down.

At 3:00 a.m. I wait for the familiar sound of the radiology team rolling the portable x-ray machine down the hallway so they can hoist me up in bed and slide a frigid metal plate under my back for my nightly chest x-ray. But they do not come tonight. I cannot tell whether that is a good or a bad omen.

For the first time, I hope that one of the many equipment alarms goes off and breaks the monotony. An empty drip bag, a clog in the dialysis machine, a crimped wire monitoring my vital signs, the motion detector in my mattress. Then a nurse will run in and perhaps I can wrangle an update. But nothing happens. Even the machines seem to have abandoned me.

I miss Helene.

* * *

November 30, 2016, 7:00 a.m.

Sunlight finally sneaks through the blinds and the nurses enter my room for the shift change handover. This is usually an exciting part of the day because the departing nurse stands next to the bedside monitors and reports to the incoming nurse my status and any changes in my treatment while I get to listen in. But there is no real update other than we are all waiting to see if I will be going into surgery.

Another nurse comes in to tell me that Helene is calling. The nurse puts the phone on speaker and holds it for me.

"Hello?" I say.

"Hi," Helene says. She sounds very tired. "My father came out of surgery and is fine and I spoke to Dr. Lee a few hours ago. I came home just to rest my eyes for a few minutes but I completely fell asleep. Is there any update on the Arizona liver?"

"The last I heard they were sending a team to look at it."

"Dr. Lee told me if it goes forward it will probably happen around noon. That's still five hours away."

"Okay. What are you planning to do?"

"I don't know. If you want I can come over right now."

"No, nothing is going to happen here for a while and things usually take longer than they say. Go check on your father and then you can come over by noon. I'm sure we'll still be waiting. If anything changes a nurse will call you."

"Are you sure?"

"Yeah, go. I'll see you later."

"It's a plan, Stan."

"Okay, Fran."

"Love you."

"Love you, bye."

I am spent. I go back to staring at the clock.

My favorite nurse Justin comes by with exciting news. I can have one small ice chip! Even better, the preliminary report on the

Arizona liver indicates that it looks good. We are still tentatively scheduled for noon. Fortified by the ice chip, I ask him to pass on a message to Dr. Lee. If possible, I would like to speak to her before the surgery.

An hour or so later Dr. Lee appears at the foot of my bed accompanied by half a dozen other members of the surgical team crowded around behind her. This may be the last time I see her. My mouth is dry but I force out some sound.

"Dr. Lee, you know I'm a partner in a law firm," I start, barely above a gravelly whisper but I begin to gain some momentum. "Whenever one of the younger associate attorneys has an important hearing coming up, I always feel it is my responsibility to give them some words of advice. It has become kind of a good luck thing. I thought that I could use some good luck now and with your permission I would like to speak the same words to you before my surgery."

Dr. Lee scoots in even closer to the side of the bed and takes my hand.

"Of course," she says, as she moves in only inches from my lips so as to not miss a single word. The rest of the team moves in closer as well. To borrow an unfortunate phrase, the room is deathly silent.

I look directly into her eyes and in as loud of a voice as I can muster, I shout at her: "Don't fuck up!"

She erupts into laughter as does the rest of the team. Dr. Lee is laughing so hard she cannot talk and simply waves at me as she leaves the room. When she is finally able to speak, I hear her say to the team as they are walking away in the hallway: "He really got me."

Nobody wants a tense surgical group. My team is now loose and ready to go.

A nurse comes into my room around 9:30 a.m. "Everything looks good. Your surgery is scheduled for 11:00 a.m. They'll be coming around in a bit to take you to get prepped."

"But they told me noon. I need to get ahold of my wife. She's with her father and I need to see her before I go into surgery," I reply with urgency.

"I'll try to reach her for you."

Now I am really worried. I need to see Helene before the first scalpel digs in and I am not sure where she is.

An orderly shows up and wheels me out of my room to be prepped for surgery. I have lost track of time. I have lost track of Helene. I have lost track of my mind. The hallways in the hospital are endless. I hear the clickety-clack of the wheels on the hard tile floor. I am pushed past the lunch food cart and the chemical smell of the boiled plastic domes. I am in an elevator with strangers staring down at me. I am rolling out of the elevator and back in a hallway, past doctors and nurses and patients on gurneys and visiting families carrying flowers and get well soon balloons. All strange faces.

Then I hear running and finally, that voice.

"Brad!" Helene cries out as she and Justin come sprinting up to my bed. The orderly stops and Helene tries to talk while gasping for breath. "I drove over here from seeing my father at his hospital, but when I got to your room it was empty and your bed was gone. I didn't know what had happened but then Justin saw me and helped me run over here."

Helene takes my hand and I squeeze it. Our eyes lock. We do not need to talk. We just give each other a smile and a look that says, well, here we go.

As they hoist me onto the surgical table, I think about the photograph that Helene brought from home and pinned to the small bulletin board on my hospital room wall the day I was admitted. The photo was taken on our last trip earlier this year when we donned tie-dye shirts and flashed peace signs at the beginning of a nostalgic 1960's Flower Power cruise. Those shirts have been out of fashion since decades earlier when Helene and I dressed up and took our first photo together before going out to Harry's Bar & American Grill to celebrate her birthday. Somehow, thinking about that Flower Power photo taken thousands of miles away makes me feel the comfort of home.

*   *   *

November 30, 2016, 11:30 a.m.

The cylindrical metal chamber is overflowing with the most impossibly repulsive and putrid sludge ever concocted. I fight to move my arms or legs but they have withered away to uselessness and I keep sinking into the fetid mire. Writhing snakelike with depleting energy, I am barely able to bring my head above the filth one last time. I gulp for air but even above the sludge there is no air to breathe. Torn strips of mold-blackened rags are suspended from above the chamber. My only means of getting air is to suck on the vile rags, but no matter how hard I struggle to push up out of the dark ooze, the life-sustaining rags remain just out of reach. Then I notice the faces. Far above in an observation room, Dr. Lee and the entire surgical transplant team peer at me through a glass window. Next to her is Dr. Bart and my kidney doctor and there is my cardiologist. In fact all the doctors that have been treating me, well over a dozen in all, stare at me from high up above the chamber. They are smiling and laughing as I futilely thrash about. All through my years of treatment they tricked me into thinking they were trying to heal me, when instead it had all been an elaborate plot to torture me for their own sadistic amusement. I gasp one last time for air but my lungs come up empty and the muck drags me helplessly to the bottom.

*   *   *

November 30, 2016, 8:00 p.m.

My eyes flash open. Not an easy task for a dead man. I must still be alive. Survival of the weakest!

As the walls of my hospital room swirl around me, I can make out Dr. Lee's voice. "Mr. Ross, congratulations, you have a new liver and it's working great. We were going to give you a good solid Buick liver but instead we got you a Ferrari!"

I try to focus and can feel my new liver chugging away flawlessly, filtering out more impurities than a Norpro Stainless Steel flour sifter. Dr. Lee says that I had given her a couple of scares over the last few weeks. However, at the last minute that perfect liver of just the right size, blood type and age, without history of disease, alcohol or drug abuse, and that had never been subjected to Kraft "cheese product," had arrived in time from Arizona. The surgical team showed off their fine knife skills by making three massive incisions down from my chest spreading out to both sides of my belly, clamped down assorted veins to stop blood flow, dragged out my freeloading liver and kicked it to the curb, and plated my new liver beautifully with a side of bile ducts nestled on a mound of freshly attached vessels and arteries. Time to prepare this deconstructed liver dish: eight hours. It was artistry with liver!

My eyeballs start to slowly move into alignment and I can now see Helene standing by one side of the bed. She gently squeezes my hand. "How are you feeling?" she asks.

How am I feeling? I have a wound the size of Cincinnati running the length of my stomach, held together by a few hundred giant black staples that would make a great layout for a Lionel train track. One of my internal organs is now an external organ. The remainder of my favorite body parts feel like they have been scrambled in a Hobart spiral dough mixer. I also cannot explain any of this to her because I have a tube running down my throat, as well as in and out of a bunch of other places.

I motion to the nurse standing near the other side of the bed that I want to write a message to my wife. The nurse finds a pad of paper, puts a pen in my hand, and supports my arm so I can try to write. There is so much that I want to tell Helene. We have been through countless glorious adventures together and most recently through a life and death challenge. But we have been through them side by side and it looks like our journey together will continue. How can I put this into words? I use my very unsteady hand to scribble a few words on the page. The nurse takes the pen from my hand and examines what I have written. "Are you sure that's what you want to say?" she asks, with a confused look.

I nod affirmatively. The nurse passes the pad over to my wife. Helene takes one look, smiles and says: "He must be feeling fine."

The note reads: "What's for lunch?"

* * *

December 2, 2016

I cannot stop thinking about my liver donor and the incredible chain of events that led me to this day. A thirty-year-old stranger in another state had the foresight and generosity to register as a potential organ donor on his driver's license. He is killed in a tragic accident within the same hour that I accept a smaller female liver from an older woman. Teams of organ procurement organizations and doctors in two states immediately mobilize to inspect and then rush the liver to Los Angeles. It is precisely my blood type and the perfect size. Had it become available an hour or two later my life would have been different.

The donor was about the same age as Jessica, just getting started in life. Did he dream of traveling or owning a house or raising a family? Had he been excited about the four-day Thanksgiving holiday but was trying not to think about having to return to work the following Monday morning? Did he spend Thanksgiving watching football games with his buddies, then later sit around a large table with his parents and grandparents, cousins and friends, eating way too much turkey with stuffing but still going back for an extra piece of pumpkin pie? Did the children fight over the drumsticks and excitedly pull apart the wishbone? Did his uncle tell the same corny jokes each year but everyone still laughed? Did they all take a moment to give thanks for the meal and the opportunity to come together as a family to celebrate their Thanksgiving traditions?

It was their final Thanksgiving together. In a few weeks it would be a very solemn Christmas Day.

A stranger had to die so that I could live. A piece of him lives inside of me. He survives not only in the memory of his family but directly through me. I am now physically and emotionally connected to him, to his family and to their traditions and heritage. I bear an awesome responsibility now to make the most of this remarkable opportunity for both of our families.

* * *

December 4, 2016

I advance to a liquid diet and Helene is there to spoon an abomination called beef bouillon through my parched lips. The hospital cook is in a particularly festive mood today and celebrates my survival with a delivery of lime Jell-O.

Not long after, the nurse tells me that I can try a cup of chicken soup. I insist on elevating the back of the hospital bed and trying to feed myself. My still shaking hand spills far more soup on my chest than ever reaches my mouth. However, it is a step in the right direction.

* * *

December 5, 2016

The doctors finally grow weary of my constant carping and begrudgingly concede that I can try some solid food. Having nothing else to do, I stare at my old friend the wall clock with great anticipation for several hours until I can finally hear the dinner cart click-clacking its way to my door. Helene takes the tray from the attendant and places it on the hospital overbed table that she maneuvers in front of me. As always, the fork and knife are wrapped in impenetrable plastic. A minuscule napkin that takes an engineering Ph.D. candidate to unfold is strategically placed just out of reach. A small plastic container of apple juice is within reach, but of no use because the tab on the corner breaks off when you try to peel it back. However, the real prize is in the center of the tray. I can smell something unmistakably food-like seeping out of the dome-topped plate.

"Your dinner is ready," my wife gleefully exclaims.

"It better not be Jell-O molded into the shape of a T-Bone steak," I threaten.

"Don't worry, I placed the order myself," Helene says. She removes the plastic dome with a simultaneous and dramatic: "Voila!"

Laying on the plate is a single grilled chicken breast, hold the sauce.

EPILOGUE

January 15, 2017

Dear Donor Family:

I received your family's lifesaving gift of a liver on November 30, 2016. I want to first express to you my heartfelt condolences for your terrible loss. Although I do not know you, I think about my donor and your family daily.

I live in California with my wife of thirty-six years. I have a son and a daughter who are close in age to my donor. My parents also reside in California near my sister. My father serves as caregiver for my mother who suffers from advanced Alzheimer's disease. My sister and I both provide emotional support for my father.

I was diagnosed with an incurable liver disease over twenty-five years ago. I was able to deal with it through medication until about three years ago when my liver became decidedly worse and I had to stop working. I have been at home for the last few years, spending considerable time with doctors, being hospitalized several times and trying to get as much rest as possible. In November last year I was taken by ambulance to the hospital where I remained for several weeks. The doctors told me that I was near death several times as I waited to see whether a liver would become available to save my life.

When the Thanksgiving holiday came and went, I wondered whether I would be able to share any more holidays with my family.

I wondered whether I would be alive to spend my December anniversary with my wife. I thought about whether I would be able to make my daughter's dream come true of traveling with her to New York for her upcoming thirtieth birthday and seeing a play together.

Thanks to this lifesaving gift I was able to open presents with my family for the holidays while shedding more than a few tears, my wife and I are looking forward to many more anniversaries, and travel plans have been finalized for that big trip to New York. Through many, many letters and emails of good wishes I have been reminded of how many great friendships I have enjoyed, how many colleagues still care deeply about me, and how I cherish more than ever spending time with them and my family. Every new day that I spend with them is a magnificent blessing.

I cannot wait to see what is in store for me in the coming years and I promise to make the most of this second chance at life. As I treasure the opportunities presented with each new day, I will never forget that this was all made possible by a caring and thoughtful donor family and your tremendous sacrifice.

With eternal appreciation and sympathy,

Bradley D. Ross

ACKNOWLEDGMENTS

With enormous gratitude I am delighted to have the opportunity to thank the following co-conspirators who made this book a reality:

Tal Taylor, who both bravely and foolishly volunteered to read the first draft. As Ernest Hemingway famously noted: "the first draft of anything is shit." Mine was no exception to the rule, but Tal persevered and provided invaluable comments and support.

Dawn Eyerly, who spared no expense to our law firm while tutoring me in the fine art of eating sushi. Without her, my grand Tokyo sushi adventure would not have been possible.

My dear friend, very first law partner and mentor Dennis Kendig, who sternly insisted that we never forego dining out daily for lunch and who instilled in me early on the value, nay necessity, of lengthy and frequent vacations.

The incomparable Fred Eaglesmith, for permission to reprint the lyrics to Ship.

The angel employees of OneLegacy, who comfort and assist recipients, donors and donor families undergoing organ, eye or tissue donations. OneLegacy acted as an intermediary to help deliver my letter of gratitude to my donor family while protecting their privacy. Visit them at: www.onelegacy.org

The world's finest editor Elizabeth Evans, to whom I initially delivered a dog's breakfast of a manuscript. But Elizabeth was relentless in her encouragement and I knew I had turned the corner when I caused her to gag at my description of eating a tarantula. Elizabeth is nurturing, funny, brilliant, thorough, joyful and a consummate professional.

Dr. Irene Kim, Dr. Tsuyoshi Todo, Dr. Nicholas Nissen, Critical Care Registered Nurse Justin Munar and the other amazing doctors, nurses, cooks and staff at Cedars-Sinai Medical Center who worked together to save my life. If you are ever unfortunate enough to require hospitalization but lucky enough to do so at Cedars-Sinai, I heartily recommend the turkey dinner.

Finally, to my doctor and hero Burton Liebross, who during the course of over thirty years continually dug deep into his doctor's bag of tricks to keep me alive and who paved the way for my successful transplant. I will forever be indebted for his unsurpassed kindness, compassion, knowledge, skill and friendship.